David Hill car[...]
in 1959 under[...]
migrant schem[...]
Some years late. he won a scholarship to
the University of Sydney, where he studied
economics before completing a Master's
degree and working as an economics tutor.

During his remarkable career, David has
been chairman then managing director of
the Australian Broadcasting Corporation;
chairman of Soccer Australia; chief executive of the State Rail Authority; chairman of
Sydney Water Corporation; and chairman
of CREATE (an organisation representing
Australian children in institutional care).

He has also held a number of other executive appointments in the areas
of sport, transport, broadcasting, fiscal management and city parks.

In 2006 he was awarded a Diploma of Arts with merit in classical
archaeology from Sydney University. Since 2011 he has been the manager
of an archaeological study of the ancient Greek city of Troizen. He has for
many years been a leading figure in the international campaign to have the
Parthenon sculptures returned from the British Museum to Greece.

Also by David Hill

The Forgotten Children
1788
The Gold Rush
The Great Race
The Making of Australia
Australia and the Monarchy
The Fair and the Foul
The First Fleet Surgeon
Convict Colony

DAVID HILL

RECKONING

WILLIAM HEINEMANN: AUSTRALIA

WILLIAM HEINEMANN

UK | USA | Canada | Ireland | Australia
India | New Zealand | South Africa | China

William Heinemann is part of the Penguin Random House group of companies whose
addresses can be found at global.penguinrandomhouse.com

Penguin
Random House
Australia

First published by William Heinemann in 2022

Cover photograph courtesy of Ian Bayliff, Fairbridge Farm School Molong Papers
Cover design by Louisa Maggio © Penguin Random House Australia Pty Ltd
Internal design by Midland Typesetters, Australia
Typeset in 12.5/17 pt Adobe Garamond Pro by Midland Typesetters

Printed and bound in Australia by Griffin Press, part of Ovato, an accredited
ISO AS/NZS 14001 Environmental Management Systems printer

A catalogue record for this
book is available from the
National Library of Australia

NATIONAL
LIBRARY
OF AUSTRALIA

ISBN 978 1 76104 552 3

penguin.com.au

MIX
Paper from
responsible sources
FSC® C009448

CONTENTS

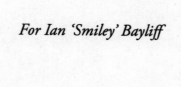

For Ian 'Smiley' Bayliff

TIMELINE

1912   Fairbridge, Pinjarra, Western Australia opens.

1936   Fairbridge, Vancouver Island, Canada opens.

1938   Fairbridge, Molong, New South Wales opens.

1940   First Molong principal, Richard Beauchamp, dismissed.
Edward Heath replaces him as principal until 1943.

1944   W. J. Garnett's critical 'Report on Farm Schools in Australia'
published.

1945   F. K. S. Woods replaces Heath as principal.
Secretary of Fairbridge Society, Gordon Green, concurs with
Garnett's report.

1946   Curtis Report into child institutions and migration
published.

1948   The Children Act passed.
Woods under investigation for sexual and physical abuse at
Fairbridge.
Princess Elizabeth donates $2000 to help former
Fairbridgians.
Fairbridge, Molong becomes semi-autonomous from London.

1951   John Moss reports on Australian child migrant centres and is
critical of conditions.

1954   Queen Elizabeth declines to visit Fairbridge on her
Australian tour.

1955   Fairbridge Council inquires into education at Molong.

1956   Ross's fact-finding mission investigates 26 Australian child
migrant centres.

June: Ross's report sent to UK Home Office, categorising the homes A, B or C.

July: Ross's report suppressed and children waiting to travel to Australia allowed to go.

1957 As a condition of funding, British government requires Fairbridge to reform.

Fairbridge allows a single parent to follow children to Australia.

1959 David and brothers leave for Australia.

December: Mrs Hill arrives in Australia.

1961 David leaves Fairbridge.

1962 Bill Phillips leaves Fairbridge amid rumours of abuse.

1964 Cottage mother Kathleen Johnstone under investigation for abuse.

1966 F. K. S. Woods dismissed from and leaves Fairbridge.

1969 Jack Newberry forced to leave Molong due to allegations of abuse.

1974 Fairbridge, Molong, closed.

1980 Fairbridge, Pinjarra, closed (last Fairbridge home to close).

1997 Inquiry into the Welfare of British Child Migrants by Commons Health Committee.

1998 Health Committee tables its report 'The Welfare of Former British Child Migrants'.

2001 Australian Senate inquiry into child migrant institutions.

2007 The publication of *The Forgotten Children*.

David and a group of Fairbridgians meet Slater & Gordon to discuss class action.

2008 Fairbridgians begin court challenge for the abuse they suffered.

2009   *The Long Journey Home* aired nationally on ABC TV.
        Prime Minister Kevin Rudd apologises to institutionalised
        children.

2010   Prime Minister Gordon Brown apologises to British child
        migrants.

2012   Prime Minister Julia Gillard announces Royal Commission
        into Institutional Responses to Child Sexual Abuse,
        including child migrants in terms of reference.

2014   Prime Minister Theresa May establishes the Independent
        Inquiry into Child Sexual Abuse (IICSA), including an
        investigation into child migration.
        NSW Supreme Court determines that class action can begin
        between claimants, Fairbridge Foundation, New South
        Wales state and the federal governments.

2015   Fairbridge case scheduled for trial but, after mediation, case
        settled out of court with a record payout.

2017   IICSA opens in London, considering evidence from former
        child migrants.

2019   British government agrees to compensate surviving British
        child migrants.
        ACT government renames William Slim Drive Gundaroo
        Drive.
        UK Fairbridge agrees to pay into an Australian government
        compensation scheme for child abuse victims.

2020   Prime Minister Scott Morrison 'names and shames'
        Fairbridge for failing to pay into the National Redress
        Scheme.

2021   Fairbridge agrees it will now pay redress directly to
        Fairbridge abuse victims.

PREFACE

Britain is the only country in history to have exported large numbers of its children. From the nineteenth century, various schemes dispatched tens of thousands of underprivileged children – unaccompanied by their parents or guardians – to the British colonies. They were sent to Canada, New Zealand and Zimbabwe (then Rhodesia). About 10,000 children were shipped to Australia, where, by the mid-1950s, twenty-six child migrant centres were operating across six states. These were run by either the Protestant or Catholic churches, or by various charities, including Dr Barnardo's (it became Barnardos in 1966) and the Fairbridge Society. Around a thousand children were sent to the Fairbridge Farm School in Molong, New South Wales, which opened in 1938 and closed in 1974. I was one of them.

Contrary to popular belief, very few of the child migrants were orphans. British philanthropic, religious and benevolent organisations drove child migration, ostensibly compelled by the idea of 'rescuing' children living in poor or broken families in Britain. The theory was that by sending these young people to the far-off lands of the colonies, their opportunities would be many and better. The migrant schemes were also motivated by a desire to convert 'a burden and a menace' into 'assets' for the Empire. Essentially, the choice presented to the children was either a lifetime of begging, thieving, disease, prostitution and early death in their homeland, or the chance to learn farming or domestic skills in a bountiful, hospitable country such as Australia.

As recently as 1997 the British government was still claiming to a House of Commons inquiry into child migration that the policy was 'a well-intended response to the needs of deprived children . . . At the time this was seen to be in the best interests of the children concerned.' The government went on to say that 'a strong driving factor in child migration' was 'the British philanthropic, religious and benevolent organisations, who were rescuing children from poverty, destitution, vagrancy, criminality or neglect and saw better opportunities for such children in the expanding colonies and Empire.'[1]

Yet what I uncovered about the lives of many of these migrants was very disturbing, as I was determined to illustrate in my book *The Forgotten Children*, and as has become increasingly clear in the years since.

It had never occurred to me, until 2005, to write about Fairbridge Farm School, much less about the years of my childhood spent there. The idea for *The Forgotten Children* began after I'd completed a Diploma of Archaeology at Sydney University, as

I had for a long time been interested in the archaeology of the prehistoric to Hellenistic periods of an area in the north-eastern Peloponnese in Greece.

Armed with my newly acquired qualifications, I thought I would test my skills by conducting a heritage survey of the Fairbridge Farm School settlement at Molong. The place was ideal for an archaeological study as it had remained pretty well unchanged from the time I had left it four decades before. The old village had become a ghost town and the farm school had received hardly any maintenance since it had closed in 1974: as I had seen on occasional visits over the years, many of its buildings had fallen into disrepair and some of the structures had collapsed.

When I started consulting some heritage experts I knew, they persuaded me that the study of the physical history of the place should include the human story of the children who had lived there as child migrants. So, using the mailing list of the Old Fairbridgians Association, I wrote to more than two hundred former Fairbridge kids asking them if they wanted to tell their story. Over the next few months I conducted audio interviews with about forty of them in New South Wales, the Australian Capital Territory and south-east Queensland. At the same time, I collected hundreds of old files, notes, diaries, unpublished autobiographies, letters and photos from about sixty others. I also caught up with my old Fairbridge friend Ian 'Smiley' Bayliff, whom I hadn't seen in years. Smiley had for ages been helping former Fairbridge kids hunt down families and relatives they had lost contact with back in the UK. At the same time, he had collected a vast amount of archival material about Fairbridge. I owe a great deal to Smiley, hence my dedicating this book to him. Smiley died in October

2021 after a long illness. A very dear friend of mine, he was also an enormous help to me with the Fairbridge research over the past fifteen years. He had a remarkable knowledge of the place and the children who went there, and helped uncover much of the truth of the Fairbridge story – particularly the dark side. I think his determination to help me finish this book kept him alive as long as it did. He was certainly excited when I gave him a copy of the final manuscript. He was a great mate. I will miss him dearly.

As I delved into the Fairbridge story, I realised that, while a lot had been written and said about the place, the stories of the children and their experiences – indeed, my own story and experiences at that time of my life – had never been told, and the pictures they painted were very different and far more disturbing than the records of the academics and historians. It was then that I decided to write *The Forgotten Children*, and from the point of view of us kids. Some good friends and I also made a TV documentary titled *The Long Journey Home*, which was eventually aired nationally on ABC TV in Australia in 2009.

I found myself both upset and angry about some of the testimony of those I interviewed for both the documentary and the book, many of whom were speaking for the first time. I wondered why seventy-five-year-old women would talk to me on the record of regular sexual abuse they'd suffered at Fairbridge when they had never discussed it with their husbands, children or grandchildren. When I asked them why they had not spoken out before, many said they thought it had only happened to them, and feared no one would believe them. Others said they had not had the strength to speak earlier, but now, as they became older, they were determined to confront the ghosts of their past. A number who had originally declined to talk to me heard that others had spoken and came forward to say they now wanted to tell their story.

There are many others for whom it is still too difficult. Susan was at the farm school when I was there; her brother was in my cottage. He later took his own life. One day Susan phoned me to say she wanted the book to be written and to tell her story but it was still 'too painful to open those doors it took me years to close'.

The wife of a man who was at Fairbridge when I was there wrote to explain why her husband could not talk to me: 'There are too many memories there. He arrived when he was barely seven years old. He really can't remember any good things to say . . . scrubbing floors every afternoon and only having a couple of hours off a week; working in the dairy at 3 a.m. in the cold frosty mornings with no shoes on.'

Another former Fairbridge boy, Allan, whom I remember as an interesting and colourful character, rang and requested I did not write any more letters asking about an interview with him. 'I've forgotten a lot of it. I don't want to remember,' he said. 'I'm happy now I have my eleven grandchildren around me. Please don't write to me again – it's too upsetting.' I told him I wouldn't bother him anymore and asked when his life had turned around. 'It hasn't,' he said. 'It never turned around.'

In addition to my own experience and the stories of others, when I first set about writing *The Forgotten Children*, I was able to access rather limited personal files about myself from the Fairbridge Foundation offices in Sydney and the Fairbridge Society archives, which are held at the University of Liverpool in the UK. A number of children who had already accessed their personal files from Sydney or Liverpool kindly made them available to me.

I also found material at the Fairbridge Foundation in Sydney, the Fairbridge Society archives in the UK, the National Library in Canberra and the State Library of New South Wales; as well as files at the Department of Education and the Child Welfare Department, which are held at the New South Wales State Archives and Records office.

From the start, however, I was thwarted in my attempts to see many of the historical files. The Fairbridge Foundation in Sydney is the successor body of the Fairbridge Farm School, which was responsible for running the school at Molong. The foundation was the custodian of the old farm school files, which it kept in a Sydney office in a number of uncatalogued boxes. While the foundation allowed me access to some of the material in the boxes, it did not let me see the minutes of Fairbridge Council meetings, which were stored in the same Sydney office. This was despite the chairman of the foundation, John Kennedy, assuring an Australian Senate inquiry in 2001 that the files would be made available to bona fide scholars. I wrote to Kennedy in July 2006 asking that the foundation reconsider their decision. Four months later he told me that the board had considered my request and decided I could have limited access to some files, but not the board minutes, and that I would not be allowed to use material that identified any child or any staff member who had been at Fairbridge. I explained I already had extensive testimony and evidence from other sources that identified improper or illegal acts by a number of staff members.

Initially, I encountered similar obstacles when I attempted to access the UK Fairbridge Society files in the Liverpool University archives, which included minutes of the UK society. I was asked to agree to a number of restrictions that the society had imposed and I had to sign a declaration that 'I will not in any way by any form of communication reveal to any person or persons nominal information or individual details which might tend to identify individuals or their descendants'. The rules stipulated I could not identify any Fairbridge child for one hundred years or any staff member by name for seventy-five years from the date of the lodgement of the files. I was obliged to 'agree to abide by the decision of the director' as to what might identify individuals.

While I was working in the Liverpool University archives, I was contacted by the chairman of the UK Fairbridge Society, Gil Wood, who had been tipped off about my research and wanted to talk to me about the project. He explained that while the organisation no longer operated a child migrant scheme, it was still active in youth welfare in the UK. I told him I had come across material in the archives that corroborated some of the more disturbing oral histories of the children I'd interviewed, and asked that Fairbridge allow me to use this material in the book. Wood agreed to consider my request but said he was concerned that any adverse publicity would make ongoing public fundraising more difficult. 'My highest priority is to protect the reputation and name of Fairbridge,' he warned.

I found there were also restrictions on the Education and Child Welfare department files in New South Wales and they too prevented me from using any material that identified any individual, which severely reduced the usefulness of the files.

At the end of the day, much of the material I used was gathered without the requisite authority. What the documents in those files helped to uncover was that the British and Australian authorities had known for years of the many serious flaws and failures of the

Fairbridge scheme, and of the maltreatment of the children it had charge of. They revealed that the governments in Australia and Britain failed to act, even though each was aware that the welfare of these children was severely compromised. They revealed that Fairbridge ignored this fact and consistently refused to introduce reforms.

Most importantly, the files confirmed much that was contained in the children's accounts. In 2005, when I began researching and then writing *The Forgotten Children*, the five very powerful institutions responsible for child migration to Fairbridge – the British government, the Australian government, the state government of New South Wales, the New South Wales Fairbridge Foundation and the UK Fairbridge Society – all denied any abuse of children had occurred, much less took responsibility for it. Sixteen years have elapsed since then, and attitudes to those who have suffered abuses of power have transformed in that time. But back in 2005, my biggest fear was that the former migrant children's accounts would be doubted. So the fact that the files confirmed so much of what I had heard in testimony was critical to me.

Little did I realise what else would come from writing the book.

Rather than being the end of a story, *The Forgotten Children* was the start of a series of events that would snowball over the following decade and a half. After its publication more people came forward stating that similar things had happened to them. In 2008 a number of former Fairbridgians and I embarked on a marathon legal case of eight years, which resulted in a record compensation payout from the Australian government, the New South Wales state government and the New South Wales Fairbridge Foundation. In 2009 we produced our documentary, and Prime Minister Kevin Rudd made an apology in the Parliament to children who had been institutionalised, including child migrants. In 2010 the British Prime Minister Gordon Brown apologised to British child migrants in the House of Commons. In 2013 Prime Minister Julia Gillard announced the Royal Commission into Institutional Responses to Child Sexual Abuse, which would include child migrants. In 2014 British Prime Minister Theresa May established the Independent Inquiry into Child Sexual Abuse, which encompassed a specific investigation into child migration. In 2018 the British government and the UK Fairbridge Society (via the Prince's Trust) agreed to financially compensate all surviving British child migrants.

After a long journey, all of the key institutions have acknowledged the widespread abuse of the child migrants, have accepted their responsibility for it, apologised to the victims of the abuse, and agreed to pay financial compensation.

This book is a companion to *The Forgotten Children*. It begins by recapping the Fairbridge child migrant story, then traces the reckoning in the years after. At the end of what has been a torrid experience for me and many of the other Fairbridge kids, I think a lot of good has come of our travails. We may not be able to change the past or undo the great wrongs, but the survivors are now believed and I think there has been a major advance in public awareness so that we are less likely to see anything like this happen again. On a personal note, it has been for me a very challenging journey – but at the same time an enriching experience and probably the most important thing I've ever done.

1

BOUND FOR BOTANY BAY

It was just magnificent . . . all the mahogany pillars and painting and high-backed chairs and the plush carpet and the white silver service tablecloths. Magnificent.

In April 1959, when I was twelve years old, I became a child migrant. With two of my brothers I sailed from England to Australia, to the Fairbridge Farm School outside the small country town of Molong, 300 kilometres west of Sydney. My mum, who later followed us to Australia, sent us because she believed we would be given an education and better opportunities in Australia than she could provide as a struggling single parent in England.

We sailed from Tilbury on the mouth of the River Thames on the S.S. *Strathaird* of the P&O line. The *Strathaird* was a grand old ocean liner built in 1932. After being used as a troopship in the Second World War, it had been beautifully restored to its original splendour and while it had been converted from a three-class ship to a one-class ship for the carriage of migrants to Australia, many of its first-class features, including the food it served, remained. None of us kids from poor backgrounds had ever been near the luxury we were to experience on the *Strathaird*.

My brothers and I were part of nearly one thousand children sent to Molong's farm school. We were like most other Fairbridge kids in that we came from a deprived background. Our mother, Kathleen Bow, was born during the First World War into a modest, working-class family in Broxburn, about 24 kilometres from Edinburgh, in Scotland. Her father went to war in 1914 and was gassed in the trenches of France before being pensioned out of the army. Her mother worked as a nurse in Bangor Hospital, to which the wounded were brought, usually from a hospital ship that berthed on Scotland's Forth River. It was said that so many of the men were terribly wounded that they were brought from the ships to the hospital at night so as not to panic the civilian population.

Mum was illegitimate and when her mother moved to Glasgow to marry a badly wounded soldier she had nursed – her second marriage – Mum was left to be brought up by her grandmother. Mum used to say that she thought her gran was actually her mother, and she only learned the truth after Granma McNally died when Mum was about fourteen years old.

With nowhere else to go, Mum went to work in the big houses in Hampshire and Surrey in the south of England, living very much 'below stairs' as a domestic servant. Within a couple years she had married local builder Bill Hill and in 1937 gave birth to Tony, who was to be the first of five sons. In 1940 Billy was born but died of meningitis a month later. My brother Dudley was born in 1944.

By the time Mum was pregnant with me and my twin brother Richard, she was separated from her husband and had been abandoned by a new partner. At that stage, she was working in a big house in Herefordshire, but as her pregnancy developed it became clear she would have to leave. She was taken in by a vicar in Eastbourne, Sussex, and lived in the basement of the vicarage until Richard and I were born, in 1946.

Then, being a single mother or a divorcee still carried a stigma. Throughout our childhood we were instructed to tell people that Mum was a widow, even though we, along with most in our village, knew it didn't ring true.

For the first six or seven years of my life we survived on charity handouts, welfare and the small income my mum generated whenever she had the chance to work while caring for four children. We lived in three rooms on the second level of a small terrace house in Dursley Road, Eastbourne. It was a very poor and rough neighbourhood with a sullied reputation. The local council, in an effort to tidy up the street's image, changed the name to Dennis Road shortly after we moved there.

The three-room flat had a coal-fired stove, which was used for cooking and heating. There was no bath but in the kitchen was a large stone sink, which for all our early childhood doubled as a bath for Dudley, Richard and me. As long as we were small enough we would sit on the draining board with our feet in the water and wash as best we could. On Saturday night Mum and Tony would bring a tin bath from out the back of the house, lug it up the stairs, heat water on the stove and take a bath in the tiny living room. We didn't have a toilet so we paraded down the stairs and through Mrs Symes' flat on the ground floor below, carrying our potties through her living area and kitchen to the toilet out the back.

In those early postwar years everything was in short supply – and we were still issued with ration books because rationing in Britain did not finally end till the limits on meat and bacon were lifted in July 1954, when I was eight years old.

Everyone in our neighbourhood was poor. It was a common occurrence just before payday for a child to go to a neighbour's house with an empty cup to borrow half a cup of sugar, flour or milk. Seldom did you ask for a whole cup for fear the neighbour wouldn't have enough – or you wouldn't be able to pay it all back. Shearer's, the little grocery store on the corner, would run up a slate for each family so they could buy food on credit between paydays, but on more than one occasion they had to halt our credit because Mum was continuing to run up a tab though she was unable to pay anything off.

From a very early age we learned how to get ourselves to school and look after ourselves in the afternoons, because Mum took any work she could get, whenever she could. From the age of about ten, our older brother Tony got a job at weekends and after school at the local fishmongers. He would come home smelling of fish but often brought back scraps they couldn't sell in the shop. Remarkably, while I still vividly remember the grinding poverty and privation of my early childhood, I don't recall ever experiencing serious hunger: Mum somehow always managed to put food on the table, even if it was only bread and dripping.

When she was sick or there was some crisis, we would be put into local children's homes, but we'd always come back together as a family as soon as things stabilised. As we got older, however, it became increasingly difficult for the five of us to live in three tiny rooms that had no toilet or bathroom. And so, when we were six years old, Richard and I were put into the Dr Barnardo's home in Barkingside in Essex. It was huge, with more than a thousand children in cottages each housing up to twenty children. Richard and I were deeply traumatised because we were told we'd be there permanently. It was a tough experience. I can remember being teased and bullied by the bigger children when we tried to write a letter to our mum – it seemed most of them didn't have anyone to write to. I also recall the awful food they forced us to eat.

After some months we were relieved to be reunited with Mum and our brothers, and in a bigger home. We had been allocated a five-room flat in a big dilapidated old Victorian terrace house in Eastbourne that had been converted into a number of smaller welfare apartments by the local council. I can still remember the day Mum came to get us back from Barnardo's, her excitement on the train trip to Eastbourne, and our arrival in the early evening to see Tony and Dudley cooking up a pan of bacon and eggs for our tea.

When I was about eight we moved into a new place on a housing estate outside Eastbourne. The village of Langney had been built on land reclaimed by Eastbourne council from the estate of an old aristocratic land-owning family. At last we had a home with an indoor toilet and bathroom, as well as three bedrooms.

Our new circumstances were part of the marvel of Britain's postwar welfare state, initiated by the Labour government. It was much maligned in later years but this phenomenal social experiment meant that for the first time the state endeavoured to ensure all classes were assured of basic food, shelter and clothing, and some level of health care and education. Prior to this, the overwhelming majority of Britons lived and died poor, in a land of appalling class rigidity and social inequality, where there was little prospect of social mobility. It is still hard to imagine that up to the mid-twentieth century many people in Britain did not have a bank acccount and owned close to nothing – no home, no assets; most felt lucky to have a bit of furniture and clothing.

By now Tony had left school and was working and paying Mum a chunk of his wages, which helped a great deal. We were still very poor but most of our neighbours in Langney were only slightly better off. In those days you paid for electricity as you used it – by putting a shilling in the meter that was under the stairs. Often we went to bed early on Wednesday nights because the last shilling had gone or we had no more coal for the fireplace until payday the next day.

We finished our primary education in a school built as part of Langney village, then went to the new local secondary school on the estate. It was named Bishop Bell School after the cleric George Bell. Bishop Bell became well known for publicly criticising the British government's bombing of civilian targets in Germany during the Second World War. However, the school was renamed St Catherine's in 2016 after the church admitted Bishop Bell had sexually abused a young girl when she was between five and nine years old.

Being on the edge of Eastbourne, Langney was a pretty good place for kids. We lived in a semi-rural environment and spent lots of time playing in the fields or on the 'crumbles', a vast stretch of pebbled beach between Eastbourne and Langney, where the pill boxes and concrete tank blocks built in 1940 in anticipation of Hitler's invasion were still standing. Television had been in Britain for a few years but no one in Langney could afford to buy one till the late 1950s, so there remained a lot of community activity. It seemed everybody was in the Boy Scouts, Civil Defence Corps, the drama club or one of myriad other community groups. Throughout the year the village would turn out for special festive occasions, including the annual summer fete.

On Guy Fawkes Night we would all march in a torchlit procession around the village before lighting a huge bonfire in the park at the bottom of Priory Road and letting off fireworks.

By the time Dudley, Richard and I reached secondary school, Tony was in the Royal Air Force (RAF). Britain still had conscription in the 1950s and Tony, who as a boy had been a member of the Air Training Corps, decided to do his national service in the RAF, though he signed up for five years instead of the compulsory two. Conscripts were paid only a small allowance, but by signing up for a longer period Tony was able to earn more and also regularly send money home to help Mum. He spent most of the next five years in Germany, where he worked on the electrical maintenance of the British Canberra bombers.

As the rest of us boys were getting older, however, it was becoming increasingly obvious that Mum would not be able to afford to keep us at school beyond the minimum leaving age of fifteen. Some years before, a woman who lived out the back from us in Dursley Road, and was struggling on her own, had sent her three boys out to Australia with one of the child migrant schemes. We knew very little about Australia at the time, other than it was big, a very long way away and had a lot of sunshine, kangaroos and koala bears. This woman boasted that her sons had done well for themselves – the eldest had become a policeman, and where we came from that constituted considerable upward social mobility.

Several things were weighing on Mum's mind. Years later she said she was worried about military conscription: in the mid-1950s Britain was involved in the 'troubles' in Malaysia and the Suez Crisis, and one of the boys we knew had been killed while he was a national serviceman in Cyprus. Members of Mum's family had been seriously wounded in the First World War and others had fought in France and the Middle East in the Second World War, and she didn't want to see anything similar happen to us.

There was also at the time a recession in Britain and she was concerned we would not be able to find good jobs. My brothers and I were old enough to know our career options were limited. Living on a council estate, the prospect of going to university or working in a profession was for people from a different universe and out of the question for us. Most of the men in our village worked on the nearby Hampden Park industrial estate, drove trucks or worked as unskilled labourers. At the same time Australia wanted to expand its population and was promoting itself as the land of opportunity where all manner of jobs were plentiful.

Mum first heard about the Fairbridge child migration scheme from a woman she worked with, who showed her an advertisement in the local paper. By the late 1950s Fairbridge, which had been operating for nearly fifty years by then, was directly marketing in the media. The Fairbridge Farm School scheme was based on a simple proposition presented by Kingsley Fairbridge in a pamphlet published in 1908 titled 'Two Problems and One Solution'. The two problems were, first, how to open up the lands of the Empire's colonies 'with white stock'; and second, what to do with the large and growing problem of child poverty in Britain. The solution was to put them together. His vision was simple: for boys from the slums of British cities to become Australia's farmers, and girls to become farmers' wives.

After Mum made inquiries about Fairbridge, we were visited by a local representative and one from London. They were good salespeople. By the late 1950s Fairbridge had become a slick organisation with almost seventy 'honorary secretaries' spread throughout the UK recruiting more children. For a poor family like ours, the offer of free transport out to Australia, then free accommodation and education once we got there, sounded almost too good to be true. The ladies told us wonderful stories about Australia: we would be going to a land of milk and honey, where we could ride horses to school and pluck abundant fruit from the trees growing by the side of the road. They told my mum that however much she loved us she couldn't provide us with the opportunities we would be given at the farm school in Australia.

They told us we qualified for Fairbridge.

The deal clincher came when they told us of their new 'One Parent Scheme', whereby a single parent could follow their children out to Australia later, to start preparing a home for when they were old enough to leave Fairbridge and get a job.

For the previous fifty years Fairbridge had sought to permanently separate children from their parents. The organisation felt it had rescued children from failed or irresponsible parents, so it did not want these children reuniting with their families. Children were sent to Fairbridge on condition that their parents (or custodians) signed over guardianship to the Australian government, who effectively delegated responsibility for the children to Fairbridge till they were twenty-one years old. But many parents did not really understand what was involved when they signed, and those who did want to be reunited found it practically impossible to get their children back.

What my family did not know at the time was that Fairbridge had introduced the One Parent Scheme out of necessity because the number of children available for migration to Australia was declining. We were also unaware that by the 1950s there was increasing opposition to child migration from sections of government and among child-welfare professionals, so it had been necessary to offer the option of family reunion in order to bolster the number of recruits.

We were almost the perfect catch for Fairbridge: three healthy boys, all above-average intelligence, from a deprived background. We were, however, a bit older than the ideal age, as Fairbridge preferred children no older than eight or nine. The stated thinking was that there was a better chance of turning younger children into good citizens because they would have had less exposure to low-class society.

I recall that at the time we talked a lot about this idea of emigrating and all of us thought it a good one. After us agreeing to go, arrangements were quickly made and within a few weeks my mother took my brothers and me on our first trip to London by train, for medical checks and filling in forms.

I still remember that first trip to London and going to Australia House on the Strand, which at the time was the biggest building we had ever been in. We were also excited because Mum had promised to show us some of the famous London landmarks, but we spent so much time being processed at Australia House that by late afternoon we had to go straight to the station to catch the train home to Eastbourne.

Several weeks later we were due to go on our way.

When the time came for us to say goodbye to all our friends and neighbours in Langney village, it was very sad farewelling people I was close to – my school friends and neighbours – knowing I would probably never see them again. We had already said goodbye to Tony a few weeks before when he was home on RAF leave from Germany. It was agreed that after he was demobbed a couple of years later, he would follow us out to Australia. However, that never happened and it would be fifteen years before we reconnected. In the decades after that, I'd catch up with Tony when I was in the UK or when he and his wife, Gillian, visited us in Australia.

After saying goodbye to our village, Mum, Richard, Dudley and I got on the train and we were off to Knockholt in Kent. Fairbridge owned a house there, where children from all over the country would be brought and put in groups before sailing to Australia.

We were naturally anxious about our journey into the unknown, but as young boys I remember we were also excited about embarking on an adventure and sailing to the other side of the world. Mum was filled with sadness when she left us that night to go back home. She would remain unsettled until our little family was back together three years later.

We were all amazed at the magnificent country home in Kent – never had we experienced such grandness and luxury. We were told that Fairbridge had bought the house with money donated by a woman whose son had disappeared after being parachuted into German-occupied France in the Second World War with the British Secret Service. It was presumed he had been captured and executed. His mother had wanted the house named in his memory, so it was called John Howard Mitchell House.

It was an imposing two-storey mansion, with an attic and cellars, gardener's lodge, squash court and stables. There seemed to be countless rooms, including a large library, banquet room, billiard room and bathrooms upstairs and downstairs. Outside, there were orchards and vegetable gardens and rolling green fields that seemed to go on forever.

There was a matron and her assistant, a cook, a gardener and a cleaner who came every day. Between them, they catered for our every need. They cooked our meals, ran our baths, bathed the smaller children, laundered, ironed and laid out our clean clothes, and made our beds.

We spent more than three weeks at Knockholt in beautiful spring weather. We played all day, as we were neither sent to school nor assigned any work.

Ian 'Smiley' Bayliff was at Knockholt four years earlier than I was, in 1955, an eight-year-old with his three brothers, and remembers it as the best time of his life:

> I remember it very, very well. Lovely place, something out of a book. The food was absolutely beautiful, you know. We'd come from a very poor family; we were just as poor as church mice . . . so coming down to Knockholt . . . there was three meals a day, breakfast, lunch and tea, there was afternoon tea, there was room to move – almost had your own bathroom there were so many bathrooms in the place. It was warm; you always had plenty of clothes . . . we were there for two months and really loved it.

Dudley, Richard and I were joined by nine other children. At fifteen, Paddy O'Brien was the oldest in our party. His sister, Mary, was thirteen and their sister, Myrtle, was eleven. Billy King from Cornwall and John Ponting from west London were about my age. Beryl Daglish and Frances Radcliff were ten, as was Wendy Harris, who travelled with her six-year-old brother, Paul.

Once our party was assembled, we were taken up to London for the day to be outfitted with a new wardrobe of clothes. Coming from poor backgrounds, most of us would occasionally have been given something new to wear but much of our clothing was hand-me-downs. In London we were each given completely new summer and winter wardrobes. The girls' kit included a raincoat, a 'pixi' hood, a linen hat ('for journey'), two gingham frocks (one 'good enough for best dress'), a coat, one tunic, a pair of grey flannel shorts, a woollen jumper, a woollen cardigan ('colours should blend with each other and with skirt'), a skirt with bodice, two aertex blouses, two pairs of lightweight knickers, two woven knickers, two lightweight vests, a pair each of best shoes, sandals and plimsolls, a pair of best socks, a pair of fawn socks, three pairs of pyjamas, a bathing costume, face flannel, sponge bag, brush, comb, toothbrush and paste, and a Bible.

The boys' kit included a raincoat, a woollen coat, khaki, flannel, corduroy and sports shorts, two khaki shirts, a white shirt, tie, belt, black shoes, three pairs of socks, three summer singlets, a winter singlet, three pairs of pyjamas, a dress jumper, a play jersey, a pair each of sandals and plimsolls, a pair of bathing trunks, a drill sun hat, brush, comb, toothbrush and paste, face flannel, sponge bag and a bible. Interestingly, the standard boys' kit did not include underpants.

This otherwise wonderful outfit, which was provided for us by the Fairbridge Society, had been a feature of the scheme since the 1930s. Len Cowne remembers being similarly outfitted in London in 1937, as a ten-year-old, before sailing to Australia in the first party of boys to Molong in early 1938. 'I was kitted out by the society with an enormous fibreboard suitcase,' he said. 'I had never seen so many new clothes at one time in my short life.'

On the last Sunday before we left Knockholt, Mum came to spend the day with us. Fairbridge had a firm policy not to have the parents wave off the ships setting sail. That Sunday was one of the saddest I can ever remember. We went to the larger town of Sevenoaks, where we sat in a Lyons tea house drinking tea and eating cakes, before going to a local cinema to watch a movie. We hardly exchanged any words and I remember walking slowly in the rain up the road to John Howard Mitchell House as it was getting dark, to say goodbye amid uncertainty as to when we would see each other again. I think it was on that bleak Sunday evening that the enormity of what we were doing hit home to me. We were going to the other side of the world, without Mum, and had no idea when, if ever, we would come back.

A couple of days later the bus came and took us up to London and to the ship bound for Australia. We all tried to keep our spirits up and remain excited, but we were undeniably anxious. Many years later, Mary O'Brien says she still remembers that day, when she was twelve and was put on a bus to Tilbury Docks, through the Blackwall Tunnel and through parts of the East End of London where she had lived.

We arrived at Tilbury late on a wet and miserable April afternoon. We were overawed at the giant size of the S.S. *Strathaird* with its eight decks. It was to be our home for the next six weeks. There was no band playing, or streamers or cheering crowds, and no families to wave us goodbye. I felt any excitement in the adventure giving way to sadness as I began to grasp the significance of our leaving. During the evening one of our two adult escorts, a New Zealand nurse, came into our cabin with her guitar. While she had every intention of cheering us up, she made us all sadder when she sang 'Botany Bay' and the words: 'We're leaving old England forever.'

The S.S. *Strathaird* had been beautifully restored to its original splendour, which included oak-panelled walls, stained-glass windows, ornate ceilings, parquet floors, artworks and Persian rugs, and antique furniture. All previous P&O steamships had black hulls, but the *Strathaird* and her sister ships (the *Strathmore* and *Strathnaver*) were painted a striking white, with buff-coloured funnels.

At home the food we ate was very basic: most of the meat was minced, a big cooked meal was likely to be sausages and mash, and our evening meal might consist of a fried egg sandwich. All our furniture was second-hand. Our bedside tables were made out of upturned wooden orange boxes, our floor covering mostly offcuts of linoleum. Having spent the last three weeks in a grand country mansion in Kent and been taken to London to be outfitted with the finest wardrobes, we were to pass the next five-and-a-half weeks in luxurious surroundings being treated like royalty.

On board we were assigned two large former first-class state cabins, one for the five girls and six-year-old Paul Harris, and one for us remaining six boys. Both were fitted out with six bunks and each had an ensuite bathroom. The two escorts had their own two-berth cabin. We were lucky to have ended up on the P.O.S.H. side of the ship; in the days before air-conditioning you paid extra to travel on the port side going out and the starboard side home – Port Out, Starboard Home – thus avoiding the hot afternoon sun of the Red Sea and the Indian Ocean.

Not all the Fairbridge children recall having luxury cabins for the voyage. Lennie Magee joked that he found himself 'in a small four-berth cabin which was so deep down in the ships bowels I could see fish looking at me through the porthole'. However, most kids recount being exposed to unaccustomed finery on board.

Our second escort for the voyage was an Australian primary school teacher. The Fairbridge Society would have recruited her and the New Zealand nurse because they came from good families and had excellent references. Having completed their customary 'grand tour' of Europe, the two young women were given a paid trip home for being our carers on the journey to Australia.

After leaving Tilbury with somewhere near 400 British migrants, we headed across the North Sea to Cuxhaven in northern Germany, where we picked up about 600 German migrants also bound for Australia. Almost as a reminder of who won the war, the Germans were allocated the less inviting cabins on the lower decks because the British migrants had already been given most of the best sections of the ship.

From Cuxhaven we steamed back through the English Channel and south through the Bay of Biscay, with its famous huge waves and gale-force winds, which made most of the passengers seasick. I recall going to the front of the top deck with my brothers, and I could lean almost forty-five degrees into the headwind without falling over.

After a couple of days we passed into the relative calm of the Straits of Gibraltar in the early dawn, and entered the beautiful, sunny Mediterranean. Of course, we missed Mum. We were able to send a postcard, which was signed by the three of us and loaded on to the mail boat that came alongside us as we passed Gibraltar. Mum kept the postcard and it remains my only surviving memento of that wonderful voyage. Over the next week we enjoyed the Mediterranean, which years later would become one of my most loved places.

Ten-year-old Wendy Harris kept a diary of the voyage and recorded the day we approached Egypt and the Suez Canal.

The sea is quite calm and the boat is a bit rocky. For breakfast I had fish and mashed potato. It was lovely. I have been sun baking this morning. All today we will be passing land, we will be passing Egypt. This afternoon I played for two hours in the swimming pool. I can float with a rubber ring on but not without one on. The sea is very blue and you can see through it if you look very carefully. Just before tea I had some sausages and potato and some lovely ice cream. I am in bed now and I am going to sleep.

The *Strathaird* was a fabulous adventure and we spent days exploring all of its secrets: its eight decks, its lifeboats, games rooms, cinema, indoor and outdoor swimming pools, sundecks, library and reading rooms, writing room, smoking room, lounges and giant staircases. We had our own cabin steward who woke us each morning with an orange juice or a cup of tea and a biscuit, in bed! He did everything for us, including making our beds, and organising the washing and pressing of our clothes.

The ship's bell rang for breakfast, luncheon, tea and dinner – in that order, which caused initial confusion as we were accustomed to meals in the working-class order of breakfast, dinner and tea. Very proud waiters from Goa, dressed impeccably in stiffly starched uniform, served our meals in a splendid dining room. Our waiter told us that Goans had worked on P&O ships for over one hundred years and that for several generations his family had been in the service of the line. Before the *Strathaird* our only restaurant dining had been egg and chips in the café behind the Gaiety Cinema in Eastbourne, where Mum taught us how to hold a knife and fork when eating in company.

The breakfast menu on the ship included tea, coffee and cocoa, steamed peaches, kedgeree, eggs to order, grilled bacon, lamb's liver with brown gravy, snow potatoes, cereals, bread and butter, and toast, jam, golden syrup, honey and marmalade.

The lunch and dinner menus varied and had a strong French influence. An example of a lunch menu was potage Windsor, fried fillets of pamphlet tartar, hamburger steak and fried egg, Malay curry and rice, potatoes creamed or Berrichronne, marrow and Portugaise or cold sideboard of roulade of veal, ham loaf or ox tongue plus a salad of lettuce, tomato, potato and caper, followed by custard or Neapolitan cream ices and cheeses, including Danish blue, Wensleydale, Kraft and gruyère.

The dinner menu changed daily and was always printed with a pleasant still life on the front. We were served dishes such as cream Pompadour, fillets of plaice, romoulade, medallions of veal jardinière, roast quarter of lamb with mint sauce, potatoes roasted or Maître d'Hotel or from cold sideboard, roast beef or savoury brawn and salade Polonaise, followed by plum apple tart or coupe Alexandra.

Adults had a selection of French and German wines and children an unlimited supply of ice cream. We had never seen such a wide range of foods so beautifully presented and in such quantities. It is little wonder that on the voyage I put on a lot of weight. On arrival at Fairbridge the children immediately gave me the nickname of 'Fatty'. While I quickly lost the excess pounds, the nickname would stick and for many years many of the Fairbridge kids knew me as 'Faddy 'ill'.

Vince McMullen came out to Fairbridge a couple of years after me on another P&O liner, the S.S. *Orion*, and said the food and dining on the ship inspired him to later become a chef.

That first introduction to the dining room, it was just magnificent, it was like the opening scene of the [movie] *Titanic*. When they swing open those doors and there are all the mahogany pillars and paintings and high-backed chairs and the plush carpet and the white silver service tablecloths. Magnificent. And, of course, you had a choice, a menu I couldn't read, let alone pick a meal. It was all in French. Amazing.

On most afternoons we would sit in giant armchairs in the first-class lounge learning to play chess and being served by waiters who put ice and straws in our drinks, while a string quartet dressed in tails played Brahms, Beethoven and Tchaikovsky. It was the first time I'd had ice in a drink, seen a violin or heard live classical music. The quartet would play requests but we and most of the other British migrants had no knowledge of classical music, so it was the German passengers who did most of the requesting.

As we sailed south and the weather warmed, we began to spend more time in the swimming pool or playing deck sports with the young Germans, mainly single men who were going to Australia to work on the Snowy Mountains hydro-electric scheme or other construction projects. We made friends with a number of them and were initially surprised by how polite and friendly they were. We had been brought up in an environment where the memory and resentment of two bitterly fought wars in the past forty years was still strong. They were very patient with us and I recall them being puzzled at the idea of a group of British children being sent to the other side of the world without their parents.

There was a lot of socialising on the ship, with parties, concerts or dances practically every night. Much of what was on offer was too adult for us – but not too adult for our escorts, who were both single and in their twenties. As the voyage progressed we saw less and less of them. By the time we were approaching Australia our general cleanliness, hygiene and routine had deteriorated and the checks to see if we had washed or bathed regularly had diminished.

For us the voyage was a marvel. We were seeing the world: the Rock of Gibraltar, the Suez Canal, elephants in the main street of Colombo. It was all like something out of a picture book: giant palm trees, pyramids through our cabin portholes, the desert, and the Union Jack flying from the highest point at Aden to remind us of the great British Empire.

Our first port of call was Port Said in Egypt. We were not allowed ashore to wander around the city because it was, after all, only three years since the Suez Crisis and the British were not popular in Egypt. Wendy Harris wrote about our approach to Port Said in her dairy:

Today I feel very excited. The sea is very calm and very blue . . . this afternoon I played and watched the shore of Egypt. After tea I watched us draw up at the dock. There were lots of palm trees. Hundreds of little boats have been selling clothes and lots of other things. They throw ropes up to us and someone has to catch it and the passenger asks for something.

We were allowed on shore in both Aden and Colombo, which were great outposts of Empire. We were treated well by the resident senior P&O managers, who appeared to attract almost vice-regal status and were living in huge houses with scores of local servants. It was the first time any of us had ever eaten tropical fruit and most of us were sick eating too much coconut. Nine-year-old John Harris remembers stopping at Colombo several years before on his way to Fairbridge:

Then we got off in Sri Lanka, or Ceylon in those days, and they took us out in to the country and we all had elephant rides and we went through tea paddies and the rice paddies and watched the elephants move logs. It was fantastic.

When everyone was getting a little bored – as you do at the end of the long summer school holidays – finally we reached the Western Australian coast. The weather had cooled by the time we landed at Fremantle on a wet, wintry morning at the end of May. We knew it rained in Australia but this was not what we were expecting. In all the photos we had seen, the place was bathed in sunshine. We were taken on a tour of Perth and for a picnic in Kings Park. This also happened when we reached Adelaide and Melbourne, where local charities put on picnics for the kids destined for the 'orphanage'. Meanwhile at each port, Perth, Adelaide and Melbourne, a steady stream of adult migrants left the ship to start their new lives in Australia and we continued to the last port of call: Sydney.

We came through Sydney Heads in the early dawn on 4 June. Full of excitement, we rushed to the front of the top deck as we sailed under the Harbour Bridge – looking up we were convinced the funnel would not fit under it. We docked at Pyrmont's Pier Thirteen, where so many migrants and Fairbridge children had landed before us.

Waiting for us was a huge man we would soon learn to fear and respect. Mr Frederick Kynnersley Smithers Woods – 'the Boss' – was the principal of Fairbridge. As soon as he introduced himself, his lack of humour and his no-nonsense manner were evident.

We spent the morning being ordered through a variety of medical checks before being taken by ferry across to the north side of Sydney for a walk around Taronga Park Zoo. After a sandwich at the zoo we came back by ferry in the late afternoon to Circular Quay and were marched all the way through the city and up George Street to Central Station for the overnight steam train to Molong.

In what could not have been a bigger contrast with dinner on the *Strathaird*, we had an evening meal of baked beans on toast in the railway Refreshment Rooms, then boarded the second-class passenger compartment of the steam-hauled, unheated Forbes mail train for the 300-kilometre overnight journey across the Blue Mountains to Molong. I remember we were still dressed in the same clothes we'd arrived in and had enough room to stretch out along the bench seating, but it was bitterly cold and we found it difficult to sleep.

The harsh thud of reality hit us after a fitful night's sleep when we stepped into the cold pre-dawn darkness of a deserted Molong railway station. It was not yet six in the morning as we passed through the little waiting room and past the dying embers of last night's fire in the fireplace. The memory of the luxury of the *Strathaird* was quickly beginning to give way to anxiety and fear.

The temperature was close to freezing as we stood huddled together in front of the station at the bottom of the main street of this little country town. We could see across the road the Mason's Arms pub, which still had hitching rails for horses.

Most Fairbridge children have similar recollections. David Eva vividly remembers the day he arrived five years earlier as a ten-year-old from Cornwall:

We got on the train and it was so bloody cold. I can remember Woods giving us a blanket. There were kids sleeping in the luggage racks and on the floor and across the seats . . . we got to Molong and it was freezing . . . I just wondered what the hell I'd let myself in for.

I recall Woods being angry that there was no one at the station to pick us up and take us out to the farm and I overheard Dudley and Paddy O'Brien whispering together about how, already, we might plan our escape. Eventually Woods' wife, Ruth, arrived driving a canvas-covered truck and I was surprised at how rude Woods was to her about her late arrival.

After being ordered into the back of the truck to sit on wooden benches down each side, with our suitcases piled down the middle, we drove six kilometres with a cold wind blowing and the canvas flapping. The twelve of us said very little, just exchanging anxious glances. The levity was completely gone.

It was still dark when we arrived at Fairbridge Farm School. We got out of the truck and were ushered into the big kitchen at the back of the principal's house, where we were all given a welcome mug of hot cocoa served by three girls who we later learned were 'trainees' working as domestic servants for Woods and his family. Nobody spoke as we stood around in a circle wondering what was to happen next.

The first bell of the day had been rung and, unknown to us, out there in the darkness the village was beginning to stir as everyone started their assigned work. Then, one after another, a boy or a girl appeared at the back kitchen door to take one of our party to the cottage we had each been assigned.

The sight of these scruffy Fairbridge kids appearing on the back porch of the house was frightening. Despite it being cold, they were mostly barefoot, wore rough, old clothing, and had unkempt hair – awful haircuts that, we found out later, had been done by other Fairbridge children. We had been given no information about how we would be accommodated and only became aware that the girls and boys would live in separate cottages when Mary and Myrtle O'Brien were taken off to a girls' cottage and their brother, Paddy, to a boys' cottage. Saddest of all was when Wendy Harris was taken to a girls' cottage, leaving her six-year-old brother, Paul. Until now the two had been inseparable – even on the voyage little Paul had stayed in the girls' cabin so his sister could look after him. After being taken away to his boys' cottage he was crying and later went looking for his sister. When he eventually found her, Wendy's cottage mother ordered him away, not to return. Paul was deeply traumatised by Fairbridge and eventually committed suicide as a teenager.

Gradually, our little group of twelve was broken up, until only my brothers and I were left standing silently in the kitchen of the principal's house. Woods eventually came back into the kitchen, angry that no one from our assigned cottage, Canonbar, had come for us. The cottage mother was away on leave and the boys, left unsupervised, had ignored the first bell that signalled everyone to their work before breakfast.

Woods grabbed a huge cane and, sternly ordering us to follow him, strode down the hill, crossed the lawn in front of the village meal hall and on to Canonbar, which we couldn't properly see in the predawn light. He led us in through the back door of the dirty cottage, which clearly had not been cleaned for a while. The cottage was made of timber and very basic.

Woods left us standing in the 'locker' (dressing) room, where there was a lot of dirty clothing hanging out of shelves and lying all over the floor, while he went into the dormitory and closed the door. We stood frozen as we heard the yelps and screams as he went round the dormitory beating the boys in their beds. It was a serious offence to be in bed after the wake-up bell. One by one the boys scurried out of the dormitory and into the locker room, wearing ill-fitting and unmatched pyjamas, rubbing their eyes and the places Woods had hit them. He shouted at them to get under the shower, get dressed and get to work – then stormed off. While we stood in shock, none of the kids who had been beaten by Woods showed much concern about what had just happened and behaved as if the episode was quite normal.

These strange-looking children asked us our names but otherwise showed little interest in us. We were, after all, just more new kids, as they all had been at some stage. They told us we were lucky as brothers to be assigned to the same cottage and that it was only possible because three older boys had recently turned seventeen and left Fairbridge, freeing up three beds in the dormitory. A short time later the village bell rang again and we were told this was a signal for the children to finish their work, make their beds and prepare for breakfast.

Then another bell rang and we were told to go with the other boys across to Nuffield Hall, where the whole village had breakfast each day. There was no induction when a new party arrived at the school. You were simply expected to tag along to learn the routine and the rules. Outside Nuffield we saw the other children from the *Strathaird*. We stood out from the other 150 children because we were still wearing the jackets and trousers from our London wardrobe. Everyone else was in khaki, blue and grey shirts and shorts. Later, we were to be issued with the same clothing and we never again saw our English clothes. Those beautiful clothes all disappeared after coming out with us on the back of the truck that morning.

In Nuffield Hall each cottage had its own long wooden dining table. There were no tablecloths; instead, each table was covered with a strip of lino. All the plates and bowls and drinking mugs were made of steel. We sat on long wooden benches, seven or eight children down each side, ranging from the biggest at the top of the table to the smallest at the other end. After prayers and grace, one child from each cottage went into the adjoining village kitchens and brought out a big steel bowl of porridge, which was spooned into individual bowls from the end of the table. The porridge was followed by a mug of milk with some butter and honey and a piece of bread made by the 'trainee boys' in the bakery at the back of the hall.

We weren't sent to school that first day. I was instructed to work in the village vegetable gardens with a fifteen-year-old 'trainee' boy named Max. My first impression of the countryside surrounding us was how drab and unappealing it looked. It was still recovering from a drought, which had left the grass dry and brown – very different from the deep green of the English countryside. I spent most of that first day with Max shovelling chicken manure on to a horse-drawn cart at the poultry farm up behind the village and then brought it down to the vegetable garden below. Max was wiry and tough, like most Fairbridge kids, and was unimpressed with my work, making no allowance for the fact that I was only twelve and had never done a day's labouring before.

We had lunch back in Nuffield Hall and at the end of the day returned to Canonbar Cottage for a shower and our evening meal. In addition to me and my brothers, there were about a dozen other kids in Canonbar, ranging in age from five to sixteen. I remember feeling frightened, and very lonely, and missing my mum. I was also physically exhausted from my first full day of manual labour.

Billy King, who came with us on the *Strathaird*, also remembers his first days at the school: 'I felt terrible. I cried for a week. And I still wanted to go home. Even then, I wanted to go home. And then I realised, like when I was on that boat, how far I was away from home.'

Derek Moriarty has similar recollections. He had been in institutions in England since the age of three and has no memory of family life. But he still recalls being scared when he first arrived at Fairbridge as an eight-year-old with his brother, Paul, who was two years younger:

We eventually arrived at the village I think around five in the afternoon. It was just coming on sundown and apprehension started to creep up on me. He [Woods] stopped the truck and we were climbing out. That's when I started to get scared. And I mean really scared . . . and funnily enough I felt homesick from . . . the moment I put my foot on the ground. And I thought, why am I homesick? I didn't come from home, I've come from an orphanage.

Despite being tired, I didn't want to go to bed that first night. There was no way I could talk to either of my brothers because there was no privacy. Besides, I didn't know what to say.

Eventually, deeply sad, I went to the dormitory at the other end of the cottage and to the bed I had been allocated, the second along on the right, with strangers on either side. My brothers were across the other side of the room and somewhere up the other end.

Much as I tried not to, I sobbed myself to sleep – but I was as quiet as possible for fear one of the other children would hear me.

2

THE FAIRBRIDGE CHILD MIGRATION SCHEME

*The average London Street Arab and workhouse child can
be turned into an upright and productive citizen of our
overseas Empire.*

The Fairbridge Farm School scheme was roundly applauded during the seventy years it sent impoverished British children to its institutions around the world.

The scheme was the brainchild of Kingsley Fairbridge, who was born in South Africa in 1885, a member of the upper middle class of the Edwardian era and a 'child of the Empire'.[1] In 1897 Kingsley's father, Rhys Seymour Fairbridge, moved his family from the Cape to Umtari in Rhodesia, which is on the border of what are now Zimbabwe and Zambia, and built a new family home that he named Utopia. As he got older Kingsley Fairbridge was struck by what he believed was the unrealised potential of land in Rhodesia for want of white settlers to farm it. Later, in his autobiography, he noted that his dream of increasing white settlement was formed long before he travelled to England and became aware of the needs of destitute children there.

In 1908, when he was twenty-three years old and at Oxford University, the young Kingsley Fairbridge first published his views on child migration, in 'Two Problems and One Solution'. The following year he addressed the Oxford Colonial Club in a Chinese restaurant in the city, where he proposed schemes for the 'emigration of poor children', without their parents or families, to the colonies:

> I propose to establish a society in England for the furtherance of emigration from the ranks of young children, of the orphan and waif class, to the colonies. I propose, therefore, to take out children at the age of eight to ten, before they have acquired the vices of 'professional pauperism', and before their physique has become lowered by adverse conditions, and give them ten to twelve years thorough agricultural education at a school of agriculture.[2]

Fairbridge went on to explain to the Colonial Club that Britain should not continue to send to the colonies its upper classes, which it needed in Britain. Rather it should send out its poor children: 'The best emigrant farmers have been the aristocracy of the English yeoman, such as England can ill afford to lose . . . the colonies should take something England does not need . . . if both sides are to profit.'[3]

At the end of Fairbridge's talk, the Oxford Club passed a resolution 'declaring ourselves in support' of child migration.

Kingsley Fairbridge began searching for a British colony in which to build his farm school and first looked at Canada. However, in 1910 some of his Australian Oxford friends arranged for him to meet the premier of Western Australia, Frank Wilson, who was in London for the coronation of King George V. Western Australia is about twenty times the size of England and at the time had a population of only 270,000 people. Wilson offered Fairbridge 400 hectares of land at a peppercorn rent, plus £6 for each child towards assisted passage to Australia. With the help of his wife, Ruby, in 1912 Kingsley Fairbridge opened the first Child Emigration Society Farm School at Pinjarra, 80 kilometres south of Perth. Fairbridge spent the next few months preparing the school for the first party of thirteen boys, aged eight to thirteen, who arrived in January 1912.

Ruby Fairbridge would later write a book about Pinjarra and in it she described the arrival of the first party of children:

> They arrived about sundown – a more incongruous, desolate bunch of humanity it would be hard to imagine. They stood in the hot evening sunlight, in their dusty thick nailed boots, cheap woollen stockings, cheap smelly suits with trousers half-mast to allow growing, with tweed caps, each boy clutching an evil-looking overcoat and a dirty white canvas kitbag. There was practically nothing suitable to wear in that climate, and everything was dirty, having been worn indiscriminately on the ship.[4]

In designing what was to be the first of many child migrant schemes to Australia and other British colonies, Kingsley Fairbridge recognised two necessary requirements for the success of the scheme. The first was that the training of the children should be entrusted 'only to men and women truly and fully able to undertake it'. Second, he noted the need for capital if children were to be able to ultimately buy and work their own farms.

In the early days of Pinjarra, Fairbridge laid out a strict routine for the school called 'Orders of the Week'. The older boys, who were called 'trainees', were taken out of full-time education at the minimum age and would be up earliest to work at the dairy and on other parts of the farm. The rest of the children would be assigned household and assorted other work around the farm and village before and after breakfast. Schooling for them followed, and then more work at the farm and in the village before the evening meal, and finally bed. Almost every waking hour at the Fairbridge farms in Australia, Canada and Rhodesia would be governed by a similar strict routine for the next seventy years.

Fairbridge, Pinjarra did not get off to an altogether good start. Only six months after the arrival of the first party of boys, Mr A. O. Neville, registrar of the Western Australian Colonial Secretary's department, said the idea behind the scheme was good but conditions at the school were substandard:

On the whole the arrangements are very primitive and some of the premises would doubtless be condemned were it a Government institution. As a training farm first . . . the place is quite unsuitable . . . it is quite certain that there is no room for any more boys until additional buildings have been erected, the premises, in my opinion, being already overcrowded.[5]

Notwithstanding the complaints, the scheme continued, with strong support in high places in England. Children kept coming, until the scheme was interrupted by the First World War. After the war there was limited interest in child migration, leading Fairbridge's friend Lady Talbot to write, 'All over England is against emigration for anyone – except perhaps tired soldiers who want a change.'[6]

Kingsley Fairbridge reinvigorated support for his scheme, however, first with a letter-writing campaign and then by returning to England in September 1919 to meet with influential supporters. He talked to MPs, met Prime Minister Lloyd George, addressed financial supporters and secured the commitment of the British government's Overseas Settlement Board.

Fairbridge was politically conservative and unsuccessfully contested the seat of Murrray-Wellington as the Country Party candidate in the 1917 Western Australian state elections. In 1919 he wrote to his good friend and supporter British Tory MP Leo Amery to say that child migration would discourage the spread of communism, which had recently become a threat to Empire following the revolution in Russia.

> These children under poor environment and their class in England are just the recruits that aren't into Bolshevism and destitution . . . the average London street Arab and workhouse child can be turned into an upright and productive citizen of our overseas Empire.[7]

In 1920 Kingsley Fairbridge returned to Australia and bought a farm on the north side of Pinjarra that was twice the size of the original one. In 1921 three new parties arrived, including girls for the first time. The new school was officially opened by the governor of Western Australia Sir Francis Newdegate in April 1923, and the new children's cottages bore the names of heroes of the British Empire: Nelson, Livingstone, Clive, Rhodes, Wolfe and Haig. Fairbridge remained first and foremost committed to the British Empire. He named his first son Rhodes, having been in awe of the colonist Cecil Rhodes when he had met him as a boy in Rhodesia.

In 1922, Pinjarra received more criticism – this time from a Miss Williams Freeman, a former matron at the farm, who alleged maltreatment of the children and 'other apparent inefficiencies'.[8] Kingsley Fairbridge sailed for London, where he successfully addressed his critics and secured more government and private funds. But he returned to Australia ill and exhausted. He struggled on for another eighteen months, and then died in Perth Hospital of a lymphatic tumour on 24 July 1924. He was only thirty-nine years old. After his death the Child Emigration Society increasingly referred to itself as the Kingsley Fairbridge School, eventually becoming the Fairbridge Society.

Throughout the 1920s and into the 1930s the Fairbridge model was regarded as a highly successful emigration scheme and was increasingly embraced by the British establishment. Fairbridge and child migration attracted further interest during the Depression. Its many upper-class supporters saw the scheme as a vehicle for rescuing destitute children and providing them with greater employment opportunities than existed in Britain.

In the 1930s the Fairbridge Society began to seriously plan for the expansion of the farm schools to other British colonies and dominions. In 1934, the Prince of Wales, who would later become King Edward VIII before abdicating the British throne, started the ball rolling. At the launch of an appeal in London to raise £100,000, he committed £1000 of his own money and echoed the words of Kingsley Fairbridge when he said, 'This is not charity. It is an imperial investment.' *The Times* reported that His Royal Highness described Fairbridge as the only 'completely successful form of migration at this time', which would give orphans and poor

British children the chance of happiness and successful careers, contribute to solving unemployment and provide a steady flow of good citizens to the colonies and the dominions.

The fundraising campaign was supported by a four-page lift-out in *The Times* on 21 June 1934 with the headline 'FARM SCHOOLS FOR THE EMPIRE'. On the front page of the supplement was a large photograph of His Royal Highness, and a picture of a Coutts bank cheque written out to the Child Emigration Society for £1000 and simply signed 'Edward'. The inside pages showed children at Pinjarra at work, school and play, with a photo of a cottage and a caption that read 'Homely scene at Haig Cottage'. Another snap of two boys working in a field had the caption 'Where labour is a delight', while another was of a boy in bare feet chopping up a felled tree, which read 'In training for the clearing of his own block of land'. On the back page, for contrast, was a photo of a large group of children crowded onto the back stairs of an old house in Britain, with the caption 'Slum warrens'. Below was a list of patrons of the appeal, including a selection of marquises, earls, countesses, ladies and lords, knights of the realm, and the famous actress Dame Sybil Thorndike.

The next Fairbridge institution to open was on Vancouver Island in Canada, in 1936, which was designed to eventually accommodate 250 children. Back in Australia a child migrant centre that was closely connected to Fairbridge was opened the following year in Bacchus Marsh outside Melbourne. The scheme was funded by the Northcote Trust, with the help of generous donations from local pastoralists. The late Lady Northcote was the wife of Lord Northcote, the governor-general of Australia from 1904 to 1908, and had left substantial money in her will to make the opening of the home possible.

During the Second World War and the cessation of migrant shipping to Australia, the number of children at Northcote dwindled and in 1944 the school was closed and the remaining children were moved to the Fairbridge farm that had opened in Molong, New South Wales, in 1938.

The farm school opened in Rhodesia was to be different from the others. In 1936 Reverend A. G. B. West of the Fairbridge Society travelled extensively through Rhodesia, meeting its prime minister Godfrey Huggins and others, before recommending the building of a farm school capable of accommodating 250 children. However, the society in London was concerned that British children from poor backgrounds would not be suitable for farming in Rhodesia, where this kind of unskilled work was usually undertaken by poorly paid African men. At the same time, it was felt that working-class British children would prove incapable of filling the leadership roles expected of white Rhodesians.

Consequently, the Fairbridge Farm School in Rhodesia was to recruit from a better class of family than the rest of us, and train its children for white-collar and leadership roles, with their families contributing financially to their upbringing. Those sent to Rhodesia were generally older – between ten and fifteen.

The start of the Rhodesian scheme was announced by the Rhodesian High Commission in London in August 1939 but then the Second World War broke out. It was relaunched in May 1945 and the first party of children arrived at the new school in Bulawayo in 1946.

In Australia a group of former Rhodes Scholars, some of whom had known Kingsley Fairbridge at Oxford, became enthusiastic about opening more Fairbridge schools in Australia. The suggestion to build one in each of the Australian states was promoted at a biennial conference of Rhodes Scholars in Melbourne in January 1935, and was enthusiastically supported by Fairbridge's widow, Ruby, who spoke at the conference.

About six months later, the New South Wales Rhodes Fellowship met in Sydney and began raising money to build a farm school in New South Wales. They had the support of Scottish-born Andrew Reid, who donated substantial funds for the building of the school. On 30 July 1936 the first meeting of the provisional committee of the Fairbridge Council was convened at the University Club in Phillip Street, Sydney, and it sent a telegram to the Fairbridge Society in London telling them of the intention to launch a scheme in New South Wales, and of the plans of the executive 'to carry on enquiries for the land and the farm'.

Initially, the Fairbridge Society was unenthusiastic about the New South Wales initiative. They were happy to leave New South Wales to Dr Barnardo's, who in the 1920s had opened a farm school near Picton, outside Sydney. At the time London was looking at Queensland, where there was considerable interest from the upper echelons of the state government, as well as in New Zealand.

There were to be ongoing tensions between the Fairbridge Council in Sydney and the Fairbridge Society in London regarding their respective powers and responsibilities. The council in Sydney was to organise much of the funding to start the school but would need ongoing financial support from London to cover its operating costs. London would be responsible for ensuring the continued support of the British government and the recruitment of British children. London would also retain the power to hire and fire the schools' principals.

For many years both organisations vied with the other for power and responsibilities. But more than half a century later, in 2018, when a UK independent inquiry was investigating the widespread sexual and other abuse at Fairbridge, both would argue that the other had primary responsibility for the running of the school.

The building and opening of the Fairbridge Farm School in New South Wales happened very quickly: it took little more than a year between the acquisition of land and the arrival by ship of the first party of children. On 8 February 1937 the society bought Narragoon, a 650-hectare farm six kilometres east of Molong. At the time there was only one timber house on the property, which was to become the farm supervisor's house.

On 24 February a public subscription campaign was launched in the *Sydney Morning Herald* and the target of £50,000 was quickly reached and passed. Among the promotional publicity was the claim that the Fairbridge children were a 'burden and menace to society that could be converted to valuable assets in Australia'. By the end of the year a windmill, water pipes and water tanks had been installed on the new farm site and the first of the children's cottages completed. The cottage was initially used by Commander R. R. Beauchamp, the school's first principal, and his family until the big two-storey principal's house was completed a couple of months later.

By March 1938, the first party of twenty-eight boys had arrived on the S.S. *Orama* after a voyage of a little more than five weeks. When the boys arrived at Fairbridge, three children's cottages, named Brown, Green and Molong, and the principal's house, were completed. The boys were split between Brown and Green cottages. Molong Cottage was used for schooling, cooking and eating until the large hall with the village kitchens and a school were built over the next two years.

Len Cowne recalls the farm school he saw when he arrived in the first party. The design of the cottages was to remain the same for all of us who went to Fairbridge over the next thirty-five years.

When we, the first party arrived, the school consisted of the beginnings of a settlement which . . . became known as the 'village', and was to become the main domestic and communal area of the farm school.

Three very large wooden bungalows . . . had been completed . . . the cottages were to be the homes of the child migrants and were solidly built of timber standing on brick tiers for both ventilation and to discourage termites. [They] were roofed with heavy duty red corrugated asbestos sheets. Apart from the bathroom, which was open to the roof, all rooms had ceilings made of a sugar cane waste product called 'canex' that looked like compressed straw but was good insulating material.

Each cottage consisted of a large dormitory at one end separated from the matron's quarters at the other end by a locker room, a dining room . . . a bathroom, and a kitchen with a wood-fired black iron stove. There was no main drainage or main sewer, so domestic waste water went into soakaways via a grease trap, and sewerage went into large septic tanks.

Our beds were made of metal tubing, somewhat like the frame of a farm gate, with unsprung diamond wire mesh between; there being no pillows, one end of the frame being angled slightly upward instead. This took some getting used to, as did having to depend on oil lighting for several months until the electricity was connected . . . Having our meals cooked on a Victorian-style wood-fired range seemed, at least to me, like being transported back into the days of my grandfather's youth.

From the outset, few of the Molong child migrants were orphans — most came from destitute and broken homes where usually a single-parent mother was struggling to survive in those years before the welfare state. Fairbridge tended to recruit children through local charities and children's homes, and many were ignorant about how they got to Australia.

Henry McFarlane was eight years old and in the first party of children that sailed in 1938. He said he'd been 'institutionalised ever since I can remember'. He came from Berwick-upon-Tweed in Scotland and ended up in a children's home at the age of 'three or four'.

My mother was Scottish. Her name was Elizabeth Stuart McFarlane, and she was a young woman that had a baby out of wedlock . . . and she paid these people to look after me . . . but they weren't really acceptable, and I think the Scottish welfare, or whatever it is, stepped in and put me in a home.'

Henry remembers the children's home where 'they belted the hell out of little children for wetting the bed'. When he was six, he was moved to Middlemore Home, near Birmingham, where many other Fairbridge kids would be sourced over the next four decades.

All of a sudden I just heard that I'm going to Australia. I didn't know. I never had no choice or anything like that . . . I know my mother must have signed this form to say 'send him', you know, 'send him over'.

The official opening of the farm school at Molong took place six months after the arrival of the first party in November 1938 and was an opportunity for the Sydney Fairbridge Council to demonstrate the strength and breadth of its support. The *Sydney Morning Herald* reported that over 700 guests arrived to witness the opening by the governor-general of Australia, Lord Gowrie. During the ceremony his wife officially opened Green Cottage, which was renamed Lady Gowrie Cottage in her honour.

By the outbreak of the Second World War, a total of 124 children (96 boys and 28 girls) had arrived on six different ships. At the time ten children's cottages had been built (an eleventh was finished during the war), as was the village hospital, village school, schoolmaster's house, staff quarters, farm supervisors' houses and the deputy principal's house.

Margaret McLaughlin arrived in 1939 when she was five, with her brother, who was a year older. They first went to the North-cote child migrant school in Victoria, but were sent to Molong when Northcote merged with Fairbridge in 1944. Nearly seventy years later Margaret remembers becoming a child migrant because nobody wanted her and her brother. She says her mother was in Scotland while they lived with their father in the north of England, and both children were neglected:

I've [still] got the reports – they're in my cupboard up there – from when I left England to come to Australia from . . . we were just little urchins, my brother and I. No one wanted the McLaughlin kids. No one wanted to own, no one wanted to adopt them. So they might as well go to Australia. And I cry every time I look at them. That's very, very sad. Nobody wanted my brother and I. After reading these reports many years later, it really distresses me to think that we are all God's children, and it can happen to absolutely anyone. And it happened to hundreds – many a thousand children went through what I went through.

The last party of children to arrive at Fairbridge before child migration was halted due to the Second World War had to sail from England to Canada and then across the Pacific, via Honolulu and New Zealand, in order to avoid German attacks on shipping. Margaret Clarke was ten years old and sailed with her three sisters, Rosemary, aged thirteen and her twelve-year-old twin sisters Joy and June. She said her father had 'gone off with another woman' and a friend of the family arranged with her mother to have the children shipped to Australia by Fairbridge:

We were in a big convoy, very secret . . . I didn't see my mother or anyone before we left . . . [we] went right up north to escape all the submarines and went past ten icebergs when submarines came into the convoy and sank two merchant ships and damaged some others, but we weren't touched.

Six-year-old Peter Bennett and his nine-year-old sister, Marie, were also on the *Duchess of Richmond*, which sailed to Canada. Peter only learned later in life that he and his sister were illegitimate and that he was in children's homes from the time he was only days old. He said his mother was taken back into her family, 'but the family would not have the two illegitimate children back with her; because [her father] was an eminent surgeon and they were Catholics, so we ended up in homes'. After years in a home in Suffolk, and found to be 'neglected, undernourished and not looked after and kept well', they were sent to the Middlemore

Emigration Home in Birmingham before being dispatched to Fairbridge.

No more children would come to Australia until shipping was available again in 1947. In the meantime, the farms at Molong and Pinjarra and the Northcote home in Victoria shrank as children progressively left the schools when they reached seventeen years of age to take up paid work.

By the end of the 1940s a number of changes were occurring in child welfare in Britain that would make it more difficult for Fairbridge to attract children to its scheme. In 1946 the Curtis Report into child welfare became the foundation of the Children Act of 1948, which gave responsibility for child welfare to local government. Also, Britain placed greater emphasis on foster care rather than institutions. The child welfare professional was increasingly replacing the philanthropic amateur, and large impersonal institutions like Fairbridge were rapidly falling out of favour. So Fairbridge was forced to devise a new recruitment strategy – the One Parent Scheme – which it announced in late 1957.[9] And that is how my brothers and I went to Fairbridge.

When my mum first inquired about Fairbridge and we were visited in our small council house by the organisation's two 'honorary secretaries', they told Mum that however much she loved us, she couldn't provide us with the opportunities we would be given at the Fairbridge Farm School in Australia. They gave us brochures, one of which explained the new One Parent Scheme:

In Britain many thousands of children through circumstances and the bad environment in which they are forced to spend the formative years of their childhood are deprived of the opportunity of a happy, healthy and sound upbringing and are allowed to go to waste. We believe that a large number of these boys and girls (plus a parent where there is one) would have a greater chance in life if they were taken out of the wretched conditions in which they live, and given a new start in life in . . . our existing Fairbridge Farm Schools . . . Here they can exchange bad and cheerless homes in drab and murky surroundings of the back street . . . for a clean and well-kept home, good food and plenty of it, and fresh air, sunshine and a myriad of interests and beauties of the countryside . . . here they are given the love and care which many of them have never known.

Stretched single parents like Mum would have been totally unaware of the debate raging within the British government about the failures of the child migration policies and of a highly critical assessment of the schemes by the Home Office three years before we signed up.

Those of us who went to Fairbridge under the One Parent Scheme were far more fortunate than the majority of Fairbridge children who were already there. We tended to be older when we arrived – my twin brother and I were twelve and Dudley was fourteen. We would spend fewer than three years at Fairbridge before we rejoined Mum and got back together as a family. In contrast, the children who came out in the decades before us, who were typically only eight or nine – some were as young as four years old – would spend their entire childhood at Fairbridge, and most of them would never see their parents again.

3

LIFE ON FAIRBRIDGE FARM

*You couldn't have any shoes. And Molong was the coldest place
in the world. And I used to get these chilblains on my fingers and
they would bleed and my feet would bleed.*

On our first day at Fairbridge we were given one set of clothes
for work and for wearing in the village and another for
school. We also wore our school clothes to church on Sunday.
Each set of clothes was laundered on alternate weeks. The work
clothes were khaki, blue or grey shorts and a shirt, with a grey
pullover in winter. The school clothes were khaki or blue shorts
and shirt, with the same pullover and a pair of shoes and grey
socks. It was 'sissy' to wear socks pulled up, so they were rolled
down around the ankles, however cold it might be, and the boys
did not wear underwear until they were twelve years old. It was
not until secondary school that children regularly wore shoes.
At primary school and around the village everyone went about
barefoot.

Lennie Magee remembers his fine English wardrobe vanishing and being issued with rough Fairbridge clothing when he arrived:

[When we arrived] each of the boys was wearing a brand new pair of shorts and a blue shirt, a gold and brown tie, a blazer, long grey socks and black leather shoes. They were taken from us . . . and we were never to see them again . . . With few exceptions all of the clothes we were issued at Fairbridge were hand-me-downs. Someone had worn them to a frazzle before us. My first trousers were short, grey and hairy, with buttons, worn with a threadbare T-shirt and bare feet, except Sunday mornings when we wore shoes. Generously, we were given an extra blanket in winter and a pullover to wear, but it wasn't until I was twelve years old that I was given my first pair of underpants. Thankfully, they were new.

There were fifteen children's cottages in the village at Fairbridge, although not all of them were occupied. Ours was fairly typical. It housed three boy trainees who were fifteen or sixteen years of age. About six of us were of secondary school age and attending school, and six more were attending the primary school at the back of the village.

The fifteen barrack-style timber cottages in the village were all of a similar design. The dormitory at one end of the cottage had fifteen or sixteen small metal-framed beds with an unsprung wire mesh strung into the frame. The frame was bent up slightly at the end because there were no pillows. Each bed had a kapok mattress, two ex-army blankets and three in winter, and two calico sheets, one of which was laundered each week. There were no bedside tables and no bedroom furniture. There was only one small light-bulb, not that reading was allowed in bed. The bathroom had two showers and a bath, but we were never allowed to use the bath. There were two toilet cubicles with short 'saloon' doors, two sinks above which were our toothbrush rack with numbered holes so we knew which one was ours, and on the side a row of numbered pegs where we hung our towels. There was also a water-heating 'donkey' stove and a pair of laundry tubs in which we washed our woollen jumpers and socks.

I was amazed on my first night to discover the windows, which were on three sides of the dormitory, had to be kept open all year round. The reason, it seemed, was that Fairbridge had more beds squeezed into the dormitory than child welfare regulations permitted. John Ponting, who, as a twelve-year-old, arrived in Sydney on the same ship as me, recalls an encounter he witnessed between a child welfare inspector and Principal Woods:

> I was on 'boss's duties' one day when the child welfare came calling. I remember this joker measuring the dormitory in Gowrie Cottage; he then counted the beds and decided that it would never do to have that many beds in such a small space. Mr Woods asked what was the reason. The guy said it had to do with each child having x amount of space. Woods showed the guy the open windows on the three sides of the dormitory and this guy nearly had a heart attack when he was told that the windows were never closed.

The bathroom allowed little privacy, which was a more embarrassing issue for many of the girls, who had never undressed in front of other girls before but had to line up with no clothes on, waiting for their turn in one of the two showers in their cottage. The toilet rolls were rationed out to each cottage. Daphne Appleby recalls the consequences: 'I can remember we used to get four toilet rolls per month for fifteen children. Four toilet rolls! So we used to use any magazines or anything we had. It was quite horrific.'

The largest room after the dormitory was the dining room where the children ate their evening meal on a large table that had been cooked on a solid stove in the cottage kitchen.

In the 'locker room', each child was allowed four shelves and a small area of hanging space for clothes. Shoes and socks were not to be worn in the cottages and were stacked inside the back-door porch, but most kids went around the village barefoot anyway as until we were older we were actively discouraged from wearing shoes.

Each cottage had a cottage 'mother', who for some unexplained reason we were ordered to address as 'sister'. The cottage mother lived in a tiny two-room apartment at the end of the children's cottage, which consisted of a small bedroom, bathroom and a lounge room just large enough for a three-piece lounge suite but little else.

Those children who were lucky enough to have good cottage mothers are likely to remember their time at the school far more positively than those who suffered the more brutal or simply negligent type. Unfortunately, most Fairbridgians remember that from the very beginning they received little love and care from their cottage mothers. Henry McFarlane, who was an eight-year-old when he arrived in the first group of boys in March 1938, recalls: 'There was no love, nobody if you felt a bit down . . . came around and put [their arm] around [you] and said, "Come on – we're here for you."'

Most of the cottage mothers were single. However, in Canonbar Cottage we had a German cottage mother named Ilse Boelter, who had come to Fairbridge with her husband Kurt and their six-year-old daughter, Ulrica. Kurt was a university graduate in agriculture and was the Fairbridge vegetable garden supervisor. His wife was a graduate in literature, including English, and we were all amazed at her grasp of English grammar when we were studying it in school.

I thought Mr Boelter was terrific. I remember when I worked in the vegetable gardens he showed us the dozens of shrapnel scars he had, which were the legacy of fighting on the Russian front in the Second World War. We had been brought up on tales of how Britain beat Germany, and had hardly ever heard of the far more significant Russian front. I was captivated by his stories; he had been a captain and a tank commander until his tank had been blown up by the Russians. He had been left to die as one of the hopeless cases until one of the German doctors decided to try to save him. After he recovered, he served out the war in the Italian campaign. He was convinced he would not have survived had he stayed on the Russian front, where the German losses were huge.

He was stern but never violent and while many of the staff at Fairbridge hit the children, Kurt and his wife were cultured and dignified. He rolled his own cigarettes, like a lot of people in those days, and told us how dangerous and addictive it was. Of course, we wouldn't listen.

The most important person at Fairbridge, the man who ruled over every part of our lives, was the principal, and the most prominent of all the principals was 'The Boss', Frederick Kynnersley Smithers Woods. He was at Fairbridge from 1939 until 1966 – most of that time as the principal – and is the single most dominant figure in the Fairbridge story.

Woods was the third principal, following the short periods of Richard 'Dickie' Beauchamp, who was sacked in 1940 after two years, and Edward Heath, who left three years later to take up a wartime job with the Red Cross. Woods was a great bear of a man with extraordinary physical strength: he stood over six feet four inches (193 centimetres) and weighed more than twenty stone (127 kilograms). He had started work at Fairbridge in 1939 as assistant to the principal, having escorted the fifth party of children from England to Molong with his wife, Ruth, on the S.S. *Strathnaver* in August 1939. I remember him as a person capable of insensitive and even brutal acts, yet on other occasions one who displayed remarkable tenderness. He was a larger-than-life character, respected and feared by all of us. Lennie Magee remembers Woods and Ruth:

He was a giant who loomed over us, filling out horizon in every way . . . he loved the outdoors and wore shorts from which protruded muscular legs of Mr Universe proportions. Behind his strong face and Roman nose was a keen and hungry intellect. There was a rocky concreteness about him. He was masculine, even boyish, except his lips. They had a slight hint of feminine softness. There was no doubt that to his own family he was probably the greatest guy in the world. From the day I arrived at the farm to the day I left I was petrified and almost speechless whenever I had to stand before him. His wife Ruth had first represented England in hockey and then went off to Africa as a missionary. She still looked and dressed like one. It was rumoured she was the daughter of the Archbishop of Canterbury. Although they were incredibly selfless and benevolent, to me they were both unap-proachable and their austerity frightened the life out of me.

Woods was accountable to two masters. The power to hire and fire the principal rested with the UK Fairbridge Society, but on a day-to-day basis he was answerable to the Fairbridge Council of New South

Wales. The chairman of the Sydney council was a regular visitor to Fairbridge but we only saw the whole council once a year when they all came to judge the annual cottage gardening competition.

Woods and his wife committed their lives to the Fairbridge scheme with almost missionary zeal. However, over the decades Woods increasingly became an anachronistic Edwardian disciplinarian and an overzealous agent of the British Empire at a time the Empire was already in decline. He upheld the values of a world that had already been largely swept away and in many respects embraced a vision that was already out of date even before the farm school at Molong opened.

Woods was born on 23 December 1906 at Bethlehem in Orange Free State in South Africa. Though his father had also been born in South Africa and his mother in Argentina, the family described themselves as British. In addition to sharing the same countries of birth, there were other striking similarities between Woods and Kingsley Fairbridge. Both had spent most of their boyhood on a farm, took rudimentary schooling and then received a Rhodes Scholarship to Oxford. Both were athletic, strong, outdoor types and married dedicated women who committed their lives to their husbands' mission. It is unlikely the two men ever met, though, as Woods was born twenty years after Fairbridge.

Woods was educated at home until the age of twelve before going to St Andrew's Diocesan School in Bloemfontein, where he was head prefect, school heavyweight boxing champion and a champion rifle shot and swimmer. He spent three years at Rhodes University College in Cape Province and was awarded a Rhodes Scholarship to Oxford in 1929. After leaving Oxford he moved to Nyasaland (now Malawi) to work as assistant aide-de-camp to Sir Hubert Winthrop Young, the governor.

In 1935 he applied for the Fairbridge job in Australia. The decision was no doubt influenced by his wife, Ruth, who had been working in southern Africa as a missionary. Many years later Ruth would tell some of the trainee girls that she saw her work at Fairbridge as a continuation of her missionary work.

Gwen Miller, who arrived at Fairbridge aged ten, did not like Woods much but felt differently about Ruth:

But I didn't mind Mrs Woods . . . I always got the feeling she liked me. She was the only one that ever told me that I was a good worker and thanked me for doing a heap of ironing for her.

Ruth Woods would be a huge source of strength to her husband over the next thirty years. When they arrived at the farm school, the Woods lived in the assistant principal's house at the back of the village, but they moved into the big two-storey principal's house when Woods became acting principal in 1942, when he was 36 years old.

Woods played a giant part in the lives of almost a thousand child migrants who passed through the farm school. He organised our days, hired and fired staff, rostered every child at work and play, set the rules and enforced the discipline, dispensed punishment and trained us in a range of summer and winter sports. He was the driver of the old Fairbridge bus, the leader of the Boy Scout troop and of the Wolf Cub pack. He ran the junior Farmers Club and operated the antiquated film projector on the odd occasion we saw a movie. He rarely took a holiday.

The village bell ruled our daily lives. It rang to wake us up and send us to work. It rang to tell everyone to return to their cottage, make their bed and go to the hall for breakfast. It rang to tell us when to go to school, to the village work muster after school, when to return for showers and the evening meal and night curfew. At the weekend it would ring for the village work muster on Saturday morning, the start of sport on weekend afternoons, for church on Sunday mornings and to signify the start times of any special events.

It wasn't actually a bell – it was a piece of steel railway line about a metre long that was suspended by a steel chain from a wooden crossbeam. One of the boys, usually a trainee working in the village kitchens, was assigned to ring the 'bell', by striking it with an iron bar. Most of us liked to ring it because you could make a sound that was heard for miles around. Fairbridge did own a proper big bronze bell, but it couldn't be beaten with an iron bar. For years it sat beside the piece of railway line before being put into the Fairbridge village chapel, which was not built until 1961.

At the wake-up bell at 6 a.m. we were all expected to have a quick shower, often in cold water, before going to work, when in winter it was still dark. Most of the younger children would work cleaning the cottages by washing and scrubbing the kitchen and bathrooms, and sweeping and polishing the wood floors, under the supervision of the cottage mother.

The older boys were usually assigned work outside, including going up to one of the two village woodpiles to chop wood. For a while I had this job. I'd join other boys on one of the two village woodpiles swinging our axes in the predawn light, racing to fill our wheelbarrows, often in bare feet, before the bell rang for us to return to our cottages, where we would strip and make our beds.

Like many others, I was surprised to find Fairbridge so cold when I arrived. We simply weren't prepared for Australian winters to be so bitter. Joyce Drury, who arrived at Fairbridge aged ten, describes her shock:

> I came in June to Molong – and I have never felt the cold as I did that first night . . . and getting up in the morning! There was frost, even though I came from England, it's a wetter kind of climate up in Lancashire in the north-west and I'd seen snow, but I hadn't seen frost on the ground, and that surprised me.

Suffering such temperatures was made worse by having to go about barefoot most of the time and not being allowed to put your hands in your pockets. David Eva, who arrived at Fairbridge as a ten-year-old, remembers his first morning: 'Of course I had no shoes on,' he said, 'and all these other bloody kids had no shoes on.'

Peter Bennett recalls how, aged only six, both his hands and feet bled:

> You couldn't have any shoes. And Molong was the coldest place in the world. And I used to get these chilblains on my fingers and they would bleed and my feet would bleed . . . and hands in pockets! Woods said to me, 'Hands out of your pockets, Bennett.' So he said, 'Come down to the machine,' so I had to take my pants off, and he sewed the pockets on the leather working machine he had down the end of the hall. So, I'm smart, I undid them. And I got caught again. So he sewed them up again and got an assistant to cut the pockets out and said to me, 'Now open them up.'

Laurie Reid remembers the effects of not wearing shoes for years:

The only time we were told to wear shoes was if you went to church or to secondary school. Now when I left the place it took years and years for me to get all that hard skin off the bottom of my feet. I could walk on bindies or anything and wouldn't even feel them.

Breakfast was the same every day. After prayers a child from each cottage would go into the kitchen and bring out a large bowl of porridge, which would be ladled into steel coupes for each boy or girl. The porridge was followed by a piece of bread and butter and honey and a steel mug of milk. In winter the milk was heated and flavoured with cocoa.

After breakfast each weekday morning the school-age children got ready to go to the local schools. The primary school was over the hill at the back of the village – a small four-roomed school-house built shortly after Fairbridge was opened. At lunchtime they would walk back to Nuffield Hall for a cooked lunch, then go back to school for the afternoon. As with breakfast, a child from each cottage went into the kitchen and brought out lunch on a metal tray, which the cottage mother served on to steel plates for each child at the table. The cottage tray had three sections: one for the meat, which was invariably mutton, one for potatoes, and one for other vegetables grown in the village gardens.

The secondary school children assembled at about a quarter to nine outside the principal's house each weekday morning to catch the bus for the trip into Molong. One or two of the boys were responsible for carrying a big basket containing the lunch sandwiches. The Fairbridge children disliked the sandwiches, which were made early each day by two of the school boys with bread that was often badly baked and with fillings like pickle or Vegemite. Daphne Brown recalls:

The girls that came from private homes would be eating lovely sandwiches. They would have apples and we would say 'Bags your core.' And they gave us their cores and we would eat the rest of the apple because any fruit we got was seconds.

Fairbridge was not geared up to care for the very young children, some of whom were only four years old. These little ones were sent out after breakfast on their own to forage for small twigs, called 'chips', to help light the cottage fires and boilers.

Stewart Lee arrived at Fairbridge as a four-year-old, with his three older brothers. He talks about being left each day as the older children went off to the little school at the back of the village:

I don't remember a great deal . . . like, it's bits and pieces . . . I used to follow them up as far as the woodpile, then they'd have to go on to school and I'd go home and start to pick up chips . . . so, you're four years of age and there's nobody looking after you and you just go out all day collecting chips of wood . . . or sitting down on the septic tank just looking down the road. There was nothing else to do.

During my first eighteen months at Fairbridge I was one of the few children thought to be bright enough to go to high school in Orange, some 35 kilometres away. Each morning the handful of us who were sent to Orange High School had to leave breakfast early and walk hurriedly a kilometre down to the Mitchell Highway to catch the overcrowded school bus. The bus carried other Molong town kids going to Orange High School and an assortment of private schools, including the Catholic De La Salle College and the exclusive Kinross Wolaroi School. By the time the school bus had picked us up it was usually already full, so mostly we'd spend the hour-long trip standing up or sitting in the aisle on our upturned school cases.

After school we all changed into work clothes for assigned work around the village or the farm. On Monday and Friday afternoons we had to present ourselves for 'village muster' behind Nuffield Hall kitchens, near the village bell. Village muster on Monday and Friday – and Saturday morning – was physically hard work around the village and farm. It could involve planting trees, cleaning drains, clearing roads, repairing fences or period- ically cleaning out our cottage septic sewerage tanks. We also spent a lot of time weeding, and painting the rocks bordering the village roads and paths in white paint. At harvest time all avail- able children would be taken up to work on the farm.

On Tuesday afternoons we worked under the guidance of our cottage mothers on the gardens. The Fairbridge village was very beautiful and well maintained, mainly by the children. The village had been built on typical Australian sparse bushland but by the time we arrived, the shrubs and trees that had been planted in the 1930s had matured and looked very much like a well-cared for English country village.

Each year the Cottage Garden Competition was judged by the board of the Fairbridge Foundation on its annual visit to the farm. The competition was fiercely contested, particularly among some of the longest-serving cottage mothers. We therefore dreaded spring, when we'd be ordered out at every possible moment to clear, plant, mow, prune and weed the garden.

The annual visits of the Fairbridge Council were quite staged. The cottage gardens had months of preparation and the village received weeks of sprucing up. We were on our best behaviour and were ordered to wear shoes for the weekend. For our lunch in Nuffield Hall we put sheets across the tables to give the impression that we normally had tablecloths and, rather than the usual mutton, we ate much nicer dishes that we would not see again till the same time next year. As Lennie Magee recalls:

> We became the unwitting partners and members of the world's biggest con. Gardens were fastidiously weeded, gleaming white sheets were placed on every table, and large pigs and chickens were slaughtered for their succulent white meat. After we worked our butts off to make every floor shine, we polished every doorknob, scoured every sink and toilet, and turned every cottage table into a mirror. The whole world became bright, sunny and genial as every child was scrubbed clean until it hurt, dressed in new clothes and made to wear shoes . . . When these well-meaning folk sat on the stage at the staff table in the Nuffield Hall and smiled down at us . . . politely eating our lunch, they were a hundred miles away . . . eventually they all stood up and waved us all goodbye as they left the hall, clambered into their cars and slowly drove away; no doubt amazed at the impact that they were making on the poor and needy. Meanwhile, as the dust was settling, the tablecloths went, the meat went, the clothes and the shoes went, and so did the glow and the smiles.

In the otherwise totally regimented weekdays we looked forward to our 'free' afternoon each Wednesday. If you were on a discipline list for some offence, though, your privileges were withdrawn and you had to work. During the couple of hours' free time after school the kids enjoyed playing or simply hanging around. There wasn't a great deal to do, but most of us enjoyed the little time when we weren't being ordered around.

Thursday afternoon was sport, which depending on the time of year meant cricket, soccer, rugby league, hockey, swimming or athletics. Many of us enjoyed sport as much as we enjoyed free time, but for those children who did not excel it could be a nightmare, as the boss would run after the boys he thought were being slack and whip them on the back of the legs with a cane to force them to try harder.

Before the evening meal back in our cottages we had a shower in the cottage bathroom, usually with hot water because the boy who was assigned to clean the bathroom each morning was also responsible for relighting the 'donkey' boiler before going off to school.

The quality of the evening meal varied. The cottage mother was responsible for 'tea', as we called it, which might be some of the lunch leftovers brought back from Nuffield Hall and reheated. Some of the cottage mothers would take the trouble to cook an interesting meal, while the lazier ones served up little more than bread and milk, or left the cooking entirely to the children. Barney Piercy remembers how his cottage mother used much of the cottage rations to feed her cats:

> She had forty cats with a cat pan in each room of the cottage. She used to feed them our meat. Spaghetti bolognaise had meat but we'd have spaghetti without meat and the meat was going to the bloody cats.

After 'tea' in our cottage, the Orange High School kids normally did the washing up because we had missed a lot of the cottage and village work during the day. It was an awful job because all the hot water had been used up with the evening showers. Cleaning mutton fat off steel pots and plates in tepid or cold water was hard and seemed to take forever. After dinner we just hung around until it was time to go to bed, because there wasn't much else to do. In our cottage there was no radio or TV and no books, except for the odd comic or Zane Grey western. Most of us simply ignored any homework we had been assigned at school as no one ever checked that it was being done.

On winter evenings we were allowed to light the one fire in the cottage and up to fifteen kids would crowd around it before going off to bed in the freezing cold dormitory at the other end of the building. A number of children recall they were only permitted by their cottage mothers to light the fires on rare occasions, and talking after lights out in the dormitory was forbidden.

The weekends were as highly regimented and organised as the rest of the week, but usually involved sport and free time. A regular feature at the end of the week was the Weekend Notice, which was roughly typed by Woods on his manual Olivetti typewriter and pinned up on one of the entrance doors of Nuffield Hall every Friday afternoon. The typical Weekend Notice began with orders for Friday afternoon village muster, and went on to give the time the bus would take trainees into Molong that evening to the town cinema. The notice would also list those whose privileges had been withdrawn as punishment for having done something wrong.

The notice would list duties for Saturday, including the big village work muster that was compulsory for everyone not authorised to work doing something else. It would list the time for lunch and the opening of the tuck shop, which would be open for half an hour after lunch for the kids to spend their meagre pocket money on a small range of available sweets and chocolates.

The sporting commitments were listed, along with the complicated plans for moving various teams for rugby league, soccer, hockey and cricket to nearby towns and back again.

Sometimes there would be an event on Saturday night in the hall, and some of us would be rostered to act as waiters for guests who were visiting the village.

Sunday was the only day we did not work before breakfast; the whole village, except the trainees, slept till 7 a.m. Attendance at church was compulsory and on most Sunday mornings the Anglican vicar came out to Fairbridge to conduct the service in the village hall. But on the first Sunday of each month we crowded on to the old Fairbridge bus and went to church in Molong.

Sunday afternoon consisted of more sport, particularly for the older boys who as 'trainees' usually worked all day Saturday. Otherwise, if you were not on some discipline list, it was free time, when you could get special permission to go down to the Molong Creek, where you might have a swim, boil a billy of tea, or go rabbiting.

Sunday night back in our cottages was usually an empty time when we would sit around after the evening meal and talk, or perhaps write a letter home – for those of us who had someone to write to. For me, a slow Sunday night was a time to reflect on how it was that I had gone from living happily as part of a family in a village in the south of England to being with more than 150 other children in a tough farm school in remote Australia.

4

A WORKING SCHOOL

'What's the matter Bennett?', and I said, 'It's got maggots in it, sir.' He said, 'They're not maggots. This is the larvae of the weevils. Good protein. Eat it.'

Most of the Fairbridge children left school at the minimum age, which was fifteen years or a little before. For the next two years they became what was known as 'trainees' on the farm, and worked twenty-eight-day rosters, rotating through different jobs around the place. When they reached seventeen they were found paid work and left Fairbridge.

One of the most unpleasant surprises I had on arrival at the school was the reality of the trainee scheme – effectively a regimen of hard labour. Although we took on the full-time workload of an adult, we were given only a shilling or two a week in pocket money.

The farm, of about 650 hectares, was roughly two kilometres wide and ran for 5.5 kilometres south of the Mitchell Highway and the Molong Creek, which formed its northern border. Fairbridge was largely self-sufficient, thanks to its sheep farming, grain growing, vegetable garden and orchard, dairy, piggery, poultry farm and slaughterhouse. All the work was undertaken by the children and only a handful of adult farm supervisors.

The Fairbridge aim of training underprivileged British boys to become farmers and girls to become farmers' wives was captured in the school song:

> We are Fairbridge folk, all as good as e'er, English,
> Welsh and Scottish,
> We have come from everywhere:
> Boys to be farmers
> And girls for farmers wives,
> We follow Fairbridge the Founder.

Though the Fairbridge schools operated for more than seventy years in Australia – from 1912 till 1980 – practically no Fairbridge child was ever able to acquire and operate their own farm. As Len Cowne recounts:

> Fairbridge Farm School, euphemistically called a 'college of agriculture', was in reality . . . built to train British migrant children to become farm workers . . . Boys were trained in most aspects of agriculture, and the girls learned all the domestic chores that went with running a house. On leaving our 'alma mater', we boys were found places as farm labourers, and the girls often ended up skivvies to some wealthy landowner.

Many of the trainees started work before the village wake-up bell. The team of six boys on the dairy roster began the first milking at three o'clock in the morning and did not finish work before six in the evening after completing the second milking, which started at three in the afternoon.

Most of the Fairbridge boys dreaded the dairy because the work was unrelenting, more than sixteen hours a day, seven days a week and for twenty-eight days straight. And Ted Begley, the dairy supervisor, was a sadist, who regularly kicked and punched the boys at the least provocation.

The dairy was the toughest place I ever worked. I found it so exhausting I didn't think I would survive the experience. I was rostered on the dairy shortly after my fifteenth birthday, during the winter school holidays. Before 3 a.m. a boy called Norm 'Goofy' Bannerman came down from Canary Cottage to wake me to go and fetch the cows for the morning milking. It was pitch black, cold and pouring with rain as we trudged up the hill beside the deputy principal's house, through the fence and across a paddock to find the cows. We had no wet-weather gear and were soaked. I couldn't see a thing, but Goofy knew the ropes so I just quietly followed him, slipping and sliding in the mud. It seemed to take ages to get the cows into the milking yard, where the other four boys had set up the machines for milking.

There were about fifty milking cows in the herd, which was one of the biggest in the central west of the state. The herd had been smaller in the earlier years of Fairbridge but increased after a donation of milking machines by the pastoral company Dangar, Gedye and Malloch in the mid-1950s.

There were six milking bays but only four milking machines so we took turns to hand-milk the other cows in the two other bays. We also had to hand 'strip' each cow to fully empty her udder after the machine had taken all that it could. If Begley found you weren't emptying all the cows properly he would switch off the machines and make you milk the entire herd by hand.

I didn't mind the hand-milking in the cold early morning. Sitting on the milking stool and nestling your head into the belly and the udders of a cow was the only way to get a bit of warmth. You could also lean forward and squirt the warm milk straight from the cow's udder into your mouth.

The milking took a couple of hours. Towards the end the senior boy on the team started separating the cream to make butter and cleaning all the milking equipment. The rest of us had various jobs around the yard and the piggery across the lane. By sun-up a younger boy would come up from the village to hitch a cart to the horse. He and one of the boys from the dairy team would load about three ten-gallon urns to take down to the village, filling jugs belonging to the few staff members and their families who lived in the tiny houses on the way, before delivering the bulk of the milk to the village kitchen. The horse would be left in harness to graze outside Nuffield Hall during breakfast.

Ian Bayliff remembers working as a schoolboy on the dairy cart:

> I loved it. It got me out of the cottage early in the morning and away from the cottage mother and the drudgery of cleaning the cottage every morning. It also got me out of village [work] muster and church on Sunday mornings. I managed to get a second stint at it . . . it was one of my best memories of Fairbridge.

Back at the dairy the rest of us still had jobs to do after milking and before breakfast. I was assigned to the piggery and had to cross the lane to feed the pigs the slops that had been cooked up the previous day. As was often the case at Fairbridge, I wasn't trained and was given the barest of instruction from one of the senior boys. I just muddled along and worked it out as best I could.

The dairy team invariably came down late for breakfast when everyone was finishing up or had already left the dining hall. Before going to eat, we would wash, take off our muddy, shitty work boots and perhaps put on some dry clothing. As trainees we usually got something cooked for breakfast, which might be a mutton chop, or a poached egg. The cook understood how hard we worked and allowed us to eat the breakfast cereal rather than the awful and by now cold porridge. We could also go up on the stage to the staff dining table and eat whatever the staff had left and drink any remaining tea and coffee, which was normally forbidden to the children. It was just as well, because our cooked breakfast was by now very cold, as David Eva recalls:

> We'd get down there about eight o'clock and then we'd have our breakfast and of course the bloody eggs were like rubber. If they got poached you could throw them up in the air and they would bounce all over the place – and your porridge stuck in the bowl.

After breakfast we would all go back up to the dairy. I was assigned to clean and feed the pig pens while the other boys cleaned the yard, washed the milking bays and fed the poddy calves. At the piggery I cleaned out the sties and boiled up the food that would be fed to the pigs the following day. There were two huge coppers. I lit the smaller one for the food scraps from the village kitchens and in the bigger one I boiled up wheat from the silo with the meat offcuts and guts from the sheep killed in the slaughterhouse behind the dairy.

The dairy gang slaughtered sheep twice a week – on Monday morning and again on Thursday morning, usually ten to fifteen sheep in each kill. We rarely killed lambs; our meat diet was overwhelmingly old mutton. Again, at the slaughterhouse we received little training. You learned to kill from the experienced older boys. On my first day the most senior boy put the knife close to hand and pulled the sheep over on its side. I had the job of holding the sheep's rear legs while the older boy pulled back the head of the sheep over his boot and plunged the knife into its throat, cutting outwards, and then breaking the beast's neck. I was surprised there was so much blood and totally unprepared for the strength of the sheep. It kicked its rear legs free as I rolled around in the blood on the floor, trying to hold it down, while the older boys cursed my incompetence. By the time I regained control the sheep stopped kicking and fell silent, dead.

Lennie Magee also remembers at fifteen years of age killing the hard way:

> We were told – not taught – how to cut the sheep's throat – cut the jugular and break its neck. My first concern, however, was not the sheep's welfare but to make sure that I didn't stick the knife through the sheep's neck and into my boot. My initial attempt found me chasing a half dead sheep down the hill with a knife sticking out of its neck.

After the kill we cut off the lower legs while the beast was still lying on the ground, then hung it on a hook, skinned and gutted it, and cut off its head. The heart and the liver were cut out and put into a bucket and the remainder of the guts sat on the floor until one of the boys cut open the intestines and emptied the grass inside on to the manure heap. I would then pick up the remains and take them across to the piggery to go into the big copper. The sheep's guts would slop around in my wheelbarrow like giant spaghetti. No one ever showed me a better way of picking up the intestines than by the armful, with slippery guts sliding through your arms and down your legs.

On about my second day on piggery duty, I was leaning on a tap while filling a bucket of water. Unbeknown to me, Ted Begley had crept up behind me and he kicked me between the legs, up into my balls. As I lay writhing in the mud he grumbled something about going to sleep on the job, and then wandered off. This was my first encounter with Begley.

Begley was almost universally despised and was aptly described by one of the boys as 'a raging, violent thug'.[1] Nearly every boy who worked for him, including me, has bitter memories of his savage and brutal behaviour. Twice, when I was working on the dairy, he kicked me without any reason and without any explanation. John Harris, who generally speaks highly of Fairbridge, singled out Begley for his violence:

Ted Begley was an out and out low life. He'd whack you, he'd kick you, knee you. If you were bending over doing up your shoelaces you'd get a number nine up your bum. You know, he'd just kick you as you went past. He was just an out and out bastard. Absolutely the lowest order.

We usually finished the morning work in time to walk down to the village and have lunch with everyone else in Nuffield Hall. Two of the boys in the dairy gang had the job of getting the cows into the lucerne paddock before the afternoon milking, but the rest of us could have a nap for an hour or so. On one of the days I was 'on cows', I herded them into the lucerne paddock before the afternoon milking then laid down and dozed off. I was woken abruptly by Ted Begley kicking me in the head. Fortunately, he was wearing rubber Wellington boots.

At three o'clock we had to start the afternoon milking, which took a couple of hours plus clean-up time. We didn't get back to the village before dark, always after everyone in the cottage had finished their tea. Although hungry, I was almost too tired to eat. I had been working for more than sixteen hours and would be lucky to get six hours' sleep before Goofy would wake me again to go and find the cows for the next milking.

Another tough roster was working in the village kitchens. A paid cook lived in small quarters behind the kitchens and supervised the work of two or three trainee boys in the kitchen and two or three trainee girls who worked as waitresses for the staff in the adjoining dining hall. The boys started work at five o'clock in the morning and were also responsible for ringing the village bell, which was located outside the back of the kitchens.

One of the first duties each day was to 'riddle' the big slow combustion stoves that operated twenty-four hours a day. After rattling out the overnight ash and opening the dampers, the boys would put on more fuel so that breakfast could be prepared for around two hundred people. In addition to cooking a large amount of porridge the boys would slice around two hundred pieces of bread, before two of the secondary school children came to use the slicer to make sandwiches for the children who were going into town for school that day.

About 5.30 a.m. the cook would come in and supervise the preparation of breakfast for the staff. Once that was done, the trainee boys would spend most of the morning confronting a mountain of pots and pans to be washed up before preparing the village lunch. There were fewer for lunch as all the secondary school children were bused to Molong and a handful of us into Orange.

The vegetable garden wasn't a bad roster and I worked there during one of the summer holidays when the garden supervisor was Kurt Boelter. The hours working on the garden were easier than most jobs. Boelter, an early riser, was usually already working by the time we joined him after the wake-up bell. We came back up for breakfast like everyone else, and were permitted a mid-morning and mid-afternoon break, at each of which we got a big mug of tea with milk and sugar, which was something of a luxury at Fairbridge. We returned to the village for lunch and finished work in the afternoon in plenty of time for a shower and the evening meal.

Much of the work in the garden involved ploughing, planting, and using the rotary hoe to keep the beds clear, watering, weeding and finally harvesting. We grew many of the crops, including potatoes, turnips carrots, pumpkins cucumbers, peas, beans, cauliflower, cabbage, spinach, tomatoes and corn. Around the vegetable garden there were apple, pear and plum trees – although many of the kids recall little good fruit coming from them, and most of it being contaminated with fruit fly.

For years all the ploughing and clearing was done entirely by horse-drawn plough, but in the 1950s, following his visit to the farm school, the governor-general Sir William Slim persuaded the Ferguson company to donate a tractor. I remember excitedly learning to drive it when I was about fourteen – but Kurt Boelter the gardening boss still preferred to plough using old Blossom the horse till he left the farm in the early 1960s to return to Germany.

Over the years there were a number of garden supervisors, most of whom the kids thought were okay. But in the early 1960s Ted Roach was hired at Fairbridge in this role, while his long-suffering wife became our cottage mother in Canonbar Cottage. Roach was the opposite of Kurt Boelter. Ill-mannered and perverted, he would grab the boys' genitals as a sick joke that made us all feel dirty and uncomfortable. He would sit at the Canonbar meal table in the evening with filthy hands that he had not washed after coming up from the garden, and roll and smoke cigarettes at the table while we were eating.

The Fairbridge children have mixed views about the food we ate. Breakfast and lunch were taken by the whole village in the giant Nuffield Hall, which had been built with a donation to Fairbridge from Lord Nuffield, the maker of British Morris motor cars.

Before each meal, all the cottage's metal plates, bowls and mugs would be brought over by the smaller children, who would set the table and take everything back to the cottage for washing up afterwards. Leftover food would be taken to the piggery and boiled for the pigs. If the food served in the hall was inedible, we would try to eat as little as possible and scrape the rest into the pig bins. But Fairbridge did not tolerate wasted food. On many occasions Woods would inspect the bins and if too much food had been thrown out, it was immediately taken back to the cottage table to be served up to the children. It didn't matter that mutton was now mixed with custard or cabbage with semolina.

Billy King recalls Woods forcing a child to eat contaminated porridge: 'I've seen him have this kid at the table eating the porridge and vomiting it back up and he had to stay there and spoon it back into his mouth until he ate it.'

Peter Bennett remembers having to eat a different kind of contaminated porridge: 'I'll never forget the porridge because . . . the rolled oats used to come in the big 200-pound bag and by the time it got a third of the way down it was full of weevils. And one morning I was having my breakfast and I wouldn't eat it.'

Principal Woods dismissed Bennett's protest: '"What's the matter, Bennett?", and I said, "It's got maggots in it, sir." He said, "They're not maggots. This is the larvae of the weevils. Good protein. Eat it."'

Not all the Fairbridge children remember the food being so bad. John Harris felt the choice was too limited, but said he would not complain about the quality. Joyce Drury also thought the food at Fairbridge was okay, particularly compared with her experiences in England when she was a small girl and food was scarce:

I found the food all right, especially when Mr Oats was the gardener and there would be lots of fruit growing on trees, and the straw-berries, and we'd go out mushrooming . . . or someone would say that a [neighbouring] farmer had rung up to say, 'We've got all these apples that are blown off the tree.' So, we'd have fruit.

While some of the Fairbridge children considered we were fed adequately, the food got the thumbs-down when it was investigated by a nutrition expert. In 1956 Sydney Hospital's Molly Baker, B.Sc., was asked by the Fairbridge Council in Sydney to examine the children's diet and after a weeklong visit she wrote a scathing report of food and food management. In the report, which was never made public, she claimed the children were not being fed enough, that the food lacked sufficient nutrition and that much of it was contaminated. She observed 'maggots floating in stewed mutton', 'moths in the porridge', 'flies floating in the custard and cream' and numerous 'live flies on food and fly blown meat' and 'decomposing organismic matter on the kitchen floor'. Some of her other comments on hygiene included: 'the kitchen walls are dirty'; 'garbage cans have no lids and are left standing outside the dining hall windows'; and 'almost without exception *all* kitchens utensils were dirty'. Milk cans, used for bringing milk from the dairy, were frequently 'improperly washed', having 'grit and gravel' in the bottom. She reported that the food was 'monotonous, unpalatable and lacking in essential nutrients' and 'does not constitute an adequate diet'.[2]

She also claimed the cottages were not allocated enough food for the evening meal and that cottage mothers had complained to her that their rations 'were exhausted days and even weeks before the next issue could be expected'. The meat, Baker said, was badly butchered by the boys. She said the variety of vegetables from the Fairbridge garden was 'very limited', particularly in winter, when children were served 'parsnips, turnips, cabbage and cauliflower for a period of about a month without change', and for months of the year there was no fresh fruit.

Baker also disagreed with the policy of staff being served a wide range of food while the children's diet was limited:

The distinction between staff and children, in the matter of food, is very great. I believe this distinction is both unnecessary and undesirable. The cottage mother had an egg for breakfast every morning and it was eaten at the table with the cottage children, to whom an egg for breakfast is unknown.

Baker concluded her report by recommending a number of changes, which could be introduced 'efficiently and quickly' and be achieved with 'very little added expense'. Principal Woods was livid. Rather than accept Baker's recommendations, he attacked her. In a seven-page response laced with sarcasm he said:

> The cook and his wife have now resigned as a result of this report from Miss Baker, since they felt that more has been asked of them than was in reason. Miss Baker has offered to help us in the matter of food and kitchen work. Perhaps she would be able to find us a cook and an assistant who can do all that she feels they should do.[3]

While Woods did accept some of the issues raised in the report, he made it clear there would be no significant changes at Fairbridge. He acknowledged that sometimes 'young and inexperienced' trainees failed to wash the vegetables thoroughly enough, resulting in 'slugs and snails' in the greens, or 'overcooked' sheepskin finding its way into the stew. He did not dispute that certain items in the kitchen were dirty: 'As to the kitchen utensils being dirty, the cook agrees they probably were so, since he had a weak team of trainees to help him, and he just could not do his and all their work as well.'

Nor did he refute Baker's claim that the kitchen walls were dirty. He said that they would not be fixed in the foreseeable future because the painting of the kitchen was 'fairly far down the list of maintenance work to be done in the village'.

In response to the complaints that cottages were given insufficient food rations, Woods wrote:

> I personally questioned seven of our eleven cottage mothers and none of the seven admitted to have made any such statement, and all expressed themselves as satisfied with the rations, and preferred to have them given out monthly.

He rejected the suggestion that the children should be served eggs or the same cooked breakfast as the staff, on the basis that it would cost too much:

> The children do not normally have eggs in the main dining hall, since the inception of the school the children have only had porridge or cereal and bread and butter etc. should it be desired to serve the children with a second cooked dish as well, the budget will have to be considerably increased to allow for the increased consumption of food.

And he refused to accept Baker's claim that there was too little variety in the vegetables served to the children, calling it a 'gross misstatement'. It was 'senseless', he said, to expect tomatoes in winter or cauliflower in midsummer. He also said that flies had always been a problem at Fairbridge: 'The cook, and all the previous cooks before him, have every year to wage the battle of the flies, and as the present cook is a new Australian, he had still to learn the menace that the Australian blowfly can be.'

The fly problem, he suggested, was made worse by the design of the village kitchen, which provided numerous ways for the flies to get in: 'These include the vegetable door, the coke yard door, the bakery and store door, the meat and milk doorway and two servery doorways. Added to this, numerous children come in and out of the kitchen before and during meals.'

Finally, Woods disabused anyone who thought the Baker report would result in more or better food at Fairbridge:

> I fear that many of our staff had presumed – quite wrongly – that Miss Baker's findings would necessarily result in everyone getting

more food supplied to them in all forms, and so there has been the very evident attempt made more or less surreptitiously to paint as black a picture as they could for Miss Baker's benefit . . . I had fore-warned the staff not to attempt to do this in a written instruction to them before I went on holiday, but had to ask them all to observe the status quo, and in no way attempt to prejudice or bias Miss Baker's mind or opinions.

So the Baker report did not result in any significant changes, and the range of food and the way it was managed remained virtually unchanged for the rest of the life of the farm school.

David Eva, who spent seven years in Brown Cottage, recalls some appalling meals:

This is true. I'm not making this up . . . I came home from school and it was the cottage mother's day off. And normally they used to cook the [evening] meal the day before their day off and all the boys had to do was to put it on the stove and heat it up. Now, this day she made this bloody soup. Now, her soup was just throwing the (mutton) flap in the bowl with a couple of onions floating on the top, and boil the Christ out of it, and leave it on the stove. Well, I came home from school this day and I looked in the bloody bowl and the bloody meat was nearly walking out of the saucepan. I took it to Woods, who was running the village work muster with the other children who had come home from school. And I went down there and shoved it in front of him and said, 'Would you eat this?' and he took the lid off and said, 'Oh, extra meat rations!' Extra meat rations? She'd just left it on the stove, no cover on it or nothing and the maggots were crawling all up the side and all over the meat and everything.

Despite this, by and large Fairbridge kids were quite healthy. There were the usual illnesses and injuries that could be expected in a residential school of around 150 children, but kids quickly toughened up when they arrived and it was unusual to be off sick. Most of the children's ailments were treated in the village by a not-always-qualified nursing sister, who lived in tiny quarters attached to the back of the little hospital near the front gate of the school. The surgery opened immediately after breakfast, and again every afternoon at 5 p.m. after the work was done, because it was assumed any health problems would not interfere with work. In more serious cases children would be taken into town to the doctor or admitted to Molong Hospital. Children were not allowed to stay in their bed in the cottage dormitory if they were ill – they had to go to the little Fairbridge hospital, where there was a four-bed ward for those who needed it. On occasions there were more serious health problems in the village, including an outbreak of hepatitis in early 1959, which forced Fairbridge to quarantine much of the farm and prevented children from going to school in town for several weeks.

There was no regular dental care or even routine check-ups. We would be taken into Molong if a tooth needed extraction. But Fairbridge kids generally had good teeth because we ate very little sugar and few sweets.

In England, like most children at that time, my brothers and I had regularly attended the local church and Sunday school, and we had weekly religious instruction at school, so we weren't surprised by the religious observance at Fairbridge, but it was to play a bigger role in our daily lives than it had in the past.

Before eating breakfast each morning in Nuffield Hall, Woods would read a prayer and then each cottage would be rostered in turn to provide a boy and a girl to read the same two prayers every day. We were all expected to say grace before every meal.

When he designed the child migrant scheme Kingsley Fairbridge said it would be 'non-denomination Christian' and that worship would be optional for the children. In formulating the plan for the Fairbridge schools, he stated that 'Priests of any Christian denomination passing through the school may be permitted to hold meetings', but the 'children will be under no compulsion to attend them'.[4]

In practice, Fairbridge was almost exclusively Anglican and attendance at church was compulsory. On most Sunday mornings we were all ordered to attend a service in Nuffield Hall conducted by the Anglican vicar from Molong. After breakfast on Sunday we would move the big cottage dining tables to one side of the hall and put the benches in rows as pews for the service. An altar kept at the back of the hall was drawn out and covered, and two candles were lit for the service. Then, on the first Sunday of each month, the whole village would crowd on to the Fairbridge bus and go to the Church of England service at St John's, which was at the top of Molong's main street.

The Fairbridge bus was famous throughout the central west of the state for several decades after the Second World War. Built in 1942 for Sydney's public transport fleet, it had a normal steel chassis, but because of wartime shortages its frame and bodywork above the windows were made of timber. Only five of these 'austerity' buses were ever made and Fairbridge bought this one when the government bus service sold them off cheaply in 1948. Although licensed to seat twenty-nine passengers, practically all the children from the village – often well over a hundred – plus staff, would be packed aboard, with most standing or hanging out of the open doorways for the trip into town.

David Wilson, who spent more than ten years at Fairbridge after arriving as a six-year-old in 1951, recalls the tedium of going into Molong for the monthly church service:

> Of course every first Sunday of the month we'd go into Molong to the C of E church there. And Ruth Woods would play the piano. And if she ever caught us talking, she'd tell her husband and the boss used to cane us. And yet he was twice as noisy, snoring away.

Lennie Magee, who had no strong religious inclination but later in life became 'born again', was equally unimpressed:

> On the night I was confirmed into the Anglican church I was with two other kids stealing chocolates from the shop next door . . . on Sundays the vicar . . . inflicted some of the dullest and [most] tedious sermons ever concocted upon us hapless kids. Unwittingly, these men in white dresses robbed God of any life and personality.

Daphne Brown also found the services excruciatingly dull:

> And then Sunday . . . we used to have to go to church and I hated it because they talked about the resurrection and all that. They never made it interesting for the children.

There were very few Roman Catholic children at Fairbridge because the Catholic Church ran its own girls and boys migrant centres in Australia. One group of Catholic children who came to

Fairbridge were the Millers – Reg, Doug, Gwen and Kathy – who arrived from Grimsby in Lincolnshire in 1951, and their brother, Huey, who followed a year later. They were part of a Catholic family of ten children. When their mother died, their father, who 'hated the nuns', sent them to Australia. Gwen recalls how they were the envy of all the other Fairbridge kids: they were able to go every Sunday into Molong in the town's only taxi for mass, where afterwards they were given a huge bacon-and-egg breakfast:

We were the first Catholics at Fairbridge and the nuns in England were in touch with the nuns in Molong. They paid for a taxi to take us in to church in Molong and bring us back again. And if we had Holy Communion once a month, the nuns fed us breakfast and it was the best meal we ever had while we were at Fairbridge.

No doubt inspired by the Miller children, the enterprising Paddy O'Brien, the eldest boy in our group, approached Woods to say that he and his sisters, Mary and Myrtle, were Methodists and he wanted the three of them to attend the Methodist Church service in Molong each week. Like many Australian country towns, Molong, despite having a population of barely 2000 people, boasted a fine range of stone churches: Church of England, Roman Catholic, Presbyterian, Methodist and Baptist. Not to be outdone by Paddy, my older brother, Dudley, approached Woods and told him we were Presbyterians and wished to worship in our own church. This was not entirely true. We had never been baptised as children and attended a number of different Sunday schools, usually the one closest to where we were living at the time, but it worked and it gave us an excuse to get off the farm every Sunday, when all the other kids were obliged to go to the

Anglican service in Nuffield Hall. To begin with we would walk or hitchhike into Molong, but eventually Paddy was old enough to get a driver's licence and he would take us and his sisters in one of the small Fairbridge trucks.

For all the religion at Fairbridge, only a few carried a serious commitment into their adult lives, such as Roland Bigrig, who became an Anglican vicar, and Malcolm 'Flossie' Field, who became a server and a deacon of the altar in the Anglo-Catholic tradition.

Beneath the strict routine and discipline at the farm school we children managed to build our own world, whose value system was in many respects at odds with the official order. Particularly among the boys, misbehaviour, smoking, thieving, defiance of authority, bullying, and absconding (with police in pursuit) were all part of life on the farm.

We gave one another nicknames, usually based on physical characteristics or distinctive behavioural traits, and many today would be regarded as politically incorrect. 'Stumpy' was squat and nuggetty, and his younger brother 'Runty' was small for his age. I was 'Faddy' because of being overweight when I arrived at Fairbridge. Other 'fatties' at Fairbridge included 'Tubby' Walker and 'Fatman' Sinclair. No one was actually overweight at Fairbridge so they too probably acquired the epithets when they first arrived. 'Muscles' had a body builder's physique and 'Shark' had fine, shiny teeth. Gwen Miller was known as 'Mini' and Geraldine Whinn as 'Jellybean' because they were so tiny. 'Whoopee' could fart at will, 'Swagman' was extremely untidy, 'Bubbles' had bubbles of snot coming out of his nose and 'Goggs' had big round eyes. 'Snowy' and 'Flossie' both had mops of very blond hair and 'Smiley' simply had a happy face. One boy was called 'Maggot' because from the time he arrived at Fairbridge as a four-year-old, he ate anything and everything he could. 'Whopper' was notorious for telling lies and 'Eggy' had a pronounced, egg-shaped head.

While Fairbridge may not have been a happy place for many, as children we managed to create a lot of our own fun. The most enjoyable times were when we were able to leave the farm and its strict routine. On Sunday afternoons it was possible to seek special permission – first from your cottage mother and then from the principal – to go down to the Molong Creek. As a treat you could take a small ration of tea leaves and sugar and some milk, light a fire and boil a billy. We also used to catch and cook yabbies, the tasty freshwater crustacean. In the warm weather we would strip off and swim in the creek, although at the risk of getting a nasty nip from a yabby or, worse, attracting leeches. On a typical Sunday afternoon there might be half a dozen fires alight along the Molong Creek below the farm school.

Rabbit hunting was also very popular, especially before myxomatosis was released in the 1950s to cull the rabbit population, which had reached plague proportions and was causing terrible damage to farmland across Australia. By the time I arrived at Fairbridge the disease had dramatically reduced rabbit numbers. When we were out hunting we could easily tell which rabbits were infected because they were so sick it was easy to run them down and they had ugly red sores, particularly around their eyes.

Michael Walker, who was at Fairbridge for more than ten years after arriving as a six-year-old, remembers the joy of time away from the farm school:

I liked free afternoons and a favourite way of spending one was rabbiting, usually with a friend. We would go to a spot where there were known to be lots of rabbits. You would take a digging tool and dig, then put your arm down a burrow until you eventually got to the nest at the end. It was a thrill to feel the animal down there and pull it out by its back legs, give it a swift chop across the back of the neck and that was that. There was no sense of death as I remember.

A lot of Fairbridge kids were taken in by local families for part of the long Christmas summer holidays and most of them have fond memories of going back year after year to the same family – and keeping in touch with their adopted holiday parents for decades after leaving the farm school. A number recall the families wanting to adopt or foster them permanently, but Fairbridge would not agree.

Those of us who were not sent to stay with an Australian family felt no loss, because a highlight of the year was the annual summer holiday, when we were taken camping for a fortnight at Gerroa on the coast of New South Wales, south of Wollongong. Sand, flies, mosquitoes, sunburn, heat, humidity and sleeping on the hard ground in old canvas tents may sound unpleasant but we loved every minute of it. As Michael Walker remembers:

> We all loved going to Gerroa. The freedom of Gerroa was exhil-arating. There weren't the usual restraints. No school, no cottage gardening, no cottage mothers! There were rock pools to explore – fascinating to a country boy – and endless beaches to wander.

At the start of the holiday we loaded the ex-army tents and marquees, pots and pans, food and clothing into the old Fairbridge bus, then drove 300 kilometres over the Blue Mountains. On the steepest slopes we were ordered to walk behind and even push the overloaded bus. Once we were over the mountains, we stopped at Penrith on the outskirts of Sydney, where the local Rotary or Lions Club put on a picnic lunch, when we would eat town bread sandwiches and enough free ice creams to make ourselves sick. Then we headed through Wollongong, Kiama and Gerringong to Gerroa to set up camp.

In those days, before Gerroa became popular, with a crowded caravan park, we had most of the campsite to ourselves. In contrast to the regimentation of Fairbridge we could do pretty much what we wanted, with a minimum of supervision. We all have memories of the boss when we were at Gerroa because he became more relaxed and better humoured than he was back at Fairbridge. Almost every day there were organised events but they were not compulsory and most of the time we preferred to do our own thing. Within about a week, in the absence of enforced rules, we became increasingly feral, taking on the appearance of the choirboys in William Golding's *Lord of the Flies*.

We were particularly excited about going out to play at night time, either canoeing on the lagoon or sneaking up on other campers hoping to catch sight of any young girls who might be staying there, although at thirteen and fourteen years of age and socially clumsy we wouldn't have known what to say to them if they had spoken to us.

Fairbridge kids above the age of about twelve were rostered to help with the preparation of food and washing up at the campsite, though most of the work was done by the girls. Lennie Magee and I were assigned to make sure our campsite had enough water for drinking, cooking and washing up. At least twice a day we would take a ten-gallon milk urn, borrowed from the Fairbridge dairy, about half a kilometre to the camp tap. Bringing the water back was difficult for two thirteen-year-olds – we had to put the heavy urn down every few metres for a rest.

We spent the days playing around, mostly without hats or sunscreen, swimming in the notoriously rough surf of Seven Mile Beach, or fishing off the rocks. There were no lifesavers then and it is a wonder that no one was lost in the sea over the many years Fairbridge children went to Gerroa.

It was always very sad to leave. The long trip home up over the mountains taxed the old bus, and the return journey was never without incident, as the worn-out machine huffed and puffed and overheated. On one trip back something snapped in the gearbox and we were all left in a bushland park at Lawson in the Blue Mountains in the searing heat with no water for four or five hours while we waited for parts to come from Bathurst.

Most of the boys at Fairbridge joined the Wolf Cubs and then the Boy Scouts; the girls joined the Brownies and then the Girl Guides. Though not compulsory it was expected of the children and actively encouraged by Woods, who was the Scout master and Wolf Cub pack leader; Ruth ran the Guides and the Brownies.

The Scouting and Guide movements reinforced Fairbridge's association with Britain and the British Empire. Their founder, Robert Baden-Powell, had been a champion of the Empire, serving in the British Army in India, Afghanistan and South Africa, where he became every British boy's hero for his leadership in the seven-month siege of the British-held town of Mafeking during the Boer War. The Scouts' oath, which we were expected to recite at every meeting, was: 'On my honour I promise/To do my duty to God and the Queen/To help other people at all times/ And to Obey the Scout Law.'

To most Fairbridge boys the Scouts provided an opportunity for adventure and an escape from the drudgery and routine of the farm school. The boss was proud of this and was always looking for ways to demonstrate that we were better than the other troops in the district. He had the Scouts and the Guides thoroughly practise marching so that when we attended the annual Cherry Blossom parade or the ANZAC Day memorial parade in Orange we would be the smartest and most disciplined of all the outfits. We normally felt like second-class citizens when we went to local towns so we were happy to show we could do something better than the town kids.

Before the Orange Country Show one year, Woods took us into the bush west of Larras Lee, where we camped and chopped down large gum trees. We then constructed a big wooden bridge over the local creek with the planks held together by only diagonal and square rope lashings. The following week we turned up at the show with a truck full of tree trunks and ropes, and within a few hours were able to construct the bridge again in front of a large and admiring local crowd.

Camping out was the most enjoyable part of being in the Scouts. Typically in winter we would load up the old Fairbridge bus or a truck with all our gear and head off to some remote spot. A particular favourite was out near the old nineteenth-century gold-mining site of Ophir, where we would pan for alluvial gold. At night on these camps, patrols would be pitted against one another in what Woods called 'wide games'. The objective of the different games varied but always involved securing or holding some territory against other patrols, and a physical contest between the boys, which Woods loved, as did we.

Many of us also belonged to the local Junior Farmers Club. A major function of the Molong-Fairbridge club was to prepare an exhibit containing all the products of a farm that would be displayed at annual country shows around the district. While I was at Fairbridge I won a prize of five shillings for designing a new backdrop for our junior club exhibit. Some of the kids took the club seriously but most of us saw it as an opportunity to get away from Fairbridge and travel in the area, assemble our exhibit and have a good time. The junior farmers gave out various certificates for farming competence and I remember being given one for lamb and sheep breeding, though I had little idea what it was about.

Many of us loved sport and there was lots of it at Fairbridge. The main winter sport for the boys was rugby league, and hockey for the girls, although the boys also played hockey and soccer. In summer we played cricket and competed in the inter-cottage athletics carnival.

We played sport every Thursday afternoon on the rough and uneven Fairbridge fields, and again on Saturday or Sunday afternoons against competition in the surrounding towns. Quite often we would travel to Orange to play one match in the morning and another, as part of a different sport, the afternoon. Fairbridge kids fondly remember being bought a meat pie from the Golden Key café for lunch in Orange. Lennie Magee remembers one Saturday morning playing a game of rugby league there, then returning to Fairbridge for a game of soccer in the early afternoon before playing a later afternoon game of rugby union in Molong.

The transport of so many boys and girls in different vehicles to and from Orange throughout the day, largely by Woods and Ruth, was a logistical marvel. I can still remember on a number of occasions Ruth was ferrying girls' hockey teams in one of the Fairbridge trucks, and Woods was cramming all thirteen members of our wet and muddy rugby league team with him into a station wagon for the very crowded drive of more than 30 kilometres back to Fairbridge.

We played in very old sports shirts in the Fairbridge colours of yellow and brown, which were supposed to represent the gold of the sun and the brown of good soil. Most of the sportswear was old, and had been repeatedly torn and roughly stitched back together. The colours had faded and looked awful compared to the town kids, who were invariably issued new kits at the start of each season. We all wore second-hand boots to play rugby league, which were also often ill fitting. Some of the boys preferred to play in bare feet.

Horse riding was popular but there were only a handful of horses available at Fairbridge. The few who somehow managed to acquire one became members of the local Molong pony club, which they attended on Saturdays with the principal's two daughters, Nyassa and Memory Woods.

An annual sporting holiday was the Forbes football carnival, a day-long knock-out rugby league tournament held in the town of Forbes for hundreds of boys' teams from all over the west of the state. The competitions were not determined by the age of the players but by their weight. The smallest boys were those under five and a half stone (35 kg), then six and a half stone (41 kg) and so on up to nine and a half stone (60 kg), before the highest, in which there was no weight limit. Forbes was about 100 kilometres west of Fairbridge and we would leave in the early morning darkness to drive the back bush roads via Eugowra. There, we were officially weighed and had our weight limit stamped on our foreheads, which was checked by the match referee before each game was played. Woods liked to have all the Fairbridge boys weighed in and stamped early before taking us to the Mum and Dad café, where we were allowed to gorge ourselves on a huge cooked breakfast of sausages, bacon and eggs, baked beans, followed by toast and marmalade. It was the best breakfast any of us had while at Fairbridge. But any advantage from playing with a bit of extra weight over and above what we had weighed in at was offset by the fact that we staggered out to play our first game of the day with a stomach stuffed full of undigested food.

We rarely did well at the carnival because at some stage we would meet a well-organised team that had been properly coached, while we had only ever been told to grab the ball and run hard when we were in possession then hit the other guy hard when they had the ball. Rugby league was new to Fairbridge kids because the only football we had known before migration from Britain was soccer. Nevertheless, our teams had a reputation for playing aggressively and being committed.

Many of the Fairbridge children say the best thing they remember about their experience was the bond they had with other children, and for them this has survived throughout their adult lives. Asked what he enjoyed the most, David Wilson says, 'I think the kids we were with – the camaraderie – it was just that. I suppose it was mainly the kids we were with. Because that's the only life I knew as a kid. Never knew anything else.'

Cigarette smoking was one facet of bonding at Fairbridge. Most of the children began smoking regularly at around thirteen or fourteen years of age and typically left the farm at seventeen with an addictive habit, even though to smoke there was a serious offence that would attract a severe caning and loss of pocket money and privileges. Woods absolutely detested smoking and it seemed to flourish in almost a direct inverse proportion to his determination to stamp it out. His efforts were all the more in vain because smoking was not then considered socially undesirable and it was perfectly acceptable for women and men to puff away in just about any social situation. An added difficulty was that practically every staff member, including the cottage mothers, smoked, and some of them very heavily.

Given the shortage of money on the farm, cigarettes became valuable in their own right as a currency with which you could buy almost anything from other children. We smoked when we thought we were safest from detection, often sneaking out of our cottage at night, in defiance of the village curfew. Most of the children had worked out the habits of their cottage mother and had a fair idea when she was likely to settle down in her quarters and be less likely to be patrolling the kids' end of the cottage. But Woods would often patrol the village at night, and being a non-smoker in the clean country air he could smell a cigarette from a long way off.

Among most of the children at Fairbridge it was acceptable to be a thief. You could steal cigarettes, money, food, or whatever you could from wherever you could, so long as it was not from another Fairbridge kid. We would break into buildings if we thought there was something to steal. Once, on our way back from church on Sunday morning some of us discovered that we could slide out a few glass louvres at the back of a service station, crawl in and steal cigarettes and chocolates. It was a lucrative source and to begin with we were not greedy, only taking a few packets of cigarettes at a time so that it would not be too obvious to the owner when he opened the store on Monday morning. Eventually more Fairbridge kids found out and went overboard. The owner couldn't miss seeing that so much of his stock was missing and reported it to the Molong police, who reported it to Woods. From then on, the store was made more secure and a watch kept on it over the weekends, making breaking in a more dangerous proposition. We were lucky none of us was caught in the act.

Those of us who attended Orange High School were acutely aware that the other kids at the school always had money to spend and we had little or nothing. To generate a bit of extra income we worked out how to break in to the stationery store at Fairbridge, which was a tiny room at the back of the small guest house next to the principal's house. We would load up our school cases, which we called 'ports', with purloined pens, pencils and writing pads, until they were bulging, and then sell them to Orange High School students at attractively discounted prices. The enterprise meant we could supplement our unpalatable sandwich lunch with a cream bun or something else exotic from the Orange High School canteen.

Unfortunately, the Fairbridge bursar, Harry Harrop, could not help but notice the dramatic shortage of stationery in the store and moved to make it more secure. We were lucky it was Harry, who was no disciplinarian, so we escaped the inquisition and retribution that normally followed such a discovery.

For some years a number of kids were aware of a small hole in the wall that separated the bakehouse from the village store. The hole had been deliberately made into the back of a locked cupboard that housed chocolates and other sweets that were brought out for half an hour after Saturday lunch for sale at the tuck shop. The hole was kept a secret from staff, hidden behind the big bakehouse trough in which the yeast, salt, flour and water were mixed to make the village bread. By moving the trough away from the wall, we could reach through, stretch and just manage to get our fingers on the booty.

To start with, access was limited to the boys who were rostered to work as trainees at the bakery, but over time more and more of us got in on the act, as long as the trainee on duty would let us into the bakehouse. Eventually, Harrop noticed whole shelves were bare – and then he found the hole in the wall. Legend has it that one day he found a hand coming through the hole belonging to bakery trainee Brian Osbourne and Harry grabbed it, and that was the end of that.

One of the boys' biggest thieving campaigns continued for some years and the target was the village pocket money supply. Every Saturday after lunch the boss came around to each cottage table with a little notebook and a metal cash tin filled with coins. He would put the cash box in front of one of the older boys, stand behind him and call out the names of the cottage children one by one, and the amount they were each to be paid. As Woods called out a name, the boy with the cash box would take out the designated amount of pocket money and pass it down the table to the grateful recipient. The youngest children received the least pocket money and the trainees the most and Woods would tick off each one in his little notebook. But, at the same time, the boy with the cash box was also stealing as many coins as possible and passing them under the table to boys either side of him. Outside after lunch we would divide the spoils. The scam, involving a number of cottages, seemed to go on for years and could only have continued undetected because Woods was a careless administrator who never attempted to reconcile the little notebook with the money left in the cash box.

Occasionally boys – and even more rarely girls – would run away from Fairbridge. It was practically impossible to escape for long because the police would immediately be alerted. Eventually the boy – with no money and, more importantly, nowhere to go – would be found, brought back to Fairbridge, punished and have his privileges withdrawn for long periods. The loss of privileges included having to work when normally there would be some free time, cancellation of pocket money, and not being able to go to the cinema on Friday night in Molong. In some cases, if a crime had been committed, the boy would actually serve time in one of the state's children's prisons: if runaways had stolen food, money or a car they would end up in the Children's Court, where they might be sentenced to serve a period in the boys' prison at Mount Penang at Gosford, north of Sydney. Even when a child had not committed a criminal offence he was sometimes sent to the boys' prison simply for running away and becoming a 'Neglected Child' under the Child Welfare Act.

Someone could be expected to run away every few months. As in a jail full of prisoners, the whispers would swirl around the dining hall at breakfast the next morning that such-and-such a cottage mother had reported that so-and-so had not slept in his bed and couldn't be accounted for. The news that someone had escaped caused great excitement and we would all speculate on where they had gone, which direction they were heading and how long they might be able to elude their captors.

Derek Moriarty ran away on a number of occasions:

> The first time I ran away, we hitchhiked, and got to Brisbane. There were four of us – Bob Wilson, Jimmy Grundy, and I think Brian Wilkes was the other one. But we got split up in Brisbane when the coppers started chasing us. And Grundy and I went one way and Bob and Wilkes went the other. And of course we eventually got caught and we all finished up back at Fairbridge. And then, some time down the track, we ran away again, just Bob and me. And we finished up down the south coast; we finished up at Milton because Bob had a good mate from Fairbridge that was living down the coast at Murchison in Victoria, and we were heading down there. But we got a ride with a guy and he dropped us off at Milton and [he] went and rang the cops and told them we were a couple of escapees from the orphanage. And of course they took us and locked us up . . . and we went to the Children's Court.

Generally, children ran away in groups of two or three. Once, six boys ran away and somehow managed to stay together until they were caught more than a week later north of Sydney. Sometimes a boy fled on his own, such as Alan 'Eggy' Taylor from our cottage. He was away for about a week and when he returned he fascinated us with his stories of survival in the bush. He told us that when his meagre escape rations ran out he survived on bush tucker; he didn't even have matches with which to light a fire to cook on. We didn't believe him when he said he had caught blue tongue and frill-necked lizards and eaten them raw, so the next Saturday afternoon he brought back a large, live lizard to

Canonbar Cottage to prove his point. With all of us standing around in a circle in the cottage bathroom he swung it by its tail and smashed its head on the laundry tub, sliced open its belly, turned it inside out and nibbled the meat inside. I believed everything 'Eggy' told us after that.

I never seriously considered running away because those who did were invariably eventually caught and brought back and punished. Also, I knew that ultimately I would get back together with Mum, which made me different from those kids who had no one there for them, and were more desperate to get away.

Another aspect of the children's value system at Fairbridge was brawn over brain. Bookish kids who showed an interest in schooling were spurned and the Orange High School kids were resented. The big and strong ruled over the small and the weak. Fairbridge was a pretty rough place where little emotion was shown. As Lennie Magee remembers:

> [Fairbridge] was marked by the absence of tenderness and emotion. It was considered by many to be stoic, and uncaring. Boys were told in no uncertain terms that only little kids, girls and sissies cry. Consequently, when kids were hit by machetes, or scraped off a horse by an unyielding tree branch as I was, or suffered broken arms, legs, wrists or collarbones as often happens, the result was either a slight limp or a glazed look – rarely were there tears.

Although few former Fairbridge children talk about it, there was a system of bullying, particularly among the boys. The little boys were called runts and expected to take orders from the older boys. Again, in this regard my brothers and I were better off than most of the other Fairbridge kids. We were slightly older when we arrived – Richard and I were nearly thirteen and Dudley was fourteen – and if you hit one of the three Hill boys you had to contend with the prospect of taking on all three, which gave us a sort of collective security.

Eric 'Chook' Fowler always felt a bit of an outsider at Fairbridge. He was only four years old when his mother died. His father was an officer in the Royal Ulster Fusiliers based in Ireland, and when he remarried he sent Eric, aged twelve, out to Fairbridge. Eric says his father thought he was going to a 'young gentlemen's school'. For the whole time he was there Eric was frightened to step out of line:

> I was worried that first day at Fairbridge that I might get into a fight – which I never did – but that's the only thing that worried me when I first got there because I had no one to turn to . . . it was survival of the fittest, really . . . I was very straight down the line. I was very careful what I did. Kept out of trouble, you know.

Despite Fairbridge being coeducational, the lives of the boys and the girls were highly regulated and separate, and there were rarely any sex scandals. Occasionally kids had boyfriends or girlfriends, but it rarely became too serious. As Gwen Miller remembers:

> I didn't know anything about the world. I mean, we had boyfriends at Fairbridge but boyfriends to us were somebody you went with to the pictures. You know, you might kiss them behind the bush on the way home but that was the extent of a relationship with a boy.

For many years Fairbridge had an arrangement whereby Legacy girls came to stay at the farm for a couple of weeks during the mid-year school holidays. The Legacy organisation was a big charity that assisted families of servicemen who had died as a result of war, so the Legacy girls were the daughters of the deceased servicemen. Their arrival created great excitement among us boys. I remember quivering with the thrill of having a Legacy girl as a girlfriend for a couple of weeks. We got to hold hands in the darkened back of the Fairbridge truck and I can still feel her breath now as she leaned over and kissed me on the cheek.

The girls were every bit as naïve about sex as the boys – possibly more so. Daphne Brown remembers:

> I never heard of anyone getting pregnant. I can honestly say if there was, I don't know of anyone. And they were pretty strict because, I mean, I got caught kissing a boy and Mr Woods took me down to the office and was telling me all of this stuff of what would happen and I didn't know what he was talking about because we didn't have much sex education. We did have a movie once; Mr Woods brought it from Sydney. It was about our reproductive organs and it was quite funny because it then showed you what would happen if you were 'a lady of the night' and it showed you this lady standing up against a public bar, with a cigarette, and then she ended up with venereal disease and she went mad. So when I left Fairbridge, I thought that anyone who stood against a bar of a pub and smoked ended up mad, so I used to walk very quickly past pubs.

Joyce Drury recalls being frightened of kissing a boy:

> I can remember one boy trying to kiss me and I ran for my life . . . and I always thought, I'm not going to get married; I'm not going to have babies – and I probably thought kissing made babies in some

way – because coming from a poor, big family, and probably in my mind I thought, I don't want that to happen . . . so when someone tried to kiss me I ran for my life.

Lennie Magee recalls how, as teenagers at Fairbridge in the early 1960s, we were clumsy and unsure mixing socially with the girls:

To put your arm around a girl required for me the same courage needed to stick your tongue in a light socket. I would sit for the whole movie thinking about it, obsessed with the thought. If I could just reach out in a sort of one-armed yawn and place my hand on the back of the seat, then I could just touch her soft slender shoulder . . . A few times each year, all the tables and benches were moved to the far end of Nuffield Hall and some elderly musicians were brought in so we could enjoy a social. The band played all the hit songs from their experiences in the Crimean War, while we stood around in small groups hoping the hall would catch fire.

Looking back, it is quite remarkable that we managed to create as much fun as we did, because Fairbridge was not a happy place and there was little to be happy about.

5

SUFFER THE LITTLE CHILDREN

As little children we lived in permanent fear, being frightened all day about going back to the cottage after school, in terror of another beating for the slightest reason, or for no reason at all.

It was the youngest children who were the least protected, the most vulnerable, and the most abused.

Linda Gidman was five when she arrived at the farm school in Molong. Her older brother and sister were already there but she was still traumatised:

I kept asking for my mother and I was saying . . . 'Mum wouldn't leave me here . . . I'm waiting for Mummy to take me home' and all that sort of thing . . . and they were saying, 'Well, she's not coming: make the most of it.'

Laurie Reid was seven years old when he arrived with an older brother and two older sisters:

After just a couple of days I started to cry. 'I want my mother. I want my mother' . . . and she [the cottage mother] said, 'I'll give you something to bloody well cry about.' And they did, they strapped me and I found every time I cried I got the strap. So I thought, hey, I'd better cut this out and grow up fast, you know.

Barney Piercy had a similar recollection when he arrived aged five, with his brother Dennis, who was just a year older:

It must have been the next day, the second day, I woke up in this strange land and I started calling for my mum and I got a bit upset and frantic, and that's when I shit myself and I was still carrying on when this bloke came along and gave me a crack between the eyes . . . I did nothing after that. I just shut everything off.

Many of the children had only scant memories of their parents. David Eva has a faint recollection of seeing his mother for the last time:

I was put into a home when I suppose I was three or four . . . I can't remember too much at all. I didn't like it there . . . One day somebody came into the place and said to me, 'David, we'd like you to go and see your mother, she's in hospital,' and I can remember so plainly going in a car and going to hospital and seeing this woman in bed. And she said to me, 'I'm your mother,' and, 'I'll give you something to remember me by.' And it was a watch. She gave me a letter case with envelopes and [the address] where I could write. I never saw her again and she never wrote to me, and that was it . . . there was no hugging or anything like that. She was sitting in bed. I don't know what was wrong with her. That was all . . . and then, of course, it was full steam ahead [to Australia].

Being forced to adapt to a life without parents, or any pastoral care to speak of, was difficult enough, but many of the children were also split up from their brothers and sisters and put into different cottages when they arrived. No attempts were made to keep families together – my brothers and I were simply lucky. Boys lived in separate cottages from girls, which meant brothers and sisters were always separated within an hour of arriving at Fairbridge.

Six-year-old Peter Bennett recalls, 'Very seldom did I see my sister, or she see me, or very seldom did we see each other . . . because we just weren't allowed to mix with the girls. That was it.'

Eddie Scott, who was also six years old when he arrived at Fairbridge, remembers being routinely beaten by his cottage mother, Mollie Gibson; knowing nothing else, he thought it was a normal part of childhood. I remember Eddie well because he was only a year older than me and later lived in the same cottage at Fairbridge.

By the time I turned seven her heavy drinking became obvious and regular incidents of sudden violent outbursts made me fearful and constantly anxious. I remember how much I wanted my mum. Some nights [Gibson] would be drinking early, and when she put me to bed at about 7 p.m. she would make me bend across the bed and flog me with [a] leather belt 'to make sure you're a good boy tomorrow'. This wasn't because I had done anything wrong, it was just a way of intimidating me . . . I remember trying to guess her moods, anxious to avoid trouble . . . But I could never get it right, and I was beaten at least weekly, so often it became normal to be flogged . . . it was a cold, lonely existence.[1]

Four years after Eddie arrived in Australia, his five-year-old younger brother, Graham, joined him and Eddie was unable to protect him from the abuse and violence:

> My little brother – whom I hadn't seen since he was a baby . . . came into my cottage. I never knew he was coming and wondered why Mum and Dad weren't there too. He was only five and he cried day and night for our mum. He would wet the bed and sometimes soil himself and I had to stand by and watch him being bullied and victimised. Sometimes I was forced to clean up his mess. I felt terribly responsible and helpless in equal measures . . . In many ways, seeing his fear and distress upset me more than all the abuse I went through. I was never able to protect him properly or help him feel safe.[2]

Henry McFarlane recalls, 'There was no love, nobody if you felt a bit down; nobody came around and put their arm around you and said, "Come on – we're here for you."'

Margaret McLaughlin can clearly see how unsuited the cottage mothers were to their jobs:

> I think they were sadists and a lot of them were very cruel and you never got a cuddle. No one in my whole life there put their arm around me and said, 'You're a good girl, Maggie,' or 'Margaret, we do care for you, and we do love you.' I was never told I was loved till I was married.

In his original design of the farm schools Kingsley Fairbridge had recognised the importance of well-suited and qualified staff. However, the organisation in Australia never paid attractive wages and as a result the standard of cottage mothers was low and the turnover of staff high. The cottage mothers were the lowest-paid staff at Fairbridge, paid less than at the going rate for unskilled farm labourers. After tax, board and lodgings were deducted a Fairbridge Cottage mother was left with only a few pounds a week.[3]

The obstacles to attracting good cottage mothers to Fairbridge were the same faced by most other children's institutions in the postwar years: poor pay, unsociable hours of work, low job status, geographic isolation and very modest accommodation. A cottage mother's quarters – two small rooms and a bathroom attached to the end of the children's cottage – were hardly salubrious.

Among the cottage mothers who stayed at Fairbridge the longest were the 'widows of Empire'. Typical of them was Kathleen Johnstone, who was at the farm school from the early 1950s till the mid-1960s. No one knew a great deal about Johnstone's past or her family, but she was believed to be a widow, having been married to a British Indian Army officer. The boys in Gowrie Cottage remember she kept a sheathed Nepalese Gurkha knife hanging on the wall of her quarters. We all knew of the extreme cruelty Johnstone inflicted on the children in her cottage. I simply kept out of her way; if I saw her in the village I would quickly turn and head in another direction.

Johnstone was given the nickname of 'the witch' because of her fearsome treatment of some of the smaller children in her care. She was also known as 'Fag' Johnstone: not only was she a chain smoker but she would leave the burning cigarette hanging out of her mouth till it burned down almost to her lips. The boys in Gowrie Cottage, where she ruled for many years, lived with cigarette ash everywhere as it fell from her mouth as she wandered from room to room. Johnstone had a perennially runny nose and the children used to watch to see if the snot would reach her mouth before she wiped it away. She was very short, standing only a little over five feet tall, had a slightly hunched back, always dressed in black, or dark clothes and carried a huge bunch of keys on her belt.

Miss Jenny Barr was Derek Moriarty's first cottage mother, and he remembers her with great affection. 'She was just one of those rare people that you come across in your lifetime,' he said. 'She was a lovely old lady.' However, when Barr left and Johnstone took her place, Derek's 'world tumbled upside down'. He recalls a morning when he stopped her from beating his younger brother, Paul, with a metal poker during the early morning shower time in winter:

We had to get in and have a cold shower and it was just a case of run in and run out sort of thing; it didn't make any difference, as long as you got wet . . . and one day my younger brother got in there and he just did the same as I did, in and out, and she said, 'Get back in there, you're not even wet,' and of course he objected.

At that point Johnstone made a lunge for the steel poker that was used with the water heater in the bathroom. Now, he's stark naked. I was . . . in the locker room which was next door and I was in there getting dressed and of course he started screaming. And I hit the panic button and I just raced in to see what was going on. I raced in there and she's got the poker up over her head . . . about to flail him again; I made a lunge for it and I got it . . . and to this day I will never know why I didn't bring it down on the back of her head because that was the mood I was in . . . I went out the back and threw it as far as I could up the back yard.

Of course she went straight to the boss and that was it. I got every punishment I could get. There was no pictures, there was no pocket money, there was no dances, no nothing, and plus the usual six of the best. She could have very well killed him. If she hit him the wrong way one more time, you know, he could have been dead.

What distressed Moriarty for a long time afterwards was that there was no one to turn to:

There was certainly no point in appealing to Woods for justice or redress; whenever he had to side with either a child or a staff member, he invariably sided with the staff member. I had nightmares over that for a long, long time. Not so much the fact that she could attack him like that, but the fact that the authorities just turned a blind eye to it. They didn't believe me and, if they did, they turned a blind eye anyway. And it sort of gave me the feeling of what would it take for them to listen to a kid with a genuine complaint.

Johnstone's behaviour provoked one of the rare investigations by child welfare authorities into Fairbridge staff. In 1964 an investigation by the New South Wales Child Welfare Department found that Johnstone had held a little girl's head down the toilet in a failed attempt to cure her of bedwetting, and regularly whipped small children with a riding crop. No action was taken against her and she continued to work at Fairbridge for several more years.

Another of the 'widows of Empire' was Margaret Hodgkinson. Like her friend Johnstone, with whom she played bridge, Hodgkinson had been in India. She was the widow of a knighted judge named Routledge and, although her husband had died, thought she was entitled to be called 'Lady', which was hopelessly out of place at Fairbridge. She remarried a colonel in the British Indian Army and was widowed a second time. Michael Walker remembers Hodgkinson as one of a number of Fairbridge staff who had a problem with alcohol:

> She had a photo of Colonel Hodgkinson, who had a huge sweeping moustache and a turban on his head. She was imperious, superior and upper class. We were just little bits of flotsam. We were there to do her bidding, slaves and lackeys on tap. We weren't thought to have any intrinsic value. 'Fetch this, do that, I'll have a cup of tea on the verandah,' etc. She had a drinking problem. Sherry was the grog she preferred. In her cups we were 'the scum of the English gutters'.

Michael Walker's younger brother, Jim, was only five when he arrived at Fairbridge, and was put in Hodgkinson's Brown Cottage. He recalls regularly being woken in the dormitory and being whipped by Hodgkinson:

> She was fucking shocking . . . She'd say, 'Bend down and say your prayers, you little heathens.' And we'd have these pyjamas on with no tops and she'd come round and flog us all with the ironing cord, you know, the ironing cord doubled over was her favourite weapon. Or a riding crop that she had.

Lennie Magee recalls meeting Hodgkinson the day he arrived at Fairbridge as a seven-year-old. He was the subject of her abuse for the next seven years:

> She tottered in reeking of tobacco and perfume, took one look at me and swept me into her heaving bosom. In a voice I could actually

taste, she croaked, 'Ah, a cuddly boy, just what I always wanted.' I couldn't have replied if I'd wanted to. I was being suffocated by tweed and powder. She always dressed in tweed. Tall and thin, she looked as if she'd just appeared out of a 1930's *Vogue* magazine. She wore thick tortoiseshell glasses over a long nose ... rouge powder and lipstick had been smeared thickly to cover a corrugation of wrinkles, folds and even whiskers ... as a leftover from the Indian Raj, where she had strutted with arrogance and wealth, she still lived her life expecting everyone to wait on her hand and foot. Her husband escaped by dying and now, as a refugee from society, Hodgkinson was masquerading as a 'mother' on a farm in the Australian bush, where she walked slowly along a dirt road with a 'cuddly boy' hanging on to her ruby-clad hand.

Lennie was one of a number of Brown Cottage boys who remembers her indiscriminate cruelty:

And she was a very brutal woman, very brutal ... she would beat the children – ironing cords, I've still got the scars on my legs from ironing cords ... she was very cruel, we had to get up very early in the morning, even as a little child, even when it was winter [and get] into the cold shower ... and she would stand there and watch.

Lennie said the children in Brown Cottage 'lived with a constant feeling of apprehension ... As if a violent storm was brewing.' He said the little children were too afraid to complain, and that the principal and child welfare authorities were largely unaware of the horrors encountered by the small children inside the walls of their cottages. He said that like many of the children he was 'too little and frightened to even dream of telling anybody'.

Lennie said Hodgkinson kept a small dachshund dog named Obadiah:

> The dog peed everywhere. It didn't seem to have a bladder . . . the smell of yellow dog urine permeated the cottage. What was worse is that we had to wipe it up. Small boys under Hodgkinson's watchful eye would follow Obadiah about with wet stinking cloths while he irrigated every . . . floor. If passionate hatred can give meaning to empty lives then Obadiah took on prodigious proportions.

Ian Bayliff said that he and other small children spent their entire childhood living in dread of their erratic and unpredictable cottage mother in Blue Cottage, Lilias Da Freitas:

> As little children we lived in permanent fear, being frightened all day about going back to the cottage after school, in terror of another beating for the slightest reason, or for no reason at all. It was absolutely miserable; it was absolute hell. Any instances in my life, not just Fairbridge, I can forgive, but one person I'll never forgive is Da Freitas because she was such a sadistic person. Not just to me, to everybody. It didn't matter what she picked up – she used to wield a riding whip, or an electric jug cord – and she used to slash and belt you on the bare backside . . . She was the most despicable person you could ever – she's dead now – I'll tell you this now – I don't know where she is . . . if I knew where her grave was, I'd go and find it and work out where her head is, and I'd piss on it. And I'd tell you what, I'd have to hope she died with her mouth open. And I'm not the only one – I'd be in a long line if I ever found it.

Discipline at Fairbridge was largely enforced by high levels of corporal punishment and most of the physical punishment – and physical abuse – was administered by the principal. Jimmy Walker, who arrived at the school when he was five, and was there for twelve years, believes Woods relished punishing the children with a variety of instruments:

> There were three of them: there was a chimney sweep broom, half a hockey stick, and a normal cane about six foot long . . . Whenever he was going to punish someone he always formed a circle and made a big deal of it, you know. He used to love it, he had that streak in him, where he sort of loved beating, beating the kids.

David Wilson remembers the brutality of the beatings:

> I had bruises for about a month after [Woods] caned me. Because you have got to understand he was in the prime of his life. He was about twenty-two stone, six foot three or something, and there no fat on him at all. All muscle. And he used to really lay into us.

Eddie Scott says that most of the male staff were brutal in their physical beatings of the children but that Woods was the worst:

> I was beaten frequently throughout my ten years at Fairbridge . . . There was always shouting, name calling and telling me how bad I was, how I would never amount to anything. The cruellest lie was when . . . Woods would tell me my mother sent me away because she didn't want me.

Woods, whose temper was legendary, regularly administered punishment in his office. If summonsed we had to go up the back steps of his house and turn right into his office, where you were ordered to bend over his desk as he brought down the cane across your backside with as much force as his huge frame could muster. Lennie Magee describes the experience well:

> I could hardly breathe. Fear like a vice had squeezed all the air out of me. He rose up to his full height . . . then he reached out [for] . . . a hockey stick split in half and wrapped tightly in black tape with the bent end sheared off. 'Bend over you scoundrel' . . . Then, *thwack*. The pain was a brilliant white and jagged and it shot from your backside to the top of your head, rebounded off the top of your skull and sprang straight down to your feet. 'Stand still, you scoundrel.' *Whack*. Because I'd lost my grip on the desk (and life itself) the combined force of twenty stone wielding a stick drove me over the desk and into his wooden chair.

Eddie Baker went to Fairbridge as a six-year-old and speaks quite positively of his experiences there. He remembers Woods was so busy running the farm he sometimes caught up on a backlog of punishments by going round the dormitories caning children in the middle of the night:

> I quite admired him, because he was a man that probably got along on two or three or four hours' sleep, if that – and he would be in his office at early hours in the morning doing his reports and so forth. But if he had to chastise a child, he would have it in his notebook . . . eventually he'd get around to it and it didn't matter whether it was midnight, or one or two in the morning . . . He'd get everyone out of bed in the dormitory, simply because he had to catch up with what he had to do in his notebook . . . he brought the canes in under his arm. You'd be all shivering a bit, not knowing which one was going to

get it . . . Then when you were all out of bed . . . the particular child would be dealt with and then you could get back in to bed.

A special status was afforded those children at Fairbridge who defied authority, and being beaten or having your privileges suspended was considered a badge of honour. This was particularly so for boys who received a public thrashing in Nuffield Hall. We were entirely unaware that much of the punishment meted out to us was illegal. The law relevant to us was the New South Wales Child Welfare Act of 1939. To prevent the abuse of children in institutions, Part XI, Section 56 of the Act, which described us as 'inmates', stated that corporal punishment should not exceed 'a maximum of three strokes on each hand' and that it 'should not be inflicted in the presence of other inmates'.

Public thrashings, which were for many years a regular feature of life at Fairbridge, were conducted for particularly serious offences, such as running away from the school and in cases where Woods wanted to set an example for everyone else. His intention was also to humiliate the child. The prospect of a public thrashing probably did deter us from misbehaving but it did not humiliate those being punished: to the children of Fairbridge being publicly thrashed was like winning a special bravery award.

Henry McFarlane remembers when eight boys who had run away from the school were recaptured and publicly flogged with hockey sticks. There were so many boys to be beaten that the work was shared by Woods, the farm supervisor and the headmaster of the Fairbridge Primary School:

They caught them and gave them a public flogging. To me that was wrong . . . he [Woods] was a pretty brutal bloke . . . .and he was about twenty-two stone – *whoosh, whoosh* . . . It was brutal. And it was wrong. They wore themselves out beating those boys. And what was the headmaster of the local school doing getting involved? It had nothing to do with him . . . and you'd always see the kids, when they were having their shower, and when the bruise comes out, it comes out purple and after a while goes yellow, you know, on the outer. It wouldn't be allowed today.

Billy King, who was about my age and came out to Fairbridge on the same ship, recalls having to witness a public thrashing:

What put the fear of god into me was when Woods announced there would be a public thrashing . . . I still have flashbacks over those episodes and [how] everyone had to gather in the [hall] to watch . . . I just couldn't cope with that at all. I was absolutely terrified. I often used to think, I am going to run away from this place, and then the public thrashings used to come into it and that used to stop me . . . it was fear; it was just . . . I couldn't handle it.

Eddie Scott also remembers those floggings:

He publicly flogged me in the hall on at least two occasions and it was violent, painful and humiliating. He made me face the children, assembled to watch, so they would see me crying. Scenes like that were done as a spectacle to terrify the children into obedience as much as they were a consequence for whatever rule I had broken.[4]

I was thrashed in front of everyone once, because three of us were caught stealing fruit from the orchard one Thursday afternoon on our way home from school. The Orange High School bus had dropped us off below the farm, and as we walked up the Amaroo Road we helped ourselves to some overripe pears that hadn't been harvested. We should have been more careful. Across the paddock, up on the sports field Woods was sitting on an upturned petrol can umpiring a game of cricket. He spotted us and a boy was sent running down to intercept us. As we came through the village gates the boy told us we had to go immediately to see Woods. The Boss went into his customary rage, calling us 'scoundrels'.

It was not until the lunch in Nuffield Hall the following Saturday that Woods announced we would be publicly punished that evening. I spent an uncomfortable, unsettled, gut-wrenching afternoon anticipating the beating I would be getting that night.

I never fully understood why Woods' was so upset about us scrumping a bit of overripe fruit. There were far worse crimes at Fairbridge, such as running away and being caught by the police, or being caught breaking into a building and stealing. I had been caned many times before, but always in Woods' office. I thought it ironic that I should be punished for doing what Fairbridge salespeople in England had told us we could do when they were painting Fairbridge as the Promised Land; eating plentiful fruit from the tree.

After the evening meal that night all the boys shuffled over to Nuffield Hall. Woods began by lecturing everyone about what a terrible crime we had committed and said we now had to be severely punished. When it came time to lash the three of us I was anxious to get it over with and pushed to the front, even though the conventional wisdom was to wait until last because Woods put so much effort into the caning that he would begin to tire himself out. God, it hurt. But while some kids let out involuntary yelps and screams I was proud because I didn't make a sound.

I was lucky to be hit with a big stick or a cane and not the hockey stick. Ron Simpson remembers being seriously injured when he was beaten by Woods with that stick. When he was fourteen and working in the dairy he slept through the alarm and was late starting the early morning milking. When the milk was delivered late for breakfast Woods gave Simpson a beating:

> He bent me over and he hit me with a hockey stick . . . He didn't hit me on the backside; he hit me on the back, just above the coccyx bone. And he pulled me [up], turned me around and then he hit me on the back again and sent me straight down the [principal's house] back steps. There were five steps, and I had gravel rash, I was crying, I wet my pants, and I had to go back to work. Back to the dairy and clean up the cow yards and that.

Simpson continued working as his back became increasingly painful. Then one day while he was working in the vegetable yard of the village kitchen, his back gave out:

> It would have been about three months after that I was on kitchen duty and I got this shooting pain in my lower part of my back. I fell down onto the ground and I couldn't feel anything . . . Nicko picked me up and ran me down to the hospital in a wheelbarrow, and they X-rayed my back and found I had a broken back, that's what really happened to me.

He went first to the tiny hospital in Molong, then to the larger one in Orange, before he was taken, lying on a stretcher, on the train to Sydney, where he stayed in hospital for more than a year. He said that in all the time he was in Sydney Hospital he received only one visitor, ex-Fairbridge boy Charlie Brown, who was in the army and on leave in Sydney. Many years later Ron said he was still troubled by the injury: 'I get a lot of pain. I have trouble getting out of bed every morning of my life.'

In 1948 Woods was instructed by the chairman of the Fairbridge Council not to use a hockey stick following an investigation by the New South Wales Child Welfare Department into complaints of his brutality. The investigation found the charges against Woods 'could not be substantiated' but noted that he had used the hockey stick to beat the children and had been ordered by Fairbridge not to do so in future. He had also been ordered to cool down and not to hit the children in fits of rage, and that there should be no more public floggings. The Fairbridge Council minutes recorded that:

> The principal was then instructed that corporal punishment was to be given to the children only with the cane, only after several hours had elapsed from the time of the misdemeanour giving rise to the punishment and only in the presence of a third person of responsibility, and that each caning was to be recorded.

However, Woods again survived the board's admonishment and would continue as principal for another seventeen years. He continued with the public thrashings. When he was finally sacked, it was not for his maltreatment of the children but for his own sex scandal.

Woods was dismissed only six months after his wife, Ruth, had died suddenly of a blood clot to the brain shortly before Christmas 1964. Within a month of Ruth's passing Woods was in a relationship with a recently divorced cottage mother, Mrs Wunch, whom

Woods proposed to marry. This did not sit well with the Sydney Fairbridge Council, and after discussions with the new chairman, the Reverend W. L. Calov, Woods agreed to postpone the marriage. Unbeknown to Woods, Calov communicated his concerns about the affair to the UK Fairbridge Society, which had the ultimate responsibility for the hiring and firing of Fairbridge principals. At the time the chairman of the UK Fairbridge Society was Sir William Slim, who had taken up the position after serving as the governor-general of Australia from 1953 to 1959. (Slim would later be accused of sexually abusing a number of Fairbridge boys when he had visited the Molong school as governor-general.)

At a meeting of the UK Fairbridge Society chaired by Slim on 22 July 1965, the decision was made to sack Woods, who, the minutes record, had 'created a scandal and besmirched the good name of Fairbridge' with his proposal to marry a cottage mother who was a divorcee.[5]

The New South Wales Fairbridge Foundation expressed 'great shock' at the decision of the UK Fairbridge Society to sack Woods after twenty-six years of service.[6] Sydney did not attempt to persuade London to reverse its decision, but did press successfully for a more generous severance package. Woods had no superannuation, no professional qualifications and at fifty-nine years of age would have had difficulty finding a comparable job.

Sydney also persuaded London that Woods be given money so that his children could finish university, which is interesting because Fairbridge never provided financial assistance to any Fairbridge children to attend university.

At the same time as a termination 'package' was being designed for Woods, Fairbridge wanted Mrs Wunch, the cottage mother involved in the scandal, 'off the scene' straightaway and instructions were issued that she 'must leave the employment of the society immediately'.[7]

Woods was given a splendid send-off befitting his huge reputation. It was widely reported and universally accepted that he had chosen to retire; there was never any suggestion that he had been dismissed. The major newspaper in the district described him as 'a great man', and the Fairbridge annual report recorded his 'outstanding service'.[8]

With the help of Fairbridge contacts Woods was able to immediately take up a job as an English and history teacher at the Illawarra Grammar School in Wollongong, south of Sydney. He subsequently married another cottage mother, Mrs Grey, and they lived together until Woods died in 1977. He was seventy-two years old.

In the years after Woods left the farm school, once in a while some of the former Fairbridge kids would visit him at his home on the south coast, and occasionally he would appear at reunions of the Old Fairbridgians Association. But most, including me, never saw him again – and nor did we ever want to.

6

FEAR AND SHAME

Jack Newberry touched me up. I had three other people sexually abuse me at Fairbridge . . . Who do you tell? Because no one wants to know anyway. And then they don't believe you and then you're accused of being a liar.

While most of the Fairbridge children were forthcoming about the physical abuse they suffered at the farm school, they were much slower to speak out about sexual abuse. When I began researching the Fairbridge story, only four or five of those I interviewed mentioned to me that they had been sexually abused. But when others became aware these people had revealed such experiences, it sparked many more to come forward. What started as a trickle eventually became a torrent. By the time the Molong Fairbridge kids won their court action against the institution in 2015, more than 160 people, or 60 per cent of the survivors, claimed they had been sexually abused while they were at the farm school.

Mary O'Brien told me one of the earliest accounts of sexual abuse at Fairbridge. Mary came out to Australia in the same party as me. She told me she was regularly sexually abused at Fairbridge and kept it to herself for decades. At fourteen, she was moved out of her cottage and assigned to live and work in Gloucester House, where visiting Old Fairbridgians and other sundry guests stayed. It was also the home of the aftercare officer, Bill Phillips, and his family.

> This was a considerable privilege, to go and live with these people in Gloucester House. I went to live with them and I shared a bedroom with their daughter, but really I was just a domestic there. I was expected to clean up after them and serve them and their visitors . . . but it was the most degrading part of my life, the most humiliating part of my life . . . He [Phillips] treated me like shit, sexually abused me. He would wait until his wife was asleep and then come into the bedroom I shared with his daughter and asleep and regularly abused me. I would then be expected to serve him breakfast and clean up after him next morning. I didn't mention it to anybody because I thought it was just happening to me. I had no idea whether other children were having problems.

In July 2017, a friend of mine from Fairbridge with whom I'd kept in touch gave more details of abuse by Bill Phillips to a British government inquiry into child sexual abuse:

> Mr Phillips made a point of slipping into our bedroom. He placed his hands under the blankets and caressed my body. The first time he did this, he placed a finger to my lips to indicate I was to be quiet while he glided his hand over me. On subsequent evenings he became more daring, fondling my chest, around my body and into my vagina. It became a frequent event that disturbed me greatly. I was sexually

naïve. I had never engaged in masturbation nor had sexual activity with another person. I would lay awake at night, unable to sleep; terrified that he would come into the room. If he didn't come into my room I would eventually fall asleep exhausted from tension. On the nights he came in to abuse me I would lay very tense, with my buttock muscles tightened, pretending to be asleep. Mr Phillips would encourage me to relax as he proceeded to abuse me . . . This sexual abuse was repeated regularly for several months. I didn't dare scream out or speak to . . . any other staff member because I was very embarrassed, thoroughly ashamed and terrified that I would be punished.[1]

Liz Sharp, who went to Fairbridge in 1962 aged nine, said she was sexually abused by a number of men while she was there, including Jack Newberry when he became principal of the school in 1966. She believed Newberry's wife knew what he was up to:

Jack Newberry touched me up. I had three other people sexually abuse me at Fairbridge other than Newberry. I must have been just one of those people that had 'victim' written on their forehead. We were in Molong Cottage and we were allowed in to her [the cottage mother's] quarters to watch . . . television with her and her husband [Newberry]. It must have been winter and there were blankets over everybody and I was sitting near my friends and he was sitting next to me and I mean, he even shoved his hands up inside me then . . . she must have known what he was like and she must have known he had me.

Liz explained why she never told anyone: 'Who do you tell? Because no one wants to know anyway. And then they don't believe you and then you're accused of being a liar.'

119

Derek Moriarty was the first of the former Fairbridge boys who told me about being sexually abused. He was angry that many people were still trying to deny the abuse had occurred, and angry with himself, because he was a victim who for many years had said nothing:

> I've never told anybody this in my life. And I thought I was going to take it to my grave. I just . . . it haunts me every now and again, and I never mentioned it before because I'm embarrassed about it. Even though it wasn't my doing . . . what I've seen and heard . . . you know, it's sort of sickening and I thought to myself, if every one is embarrassed and nobody says anything, it will go on . . . and it has to be stopped . . . so, while we've all been in denial, I bet there are a lot of people besides myself that are in the same denial – and I've stated it publicly many, many times, you know, 'It didn't happen at Fairbridge.' It did, and I don't know to what extent. But it happened to me and I would say I'm probably too embarrassed about it. I shouldn't be but I'm probably more embarrassed now I've kept it under my hair for so long.

In every case where a former Fairbridge child told me about being sexually abused, they said I was the first person they had ever told. Some talked to me about it over the phone; some told me at Fairbridge meetings and reunions. Often they were reticent to discuss it in detail and simply wanted to confirm it happened to them. Typically, they might say, 'It happened to me too, you know,' or 'So and so wasn't the only one you know, he [the perpetrator] did to me, and others too,' or 'A lot more happened than you know, let me tell you.'

At first I was surprised that it had taken the victims so long to talk about it, but I subsequently learned that it is common for victims of child sex abuse not to discuss it for many years. Many never disclose it, even to their partners. The Australian Royal Commission into Institutional Responses to Child Sexual Abuse found that typically it takes decades for people who have been sexually abused to disclose the abuse.[2]

While only a few Fairbridgians told me about being sexually abused when I was researching *The Forgotten Children*, more spoke out when we interviewed them for the television documentary *The Long Journey Home*. I had first thought about making the documentary about Fairbridge while I was researching the book. In 2006, I arranged three crews to film some Fairbridge children at the old farm school village on the occasion of a Fairbridge kids' reunion, which is held every two years. I had the help of Emily Booker, an accomplished film maker and former director of communications with UNICEF in New York, and my old friends from the ABC Stewart Burchmore and Peter Morton. We recorded about thirty hours of interviews and I was still pondering how to raise the substantial funding needed to produce the documentary when fate intervened in the form of another old friend, Gordon Elliott. Gordon was a famous TV presenter in Australia in the 1980s and went to America, where he also became a highly successful presenter and then a major TV program producer and Emmy Award winner. When we caught up on one of his visits to Australia, he was taken by the Fairbridge story and generously agreed to back the venture with his own considerable talent and the formidable resources of his US TV production company. With Emily Booker as his co-executive producer, the powerful and moving documentary was aired nationally on ABC TV in November 2009, to good reviews:

Inspired by Hill's pioneering research into the story behind the farm where he spent much of his childhood, *The Long Journey Home* is a compelling, disturbing, admirably balanced and unerringly humane account of the often inhumane treatment many children endured in what was essentially a slave labour camp. Former Fairbridge children recounted the beatings, psychological cruelty and sexual abuse they received. The tales are harrowing, with several women speaking about their horrific experiences for the first time.[3]

Margaret McLaughlin and another former Fairbridgian, Christina Murray, by then both in their late seventies, insisted on being interviewed on film together, talking to Emily Booker. They had been friends at Fairbridge more than fifty years earlier but had never told their families of the abuse they had endured. They had not even talked to each other about it until that morning.

Maggie: They just took liberties. You'd have to go to their house or their rooms . . .

Christina: And if you gave them sexual favours, you were thought better of, I'll let you know that.

Maggie: This is the first time I've really spoken . . .

Christina: We don't talk about it.

Emily: You've never told anybody?

Christina: We're the first ones . . .

Maggie: Ever in my life.

Emily: It's an awful secret to live with, isn't it?

Maggie: Yes [crying].

Christina: Sshh. Come on . . . We've never, I've never talked to Margaret about it; she's never talked to me and you'll find half the others haven't talked about it either.

Seventy-nine-year-old Ron Simpson was another who first described being sexually abused when he agreed to be interviewed for the documentary. He was in tears on film when he described being raped as a thirteen-year-old by the village kitchen supervisor:

> I was working in the kitchen with a man by the name of West – he had three children, he was married. There was an area where we used to have to peel potatoes, just clearing up the peelings to put in the pig bins. And this man came out, this West, he was the cook there and he grabbed me and pushed me into the toilet – there was a small toilet in the area – and he tore my pants off, and he sodomised me. I was about thirteen. I don't know how they could do it to people.

Asked if he had reported the incident to anyone at the time Ron said, 'Yes. I told my cottage mother and she said, "Mr West's not like that. He's got three children and he's a married man." And she beat me with a stick. That was her answer.'

A number of other girls – and boys – later came forward to say they had been abused by Bill Phillips, who as the after-care officer found jobs for Fairbridge kids when they left the farm school. Eddie Scott later said that he had also been sexually abused by Phillips:

> One day when I was about thirteen, another boy and I were caught smoking and we were sent up to [Phillips] for punishment. He told the other boy to wait outside and called me into his office where he told me: 'I am going to give you an old-fashioned punishment'. He told me to take down my trousers and my underpants,

and made me lay across his lap. I was expecting he would belt me with his hand or maybe a cane, but instead he began rubbing and fondling my backside. He slipped his hand between my buttocks and put his finger into my bottom. The whole time I could feel his erection pushing into my belly while he was rocking and touching my backside, and rubbing his hands all over my body. Every so often he would give me a slap and I could sense him becoming excited. All the time he never said a word. When he was finished with me, he told me 'Behave yourself!' and sent me out of the room. He never called the other boy in for his punishment and I was too shocked and humiliated to tell the other boy or anyone else what happened. He tried it again a few months later, but that time I threatened to tell Mr Woods and he let me go. But I would never have told Mr Woods. He would have belted me for lying. I would not have been believed . . . Later, I heard other child migrants from Fairbridge refer to Phillips as the 'bum rubber'. So I suppose I was not the only one he did that to.[4]

Eddie Scott was one of a number of Fairbridge children who spoke of the sexual perversity of Bill Mott, who was the principal of the small primary school at the back of Fairbridge village:

[Bill Mott] was . . . another sexual pervert who behaved badly towards me and lots of other children. He was always following us boys into the toilets, and would push between us at the urinal, expose his erect penis and begin rubbing himself in front of the boys. I saw him do that many times and sometimes I ran away before I'd even finished urinating. He would stand at the front of the classroom and rub himself through his clothes, with one leg up on a chair so we could all see the outline of his genitals.

I don't know if any of the staff at Molong knew what he was doing, but the other kids certainly did. I didn't tell any of the staff, it wasn't a place where I felt safe or trusted enough. I heard years later he was eventually convicted of child sex offences after he left Molong.[5]

One of the worst accounts I encountered involved Vivian Bingham, who recalls first being sexually abused when she was five or six years old. Vivian turned up unannounced at Fairbridge when we were filming interviews for *The Long Journey Home* and insisted on telling her story. I interviewed her that day and am still shaken by the story she told.

Vivian: I was sexually abused when I was five years old. And it was down there [in the village vegetable garden shed]. So, I've been holding it all this time.
DH: Who sexually abused you?
Vivian: Mr Newberry . . . I just kept it in. And I suppose, in a way, I felt like it was my fault that it happened. But as I got older, I realised it wasn't my fault.

After the interview I visited her at her little house outside the country town of Yeovil, in New South Wales, where I recorded her full story. When the Fairbridge children later took legal action for the abuse they had suffered at Fairbridge, Vivian was a lead plaintiff in the court case and provided a full sworn statement to our lawyers. However, because the case was finally settled by mediation, Vivian's statement has never been made public till now.

In 2019 I heard she had suffered a massive stroke and was in a Salvation Army nursing home at Parkes, which is about

75 kilometres west of the old Fairbridge Farm School. I went to visit her with my friend Michael Georgeson and although she had difficulty speaking, she was pleased to see me and squeezed my hand tightly. She gave permission for me to use the full statement she had made to the lawyers for the subsequent court case. Vivian died in 2020, a few months after my visit. I already knew a lot about her story from my earlier interviews, but the affidavit gave me the full picture for the first time, including, tragically, an account of how the experience of abuse followed her after Fairbridge and through much of her adult life.

I remember her arriving at Fairbridge only a few months after me, when she was so young. She was tiny – less than a metre tall and weighing 24 kilograms – confused and frightened. She had a brother, Arnold, who had been sent out the year before her in 1958 aged five. He was in one of the boys' cottages so could offer her little support or protection.

Vivian was reportedly a happy little girl when she arrived at John Howard Mitchell House prior to sailing to Australia. The matron's report at the time described her as a 'dear little girl', 'attractive and amusing', 'a loveable little girl – never lost for conversation'. According to the matron, Vivian asked many questions, 'was very popular with other children' and had a 'carefree' attitude. In one of the reports the matron recorded that she regularly wet her bed, 'But this will quickly clear with care and training, I feel sure.'[6]

When she arrived at Fairbridge farm Vivian remembers wanting her mum:

I missed my mother . . . I felt really alone and scared . . . because I was such a tiny thing . . . Whenever I was flogged, whenever I got hurt, I used to think, where's Mum? So I could run to Mum. And my Mum wasn't there . . . I couldn't run to Mum.

Within months her reports at Fairbridge began to include comments such as 'intellectually dull', 'quiet and rather nervous at times', 'lacks ability to concentrate' and 'Vivian does not seem to show any progress at all'. When she was only six years old the local headmaster at Fairbridge Primary School reported, 'Vivian is a real problem child'.

Vivian recalls being physically abused by the sadistic Kathleen Johnstone. She said she was forced to scrub the cottage floor with a toothbrush and whipped with a riding crop that left 'welts and bruises'. When she wet the bed, Johnstone beat her with an electric cord. Vivian also remembers having her head held down the toilet to cure her of bedwetting. She said she was confused about the punishments. 'I did not know what I had done wrong,' she said, 'or if I'd done anything wrong.'

Vivian said she was first sexually abused when she was about five by Jack Newberry, whose wife worked as a cottage mother. Newberry worked at Fairbridge in the early 1960s as the after-care officer, responsible for finding the kids jobs when they reached the age of seventeen and left the farm. In 1966 he became the principal when Woods retired.

One day when I was about five years old I wandered down to the shed near the vegetable garden. I walked into the shed and whilst I was inside, Mr Newberry walked in. He dropped his pants to the ground and asked me to touch his penis. I was young and afraid. I did not understand what was happening. I did what Mr Newberry told me to do. Mr Newberry also touched my vagina. This was very painful. I cried when Mr Newberry touched me in this way. He eventually stopped touching me and stood up and walked away. Before he left the shed, he turned around and said to me words to the effect 'If you say anything about this, it will be worse for you next time.'

Vivian shared many of the symptoms of victims of abuse, including shame, remorse and guilt, low self-esteem, and a lack of confidence.

I was afraid to tell anyone about what Mr Newberry did because of his threats; also, I did not think anyone would believe me. I felt like somehow what had happened was my fault. I did not tell any adult at Fairbridge about what Mr Newberry had done to me in the shed next to the vegetable garden, as I was afraid about what else Mr Newberry would do to me. Although I did not understand what happened, I felt somehow I had done something wrong.

She said the abuse shaped her world view throughout her adult life:

After that I was scared that anyone could do anything that they wanted to me. I withdrew and tried to keep my distance from people. For years I have had nightmares about what Mr Newberry did to me.

Vivian's case is a typical example of how the pattern of abuse experienced in childhood follows survivors into adulthood. After finally leaving Fairbridge Vivian found work, but was soon pregnant and back at the farm school, having no family and no one else to turn to. 'Even though I hated Fairbridge,' she said. 'It was the only home I knew. I had no one else.'

Having given birth to a baby girl but with no home, no job and nobody to support her, Vivian was pressured into signing the child for adoption. 'Doing so caused me enormous grief and mental distress for decades thereafter. I felt everything had come the full circle – I was taken away from my mother and then my baby was taken away from me.'

Vivian found somewhere to live and a variety of jobs, in a shoe shop, a clothing boutique and a restaurant as a waitress. Suffering severe mood swings she said she tried to 'shove all the memories deep inside . . . and not think about them'. She said she 'did not feel good about the person who I was', and attempted suicide by slashing her wrists.

In Orange she met and married, but she and her husband only stayed together for about a year and a half. 'He hit me and abused me during our marriage,' she said. 'I think I had come to accept being abused was my due since my time at Fairbridge.' Vivian had a daughter during the short marriage, whom she named Heidi.

I lived in Sydney for a short while with Heidi before attempting to reunite with my husband in Wollongong. His parents were nearby and accused me of being an unfit mother. I felt extreme pressure from my former husband and his parents to leave Heidi with him, and reluctantly did so. I felt I had no power. I believed I had to do what other people told me to do. This was devastating to me. I loved her dearly. I thought I would be able to get her back, but I never did.

Vivian was aware of the long-term consequences of childhood sexual abuse and how it plagued her all her life.

I now believe that the physical and psychological abuse . . . had a very bad effect on the latter course of my life. I still have a hard time trusting people. I have to accept now that I am and have been chronically depressed. Looking back, I believe that my depression contributed to the failure of my marriage . . . and the breakup of my family.

She said that she has always had difficulty with sex – and it worsened after she confronted her past:

I have never liked sex. The only reason I had sex is to get it over with. I still freeze up sometimes. It has gotten worse since I have been thinking about what happened to me at Fairbridge. My husband will try and touch or cuddle me and I push him away and he becomes angry. He cannot understand why I reject him.

Like many other child migrants Vivian never lost the memory of her mum and describes how in her forties she resumed the search:

In the early 1990s I again tried to track down my mother. I asked for information from Fairbridge but could not find her. Each time I tried and failed to find my mother felt like another blow. I thought that maybe I could make more sense of things if I could see her again.

In 2006 she visited the Child Migrant Trust. The trust was set up in the late 1980s and for many years has done a remarkable job in restoring severed connections of former child migrants with their families back in the UK. The trust helped arrange a trip back to the UK for Vivian, but shortly before she was to fly to London she was told her mother had died. 'I found out that she had tried to find me, too, but we never found each other. I feel a great loss at never having been able to meet my mother since I left England as a four-year-old.'

Lord Slim, or Sir William Slim as he was at the time, was the most prominent man to be accused of sexual abuse at Fairbridge. In 1953, when he was serving as governor-general of Australia, the then sixty-two-year-old Slim visited the farm school, where it is claimed he sexually molested a number of the young boys. Slim later returned to England and in 1960 became the president of the UK Fairbridge Society.

Field Marshal William Joseph Slim, 1st Viscount Slim, KG, GCB, GCMG, GCVO, GBE, MC, KStJ, was one of Britain's most feted war heroes. From a relatively modest background, he was born in 1891 at Bristol, England, the son of John Slim, a commercial traveller and his wife, Charlotte. Educated at St Philip's Grammar School, Edgbaston, and King Edward's School, Birmingham, he taught in an elementary school, then worked as a clerk before joining the University of Birmingham Officers Training Corps. At the outbreak of the First World War he enlisted as a private but was quickly gazetted as an officer.

Fighting alongside Australian troops, he was wounded at Gallipoli and repatriated to England. On recovery in 1916, he rejoined his battalion in Mesopotamia (modern-day Iraq), where he was again wounded and awarded the Military Cross. He was transferred to the Indian army in Delhi in 1919 and later posted to the Gurkha Rifles, the beginning of a long association. At the outbreak of the Second World War, Slim commanded the 10th Indian Brigade, which distinguished itself by capturing the East African outpost of Gallabat from the Italians. In March 1942,

Slim was given command of the Burma Corps, then fighting a retreat from Rangoon as the Japanese army swept aside most resistance in South-East Asia. It was his successful battles with the Japanese in Burma that boosted his already impressive reputation. His helping to destroy the myth of Japanese invincibility and victories in battle prompted Louis Mountbatten to describe him as the finest general the Second World War produced.

After the war he was showered with decorations and honours and appointed to the highest rank of field marshal. By 1953 he had so impressed Prime Minister Robert Menzies that he was invited to take up the position of governor-general.

I first became aware of the Slim allegations when I was writing *The Forgotten Children*. In the course of researching the book I interviewed Malcom Field in his apartment in Corrimal, a suburb of Wollongong, south of Sydney. Known to us as 'Flossie' because of his crop of fine blond hair, the interview was fascinating but not exceptional. However, at the end, and after I had packed away my recorder and notebook and he was showing me the door, Malcolm asked me if I knew that Sir William Slim had visited Fairbridge. I said I did know, though his visits had been a few years before my time there.

Malcolm then said that on one of Slim's visits he had invited Flossie, who was around eleven at the time, for a ride in the back of Slim's chauffeur-driven Rolls-Royce. Flossie said that as he sat with the governor-general in the back seat Slim had run his hands up Malcolm's trousers and played with his genitals. I asked Flossie if I could restart our interview to include the story on my recorder but he said he wasn't comfortable with me doing that.

While I believed Flossie's tale, I decided not to include it in the first edition of *The Forgotten Children* because he wasn't prepared to say anything on the record and I had no other evidence or corroboration. I thought that to publish with what little evidence I had would have been unprofessional, and possibly unfair to Slim's memory (he died in 1970).

The matter was not raised again until the launch of *The Forgotten Children* in April 2007, when I was being interviewed by the media. In an interview with the *Sydney Morning Herald* I was asked how sure I was of the accuracy of some of the many controversial claims made in the book. I replied to the journalist that I'd only included material where there was supporting documented evidence or independent corroborating testimonies. To demonstrate this, I told him off the record why I had not included the claim I heard about Slim — because it was not on the record, there was only one claim, and the person making the claim was not prepared to publicly defend the allegation.

The *Herald* did not share my reticence, though, and the next day it ran a full page-three story. Along with a large photo of Lord Slim in a Boy Scout uniform and a headline that read 'Hero, villain and the school for scandal', the piece opened:

Sir William Slim, one of Australia's most revered governors-general, has been accused of attempting to sexually interfere with a young, impoverished British boy sent to an institution in western NSW.

David Hill, a former managing director of the ABC and a staunch republican, has claimed that the war hero and 13th governor-general of Australia had groped students at the Fairbridge Farm School in Molong when he visited in 1955.

Mr Hill said the student concerned had told him, while he was researching a book on Fairbridge, of being attacked in the vice-regal vehicle.[7]

My concern about the *Herald*'s lack of journalistic scruples in running the story was short-lived, when, totally independent of Flossie's claims, two other former Fairbridge boys promptly came forward and publicly alleged that the same thing had happened to them.

The first was Bob Stephens, who talked to the *Australian* newspaper a few days later. Bob later told me that the *Australian* contacted him shortly after the *Herald* story. I had interviewed Bob for the book the year before and while he had not mentioned Slim to me, he had been one of the few Fairbridgians who had talked about sexual abuse at the school. When I later asked him why he had not specifically mentioned Slim at our earlier inter- view, he said he feared he would not be believed. But, he said, when he saw the allegations in the *Sydney Morning Herald* he decided to talk.

Under the headline 'Slim Pickings' the *Australian* wrote:

It has been revealed by former Fairbridge pupil and former managing director of the ABC, David Hill, that Slim – later to become a peer of the realm – groped pre-pubescent boys at Fairbridge Farm School at Molong, in the central west of NSW, when he visited in 1955.

The allegations have this week been supported by a number of former Fairbridge boys. One of these, Robert Stephens, told *The Australian*: 'Other boys spoke of fondling in the back of cars as he toured the farm,' Stephens, 64, said. 'In my case . . . two of us were picked to go in his car as it was leaving.'

Stephens was forced to sit on Slim's knee while another boy sat on the knee of a second adult, he said. As they drove 1km to the main road, Slim slid his hand up inside Stephens's shorts (appar- ently Fairbridge boys were not allowed to wear underpants).

'How do you explain it?' Stephens asked. 'We were innocent kids. I guess we were vulnerable and in a position where no one could really speak out.' Stephens did not speak to anyone about the incident until Hill's revelations at the weekend . . . When Stephens saw the allegations . . . he decided to speak about his own experience. 'No adult would believe these things happened so you didn't talk about it. You think you are the only one. Like so many things that happened at Fairbridge, they don't go away. They live with you all your life.' [8]

Bob later elaborated on the incident in an interview on ABC radio:

On the day that he was leaving, we were asked who would like to ride in the governor-general's car down the driveway . . . Before I knew it, we're at the front gate and I'm pulled down onto his knee and he did things that were totally inappropriate. Somehow or another, I was sat on his [Slim's] knee and, ah, um, these silky white hands were right up, because I was wearing shorts, right up my trousers and yeah, it was not . . . not very nice.

The other boy to speak to the *Australian* was David Cinis. Initially, he wanted to remain nameless but later agreed to be identified. He was eleven years old at the time of the abuse.

'[Slim] came in a big black Rolls-Royce when I was about 11. He offered to drive some of the boys around – the pretty boys, I think. I was white, blond, blue eyes, skinny as a rake. He put his hand up my pants,' the man, now 63, says.

Both sexual and physical abuse was common at Fairbridge at the time. The trauma of what they suffered there was so great that a number of the boys later killed themselves. 'It was like Belsen. The worst place I could possibly imagine,' the man says.[9]

Not everyone was shocked at the Slim allegations. A week after the original *Herald* article, the *Australian* published a letter from a reader, Ivan Goozeff, who claimed he witnessed a similar incident:

> Robert Stephens's allegations regarding the sexual behaviour of former governor-general William Slim came as no surprise to me, as I well remember the occasion of the Queen's visit to Gosford in 1954.
>
> The local Gosford schoolchildren were lined up in Graham Park to watch the passing of the Queen's train, and were at the same time being inspected by the very grand Sir William. As he passed through the rows of young boys I, and others, witnessed him fondling the genitals of a boy adjacent to me, resulting in much discussion amongst the boys later at school. It left me very confused, as I knew that even my doctor would not behave in this way.[10]

The allegations against Slim were also big news in Britain. Slim's son, John Douglas Slim, who inherited his father's title and seat in Britain's House of Lords, dismissed them:

> If any proper research is done these allegations will be found to be quite untrue . . . All of us abominate any interference with children, it is an awful thing to say about anybody and I really don't know why these allegations have cropped up now after all this time.[11]

Many of Slim's supporters refused to believe the allegations and others wanted to believe that his towering military reputation would overshadow them. Russell Young, who served under Slim as a lieutenant with the Royal Lincolnshire Regiment during the Burma campaign, and who was president of the veterans' group the Burma Star Association, said he believed the accusations against Slim of child abuse will be forgotten in time:

> It has been said that he was probably the greatest army leader since the Duke of Wellington . . . You never know what people do in their private lives but we can't believe that of our great leader. I think it will all waft over and everyone will forget about it.[12]

However, Bob Stephens has continued to speak out about Slim. After first talking about the abuse, he said he was so offended at the family's sense of entitlement that he would call on the British House of Lords to end the former governor-general's hereditary peerage:

> I don't care how brilliant a man he might have been militarily, if he abused children the way I was abused, and others, I don't think people like that have the right to continue . . . in terms of peerage that goes on from family to family to family. I think that it's outrageous.

Stephens was not successful in persuading the Lords to strip Slim of his peerage posthumously; however, he did get the name Slim stripped from a major road in the Australian capital of Canberra.

In June 2019 the *Canberra Times* reported that the Australian Capital Territory government had agreed to rename the road that had been known as William Slim Drive. The ACT government said it was responding to calls for the change from Stephens, who had an art gallery in Canberra and had driven down the road almost daily for nearly two decades.[13]

The decision was announced by Planning Minister Mick Gentleman. He said the government had considered both the allegations against Slim and a submission from the Slim family, which strongly objected to the change 'as a result of the allegation of child sex abuse against our grandfather by less than a handful of people'.

Stephens said he campaigned for the change of name because the impact of child sexual abuse is 'with you forever'.[14] 'William Slim Drive has an association and legacy that contravenes our values . . . as a modern, inclusive city,' Stephens said. 'Child sexual abuse is abhorrent and we need to ensure our public space naming does not cause ongoing hurt to Australians.'[15]

Another member of the ACT government, Bec Cody, said the decision to rename the road was a 'victory for truth and honesty about our past'. 'While Slim will never face the trial he deserves,' she said, 'we should not be running a protection racket for his legacy.' Stephens was reported to have been 'in shock' when he heard of the government's decision.

> It's very raw, I don't often get emotional but this has really hit me . . . it is a huge relief. And not just for me. This is really recognition for all of us about what happened. It's been gnawing for a long time.[16]

The move to rename William Slim Drive was not universally supported and Slim, it seems, still has some influential supporters. In a letter to the *Canberra Times*, Heather Henderson, the ninety-two-year-old daughter of the former prime minister Robert Menzies, who appointed Slim as Australia's governor-general, said

Kingsley Fairbridge's scheme to send poor British children to the colonies was supported by the British government, which claimed child migration provided a choice between 'begging, thieving, disease, prostitution and early death in the British Isles, or learning farming or domestic skills in Australia'.

OUR "GUTTER CHILDREN"

A less charitable view of British child migration, from *Punch* magazine in 1869. A woman with a whip is saying, 'I am greatly obliged to you Christian ladies and gentlemen for your help and as soon as I have filled the cart [with these swept-up urchins] I'll drive off to pitch the little dears aboard of a ship and take them thousands of miles away from their native land so that they may never see any of their relations again.' (Print made by George Cruikshank, published by Charles Hancock, 1869, © Trustees of the British Museum)

What are these brothers worth?

THEY certainly looked, while discussing their future with such confidence, as if they would make the most of any opportunity which came their way. They may not have realised that their opportunity depended on YOU and ME.

From the shelter of a good home in one of our Farm Schools in Australia, we are now giving them a fine upbringing and training and the chance of full and happy lives which they so richly deserve.

Please send something—if only a little—towards the £30 it cost to prepare and equip each of these children—and every other unwanted or neglected child we send overseas.

This appeal is made through the generosity of a friend to prevent possible curtailment of the Society's work.

THE FAIRBRIDGE SOCIETY

President:
H.R.H. THE DUKE OF GLOUCESTER, K.G., K.T., K.P.
Director: W. R. Vaughan, O.B.E.
38 Holland Villas Road, Kensington, London, W.14.
Tel.: Park 6822

Eight-year-old Doug Miller and his five-year-old brother, Reg, feature in a Fairbridge fundraising advertisement poster of 1954. In the postwar years Fairbridge increasingly used local newspaper advertising to recruit children to its child migration program. (Courtesy Alamy)

'This is not charity, this is an Imperial investment'. In 1934 the Prince of Wales (later King Edward VIII) launched a fundraising appeal in London for Fairbridge with a personal donation of £1000.

Excited and anxious: four children from one of the earliest groups to sail from England to the Fairbridge Farm School in Molong, in 1939. In new outfits, and carrying their new wardrobes, are eleven-year-old Ted Gamsby from Durham, eight-year-old Clara Park from Renfrewshire in Scotland, seven-year-old Mary Simpson from Harrow, and Cyril Lloyd from Cricklewood, London. This picture became the face of the migrant program – for good and bad. (Ian Bayliff Fairbridge Farm School Molong Papers)

The party of children with whom, aged twelve, I went out to Fairbridge. We are outfitted in our new clothes and standing in front of John Howard Mitchell House, Kent, shortly before leaving England for Australia in 1959. *Back row from the left:* Mary O'Brien, John Ponting, Richard Hill, Paddy O'Brien, Dudley Hill, Billy King, me. *Front row:* Myrtle O'Brien, unknown, Wendy Harris, Paul Harris, Beryl Daglish, Francis Radcliff. (Ian Bayliff Fairbridge Farm School Molong Papers)

(*Left*) Four-year-old Stewart Lee on the S.S. *Strathnaver* was the youngest child sent to Fairbridge. (*Right*) Stewart Lee's eight-year-old half-brother Ian 'Smiley' Bayliff in his new outfit, shortly before sailing with his brothers to Australia. His parents tried unsuccessfully for years to get their boys back from Fairbridge. (Ian Bayliff Fairbridge Farm School Molong Papers)

We had never before experienced anything like the luxury of the S.S. *Strathaird* – the ship that took us to Australia. In addition to its first-class cabins and fabulous food menus, its eight decks included two swimming pools, reading and writing rooms, a library, concert and dance hall and the magnificent Forward Lounge, where every afternoon a string quartet played classical music, while waiters in starched white coats brought us drinks with lots of ice. (Courtesy of the State Library of Victoria)

Children eating lunch off steel plates in Nuffield Hall. The boss is silhouetted on the stage at the head of the staff dining table. (Ian Bayliff Fairbridge Farm School Molong Papers)

Church in Nuffield Hall on Sunday morning was the only time in the week when everyone in the village wore shoes. Well ... almost everyone. (Ian Bayliff Fairbridge Farm School Molong Papers)

(*Left*) 'Trainee' boys Mickey Mitchell and Derrick Pinnock at the Fairbridge slaughterhouse. (*Right*) Derek Moriarty in the Fairbridge village bakery. Derek was one of the first boys to speak out about being sexually abused. 'I thought I was going to take it to my grave … it haunts me.' (Ian Bayliff Fairbridge Farm School Molong Papers)

Children lined up awaiting labour assignment at the afternoon Fairbridge village work 'muster', many in bare feet. (Ian Bayliff Fairbridge Farm School Molong Papers)

(*Left*) Kitchen trainee Michael Walker rings the bell to summon the village to breakfast. The bell ruled our lives. It rang morning, noon and evening. (*Right*) Robert Kirkby brings the eggs down to the village from the poultry. (Ian Bayliff Fairbridge Farm School Molong Papers)

Robert Kirkby on village laundry duty, helping trainee girl Janet Wilcox hang out washing behind the girls' Lilac Cottage. (Ian Bayliff Fairbridge Farm School Molong Papers)

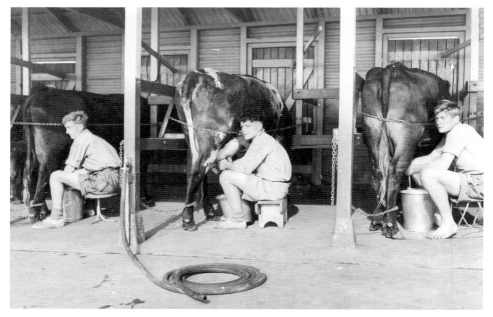

'Boys to be farmers ...' The dairy was the boys' toughest job, involving milking at 3 a.m. and again at 3 p.m., seven days a week. (Ian Bayliff Fairbridge Farm School Molong Papers)

'... and girls for farmer's wives'. Trainee girls Nellie Lee and Christina Murray making butter outside the principal's house. (Ian Bayliff Fairbridge Farm School Molong Papers)

(*Left*) Four-year-old Vivian Bingham shortly before sailing to Australia. She says the sexual abuse there began when she was five years old. (*Right*) Robert Stephens was one of the boys who claimed Sir William Slim sexually abused him while the Australian governor-general was on an official visit to Fairbridge. (Ian Bayliff Fairbridge Farm School Molong Papers)

Bob Stephens lobbied for years to have Slim's name removed from a major road in Australia's capital city and in 2021 the road was finally renamed Gundaroo Drive. (Dion Georgopoulos/*Canberra Times*/ACM)

Junior Orange High School rugby league team of 1960. I'm in the back row, third from the right. My twin brother, Richard, is the first on the left in the back row. Both my brothers and I were decent rugby league players and went on to play the sport seriously as young men in Sydney – I was awarded a Blue in league at Sydney University in 1968. (Ian Bayliff Fairbridge Farm School Molong Papers)

The man who ruled every aspect of the children's lives at Fairbridge for almost a quarter of the century was 'The Boss', Frederick Kynnersley Smithers Woods. Here he stands on the steps of the Fairbridge chapel with his wife, Ruth. Widely respected and widely feared, he was repeatedly investigated – and cleared – of charges of sexually abusing girls and brutally beating boys. (Ian Bayliff Fairbridge Farm School Molong Papers)

(*Left*) Bill Phillips was the aftercare officer who sexually abused both boys and girls. He left Fairbridge abruptly but was never charged with any offences. (*Right*) A 'widow of Empire', cottage mother Margaret Hodgkinson is remembered by the boys in Brown Cottage for her heavy sherry drinking and waking them in the dormitory to whip them with an ironing cord. (Ian Bayliff Fairbridge Farm School Molong Papers)

Maggie McLaughlin and Christina Murray were both in their mid-seventies when together they spoke for the first time about being sexually abused almost sixty years before as teenagers at Fairbridge. It is not unusual for victims to keep their abuse a secret for decades. Many never tell their story. (Ian Bayliff Fairbridge Farm School Molong Papers)

War hero, Field Marshal and Knight Grand Cross of the British Empire, Sir William Slim (later Lord Slim) sexually molested a number of young boys in the back of his vice-regal Rolls-Royce on a visit to Fairbridge when he was Australian governor-general. (National Archives of Australia)

Sir Arthur Douglas Dodds-Parker, British under-secretary for Commonwealth Relations, lobbied the British government in support of Fairbridge after he was leaked an official report criticising the farm school at Molong as being 'unfit' for children. His wife, Lady Aileen, was on the board of Fairbridge. (National Portrait Gallery)

Former child migrants Linda Gidman, Derek Moriarty and I listen to the British High Commissioner reading a formal apology made by the UK's then prime minister Gordon Brown, in Sydney on 25 February 2010. (Paul Miller/EPA, courtesy AAP)

(*Left*) New South Wales parliamentarians give a standing ovation to the Fairbridge kids in the public gallery of the parliament after state premier Mike Baird reads a tearful apology in 2015. (Sarah Gerathy © 2015 ABC) (*Right*) State Crown Solicitor Ian Knight was compelled to apologise to a number of survivors of child abuse following his admission to the Royal Commission that, in a parallel case to Fairbridge's, the government should have agreed much earlier to mediation rather than engage in protracted, delaying litigation. (Chris Pavlich, Newspix)

'The abuse of child migrants was Britain's worst ever sex scandal'. Former British Prime Minister Gordon Brown arrives to give evidence to the UK's Independent Inquiry into Child Sexual Abuse (IICSA). Brown told the inquiry in 2017 that child migration was a 'huge' violation of human rights. (Jonathan Brady/PA Images via Getty Images)

I gave extensive testimony to the IICSA into the sexual abuse of British child migrants. In an emotional opening statement in London I said the inquiry was welcomed but made it clear, 'We'll never be able to undo the great wrong that was done to these children.' (Courtesy of IICSA)

Social worker and academic Professor Alexis Jay was appointed chair of the IICSA in 2016, following the departure of three previous chairs. She rejected calls for the inquiry to be scrapped and chose to open it by scrutinising British child migration. (Courtesy of IICSA)

Henrietta Hill QC questioned me and other witnesses at the inquiry. She commanded the court room and addressed us with authority but kindness. (Courtesy of IICSA)

In sworn testimony to a House of Commons committee, former UK Fairbridge Society director Nigel Haynes claimed the Fairbridge archives revealed no evidence of child abuse. When later asked by the IICSA about the evidence of abuse found in the archives, Haynes claimed he had never read the files. (Courtesy of IICSA)

In 2020 a group of former child migrants who attended Fairbridge Farm School in Molong built a beautiful memorial park on the northern border of the old Fairbridge farm and the Molong Creek. (Brenton Cox Photography)

Old Fairbridgians cut the ribbon to officially open the park in March 2020. I'm fifth from left, and to my right are ninety-two-year-old Jimmy Napper, eighty-eight-year-old Maggie McLaughlin, eighty-year-old Peter Bennett and seventy-eight-year-old Margaret Clarke, who all arrived in Molong as young children shortly before the outbreak of the Second World War. (Carla Freedman/*Parkes Champion Post*/ACM)

she didn't dispute the boys were sexually molested but she didn't think it was by Slim:

> I am appalled to hear that the name of William Slim is to be expunged from Canberra because he was accused of being a paedophile. Accused. Not found guilty. Not for a minute do I doubt that those boys were sexually assaulted: that is something they could never forget. The question is: who was the perpetrator?
>
> The boys say it was a man in uniform who drove them down to the river . . . William Slim, as governor-general, would not have been wearing a uniform . . . He would never have been left alone . . .
>
> Lord Slim continued to be interested in Fairbridge for many years . . . you couldn't find a more decent, honest and inspiring man and leader . . . he is one of the most impressive people I have ever know, and after the extraordinary life I have led, that's saying something.[17]

Nonetheless, the territory government pressed on and on 16 March 2021 the Canberra media reported that Lord Slim Drive was now to be known as Gundaroo Drive:

> William Slim Drive in Belconnen has been renamed, as promised in 2019 by the ACT Government, in response to claims that the former governor-general, in whose honour the road was named, sexually abused boys at the Fairbridge Farm School in NSW in the 1950s . . . Dr Cathy Kezelman, CEO of the Blue Knot Foundation – Australia's National Centre of Excellence for Complex Trauma, said that the minimal act of changing the name had a significant effect on survivors. Each time a survivor confronts a reminder of their trauma, it can throw them back and be a trigger. Seeing William

Slim Drive would be a fairly significant trigger for many people,' she said.[18]

Bob Stephens' victory in having Slim's name removed from a major road in Australia's capital city in 2021 was undoubtedly achieved because of Bob's persistence, and that of others like him. I doubt, however, that it would have happened twenty years ago. I like to think the fact it was done is a sign of broadening awareness and acceptance that amends must be made – in whatever form they can be – for the sexual abuse that was inflicted on so many children in times past.

7

EVERY CHILDHOOD LASTS A LIFETIME

*My children missed out on the most important thing in a child's
life . . . I didn't kiss them and cuddle them enough as they were
growing up. I didn't show any real emotion . . . I wish I had been
able to tell them they were the most important thing in my life.*

As with all children who spent a large part or all of their childhood in institutions, Fairbridgians felt the effects of their
disadvantaged early years throughout their adult lives.[1] Most left
school at the minimum legal age, without qualifications, and
many would complain of ongoing reading and writing difficulties.
Many have spent their lives working in unskilled and semi-skilled,
low-paid occupations. They are less likely to own their own home
and more likely as adults to live in substandard accommodation.
They have greater difficulty in relationships and have issues with
trust. They have difficulty communicating and many have found it
more difficult to bond with and meet the emotional needs of their
children. They are also likely to suffer more physical and mental
health problems, experience higher levels of drug and alcohol abuse

and to end up in the criminal justice system. Those who were sent to Fairbridge when they were older and stayed there for the shortest period of time would do better in Australia. The ones who struggled through life tended to be those who spent most of their childhood in the care of the farm school.

The promise of a good education was a big factor in my mother's decision to sign up for the scheme, and a regular feature of Fairbridge's promotional brochures:

> The Fairbridge children who qualify for higher education and wish to carry on are encouraged and permitted to do so. They continue their education at High Schools, Technical Colleges, Business Colleges and such like establishments and if they qualify further and wish to continue, are helped to attend Teachers and Agricultural Colleges and would be helped even to university if they win scholarships.

Little did we know that for some years before this undertaking was given to parents in England, a financial crisis had forced Fairbridge to cut back the children's schooling. In February 1953 the chairman of the Sydney Fairbridge Council, William Hudson, wrote to Woods instructing him to shed paid staff and replace them with children, who should be taken out of school at the earliest possible date. 'Only children of exceptional ability,' Hudson ordered Woods, 'should be left at school after the compulsory age.'[2]

The practice of pulling students out of school to work on the farm began with the first party of children to arrive in 1938 and continued throughout the life of the farm school. Henry McFarlane recalls:

We left at fourteen: we had no choice. They'd just say, well, everything on the farm has to be done, the harvest is coming on. Big strong blokes, you'd better go up there and help them on the farm. See, what happened, being illiterate . . . couldn't read or write, you know – I just used to, when my mother sent a letter, I used to go on what they'd read out to you.

Nearly thirty years later, children were experiencing the same thing. Ian Dean, who was sent over when he was ten with his brother, turned fifteen in July 1965. He says:

I wanted to stay on at school and sit for the School Certificate at the end of fourth year [Year 10] but Woods just laughed. He said my marks weren't good enough and that I was needed as a trainee.

However, there were cases where Woods felt children could stay at school – when the farm was not short of trainee labour – but was overruled by the Fairbridge Council Board. On one occasion the headmaster at Molong Central School recommended four Fairbridge boys be allowed to stay beyond their fifteenth birthdays to complete the third year of high school (Year 9) and sit for the Intermediate Certificate. Woods agreed and sent the headmaster's recommendations and school reports to the council, reminding the board of Fairbridge's policy that 'all of our children must aim to reach at least the Intermediate Certificate standard'.[3] The council was unmoved and allowed only one of the boys to sit for the certificate. The others, it said, had only a 'remote chance' of passing and have 'not made the best of their opportunities'.[4]

Fairbridge's betrayal of the children was compounded by the New South Wales Education Department, which kept many of

the children out of mainstream classes at school. A high proportion of those who were sent to Molong Central School were put in
what was called the General Activities (GA) classes, which were
designed for children who had learning difficulties or were intellectually disabled. The children were in a composite class called
1G-2G, crammed together into a tiny classroom. Nearly all the
Fairbridge children who spent their secondary school in this class
have struggled through life with problems reading and writing.

Daphne Brown, who arrived as a seven-year-old with her nine-
year-old brother, says that as a result of her poor schooling she has
struggled ever since:

> My education was poor . . . we were in a class at Molong School
> called 'an opportunity class' and out of that class all of us were from
> Fairbridge except for two [town] children. Now, that should have
> told them something – we needed help – we missed out on that
> basic education . . . we had to write compositions. It was all in my
> mind but I could not spell – no one could understand what I wrote.
> So, therefore, I was disadvantaged right though life . . . I tried to
> learn . . . so, I was a bit resentful.

Stewart Lee remembers being in 1G-2G:

> [It] was known as the 'dumb class' . . . We were in one little segre-
> gated mob . . . the idea is that you're basically waste, you've probably
> been kicked out of your home or you're from broken families . . .
> we weren't expected to pass, put it that way . . . so if you had any
> potential whatsoever, you weren't going to go nowhere anyway.
> Fairbridge was exactly the same. They didn't let you get to the top
> of your own potential.

It remains a mystery why so many Fairbridge children were locked up in this class by the Education Department. A 1951 Department of Education report assessed fifty-four children who would begin at Molong Central School the following year and concluded a staggering proportion were incapable of normal schooling. According to the report, 'the existing intelligence scatter shows that approximately 40% of Fairbridge children will require Opportunity . . . type of teaching and courses,' which meant going into the 1G-2G class.

However, it is not clear what the department used to measure the 'intelligence scatter'. It could not have been IQ, the widely used measure in those days, because those test results for the same fifty-four children – which also survive in the Education Department files – show that the range of their IQs was fairly normal. Twenty-nine registered an IQ of over 100 and twenty-five below 100. Of those who measured above 100, six registered IQs of above 120, eleven were between 110 and 119 and twelve were between 100 and 109. Of those below 100, fifteen measured between 90 and 99 and the remaining ten measured below 90.

An IQ above 100 was considered to be about average. But Ian Bayliff, who registered 112, spent all of his secondary school in 1G-2G. Ian was taken out of school before his fifteenth birthday to become a trainee and when he left Fairbridge was 'unable to write two words together'. It was only in his thirties, and at the prompting of his wife, that he went to evening college to learn to read and write properly.

David Eva went from the primary school at Fairbridge to the 1G-2G class at Molong:

I was in classes 1G-2G . . . and I stayed there all the time . . . as I turned fifteen they kicked me out. When you got to that age, you were told you had to do years as a trainee . . . Education-wise, it was shocking. I think a lot of people who went through that place – if they'd had a decent education, I think a lot of them would have done better.

The Fairbridge Council was aware from the earliest days that there was a problem with the education of its children. In February 1944 the chairman in Sydney, Sir Percival Halse Rogers, wrote to the chairman of the UK Fairbridge Society, Sir Charles Hambro, to express concern about the failed education programs at Fairbridge. Halse Rogers was the chancellor of Sydney University, a Supreme Court judge, and had been a Rhodes Scholar at Oxford at the time of Kingsley Fairbridge.

> We have been conducting a review on our own account and after a consideration of results to date have left some of us with a definite feeling of disappointment and a desire to inquire whether our failures are due to ourselves or are due to defects in the selection and methods in Britain – or to both.[5]

At around the same time, the New South Wales Education Department was also expressing concern about the poor education of children at Fairbridge. In a report in February 1951 it referred to 'varied disciplinary problems at the school and the retardation of the children' and the strain and ill health of the teachers. However, other than adding a fourth teacher to the school, nothing was done to significantly improve the educational outcomes for the next two decades.[6]

Until 1951 Fairbridge children completed their schooling in the tiny school built behind the village. The three or four teachers taught more than 120 children, covering nine years of curriculum in classes averaging between thirty and forty children each.

From 1952 the secondary-school-age children were sent to Molong. Fairbridge had opposed sending the children into the town school each day and had argued for the construction of a bigger school building at the farm. However, the Education Department insisted the children attend Molong, arguing they would benefit from more integration with the local community:

A broader social experience so necessary to migrant children would be available to them. They would be eased in to the general community, rather than as now happens, thrust into a social scheme different entirely from that developed within the Fairbridge Farm community.

Had a bigger school been built on the farm, the children would have spent almost their entire lives on the site till the age of seventeen. As it was, usually they went to Molong Central School for only two or three years, which meant many, particularly those who went to Fairbridge at a very young age, hardly ever set foot off the farm. Stewart Lee recalls:

The only times [I left the school was] when Woods took us in to the Molong swimming pool – and one Sunday a month they had a church service in Molong . . . and the thing about it is – and this is what a lot of people don't realise; that's why we kept our English accents for so long, because we were still only talking to other English kids. We weren't talking to Australian kids. Simple as that.

The superintendent of the state's secondary school education reported Fairbridge kids compared poorly with the Molong town children in terms of cleanliness and appearance:

I was impressed by the general high standard of the dress and personal neatness of the school children at Molong and by the fact that Fairbridge Farm children suffer much by comparison. Until such time as the farm authorities recognise the importance of training their children in personal hygiene and neatness, and until they provide them with clothing and footwear appropriate to secondary school pupils with due regard to neatness and care of hair, the Fairbridge children will look out of place in a normal public school.[7]

Three years after Fairbridge children began going to secondary school in Molong, and in the absence of any improvement in their academic achievements, in 1955 the Fairbridge Council established an inquiry to look at education at the farm school.[8] The inquiry was prompted by the high level of academic failure of the children, and a concern that this was reflected in problems such as children running away, being involved in crime and antisocial behaviour, failure to hold down jobs and 'mothering and fathering illegitimate children' after leaving Fairbridge. A copy of the report, which was never made public, had been locked away in the Sydney offices of Fairbridge for decades. Of course, none of this information was ever made available to families in the UK like ours.

The inquiry found children from Fairbridge did fewer tertiary courses, and the absconding rate from the school remained high. The failures of the school were made all the more stark when Fairbridge at Molong was compared with the results of the older Fairbridge farm school at Pinjarra. Only 14 per cent of Pinjarra children failed to complete second year (Year 8). At Molong it was 50 per cent.

In 1955 Mr Philip Le Couteur, a member of the Fairbridge Council, made a number of suggestions aimed at improving this poor educational performance.[9] One was that the children be encouraged to take up hobbies, and that the farm school make facilities available to do this. Woods said that while it was a good idea, it would require significant additional funding. A bigger problem, he added, was that unlike children who attended Knox Grammar, the exclusive private boys' school in Sydney that Le Courteur had used as a comparison, Fairbridge children worked too hard to have time for hobbies:

> The Fairbridge child must make his bed every day . . . chop and fetch in a load of firewood . . . clean, set and light a boiler fire and fetch coke for it . . . dust, sweep and polish the dormitory . . . do the same for any other rooms in the cottage . . . fetch milk, meat, stores, vegetables . . . take down mail, messages to the office and elsewhere . . . help do the ironing, mending, washing of clothes . . . gardening, working bees on the village and the farm.[10]

Woods said it was even harder for trainee boys because they had to start work very early and by evening had little energy to give to homework or hobbies. To illustrate how inappropriate it would be to encourage hobbies among children who could not even read or write properly, he provided a profile of three trainees in Gowrie Cottage:

> Peter Bodily, fifteen years and 8 months. He reads with difficulty and writing is an effort. Graham Salisbury, fifteen years and 7 months. Reading and writing are both difficult for him. Glenwood Jory, fifteen years and 7 months. Reading and writing are both tedious for him.

My own schooling at Fairbridge ended rather ingloriously. For the first year and a half I was one of a handful of children sent by bus each day to Orange High School, which taught up to Year 11 and matriculation level. Molong Central School only taught to Year 9, which was described as intermediate level. While my brothers were faring well at Orange, my results at the end of the first year were very poor and in the following year continued to plummet as I became increasingly rebellious and less engaged with school. My end-of-year report card showed I had failed in almost every subject.

At the start of my third year at Orange High I was summoned to see the legendary headmaster Leo ('the Lion') O'Sullivan, whom I knew well from my regular visits to his office for a caning. He seemed to enjoy telling me that I was being thrown out of the school. 'We deem you to be uneducable,' I remember him saying.

'Don't you mean "uneducatable"?' I asked, not very helpfully, and not realising that 'uneducable' was correct.

I hitchhiked back to Fairbridge that morning, to be confronted by an angry Woods, whom O'Sullivan had phoned with the news. Woods was waiting to berate me for the huge and wasted cost to Fairbridge of sending me to the high school for the best part of the past two years.

Because I was only fourteen, still below the minimum school leaving age, Woods couldn't put me to work full time on the farm as a trainee. The next day I was back at Molong Central School, where I stayed until I ended my school days later that year.

Ultimately, Fairbridge blamed its poor educational results on the children – whom it described in reports as 'retarded' – and on their deprived backgrounds and failed education in Britain before they came to Australia. At one stage, the Fairbridge Council invited the headmasters of Fairbridge Primary and Molong Central to their meeting to discuss the continuing poor results of Fairbridge children. The minutes of the meeting record:

> Mr Mott and Mr Heyes gave very enlightening and instructive addresses on the educational qualifications and scholastic ability of Fairbridge children, from which it was learned that generally these children are educationally retarded, but in the last two years or so the standard is improving.[11]

Not only were the Fairbridge kids given a poorer education, but we were made to feel second-class citizens outside the farm school. We were acutely aware that most town people didn't want their kids mixing with us or becoming our friends. When the old Fairbridge bus full of kids arrived at the Molong swimming pool on a hot Sunday afternoon in summer, many gathered up their children and left. Years later I was told by a girl in my class at Molong that her mother insisted we were dirty, didn't wash enough and were a health hazard to the other local children.

At seventeen years of age the children of Fairbridge were found jobs. Most of the boys became farm labourers on remote sheep stations and the girls domestic servants. They left as they arrived, with a suitcase of clothes and on their own. They typically had very little money – about a week's labourer's wages – and a new outfit of clothes, which for boys usually consisted of two sets of work clothes, pyjamas and a smart coat, a tie and trousers. The jobs the children were found by Fairbridge were mainly in the west of the state, where lodging was included, usually on a farm.

Most of us remember leaving with little or no social skills, unable to use a telephone or open a bank account.

The stigma of being a Fairbridge kid followed us after we left the school and most of us tried to avoid mentioning our connection with the place. Laurie Reid remembers how after leaving, and while he was working on the railways, he was going out with a nice local girl. As soon as her parents discovered he came from Fairbridge they put a stop to their relationship:

I met a girl. She was a nursing sister in Orange. Anyway, a girl-friend, and we were going like a house on fire for a couple of months then and she said, 'Come and meet Mum and Dad, they want to meet you.' And they asked me what my father had done and I said he used to be in coal mining. And they said, 'In Newcastle?' And I said, 'No, over in Great Britain.' 'So, you are a Fairbridge boy?' they asked, and when I said 'Yes', that was the end of the relationship.

Most Fairbridge kids remember the day they left the farm school (in the same way as many vividly recall the day they arrived). Lennie Magee describes how he knew nothing about where he was heading, except that he was 'to be ready' to go to a job he had been found on a sheep station beyond Coonamble, nearly 300 kilometres to the north-west of Fairbridge. 'How do you get ready to leave for the unknown? I'd been in the grip of a bad dream for over ten years. I'd never held more than a one-pound note in my hand. I had no certificates, references or letters of introduction.'

He said he felt totally empty when he left Fairbridge Farm and was driven into Molong to catch the overnight steam train to Coonamble: 'As we drove through the open Fairbridge gate for the last time, I tried to feel something of what had been my absolute dream for the last ten years. Freedom, escape, pleasure. I felt nothing but stomach-churning apprehension.'

Left on his own at the railway station Lennie had half an hour to kill, which he used to go and buy a packet of cigarettes at Cassimaty's café in Molong's main street:

The train rumbled in, wheezing and clanging. I climbed into an empty compartment and sat, bleakly staring out of the window into the dark, gusty night. After a few minutes, a whistle blew and the train coughed into motion and clattered on to the west, further than I'd ever been before. I sat alone, perplexed. This was supposed to be the greatest day of my whole life, yet somehow I hadn't been able to conjure up the ability to sense or feel a single ecstatic emotion . . . I had arrived in Australia, a small and frightened little boy, looking out of a ship's porthole. Ten years later I was still a frightened little boy looking out a train window. Apart from a suitcase and a new outfit all I had to show for it was a head full of strange, mixed memories . . .

On leaving Fairbridge most of the children had to deal with a whole new terror – loneliness. Having spent their whole childhood with other kids and sleeping together in a dormitory, many now found themselves alone. David Wilson spent more than ten years at Fairbridge before he was found a job in the remote northwest of the state:

My first job was at Collarenebri [on a sheep station], working anything up to fifteen hours a day . . . I lived in the shearers' quarters, by myself . . . it used to get lonely there, yeah. Another job they sent me to when I was seventeen and a half – and I'll never forget it – it was at Narromine . . . I used to live in a shed at the back of the house and [his employer] used to just throw rocks at the thing to wake me up in the morning – about four o'clock in the morning . . . to go and milk the cow and feed all the pigs. Then I'd come and have breakfast, and he used to give me the tractor and say, 'Come in when you can't see no more.'

Joyce Drury remembers the terrible loneliness of leaving Fairbridge to work as a domestic servant, and living in the tiny attic store-room of a large farm homestead:

They showed me where I was to sleep, and it was in the attic, which was a box room, and there was a bed in there and all these boxes and boxes . . . it was the loneliest part of my life, I would say. That was the first time I'd been in a room by myself. Now, Fairbridge had not prepared us for those kinds of thing . . . Suddenly, after living for years in a dormitory, and here you are . . . And also I was treated as a servant and I wasn't prepared for that either – I expected to be with a family. [One] Sunday night Mrs Le Courtier said to me, 'Joyce, would you like to come down and listen to the radio play?' and I thought, I've made it. I'm going to sit in a living room and be with a family. And I came down and she had put a chair outside the living room door and the door was just ajar and she said, 'You'll be able to hear it from there. And of course, I walked up the stairs and cried my little heart out and thought, how could people be like that?

Gwen Miller talks of the trauma of being sent out on her own to work as a domestic servant for a doctor and his family in the town of Parkes, in the west of the state:

The first night I went to my room for the night was the loneliest night of my life – totally alone with two sets of clothes; I remember wishing that I had died with my mother . . . I was sixteen and three-quarters . . . I was a domestic, a cheap servant. And I tell you the first night that I left Fairbridge, I think it affected me more than leaving England . . . they showed me my bedroom and I don't know what I did between then and going to bed that night. But I remember going back into that room at night and the incredible loneliness. It was terrible.

Derek Moriarty said that most Fairbridge kids had difficulty fitting into an adult world for which they had no preparation and no guidance:

Most of us felt totally inadequate when we were sent out by ourselves into the world. We'd had practically no dealings with adults other than a small number of staff at Fairbridge and a handful of teachers at school. I felt uncomfortable around grown-ups and absolutely terrified approaching older people.

He said that when he tried to find a job, he had no idea how to conduct himself and was 'petrified' at the thought of being interviewed, or dealing with professionals such as doctors and lawyers.

Derek had run away from Fairbridge twice and ended up in juvenile prison aged sixteen, before Fairbridge agreed to find him a position as a pastry cook. He was one of the few kids found a job in the city, where he would have to pay separately for lodgings. The bakery was in Chatswood, in the north of Sydney, and involved working night shifts for a little more than £7 a week. The boarding house room where he lived alone cost him £5 a week and included only a Sunday roast lunch, leaving him with very little to feed himself for the rest of the week.

He enjoyed the work but after three months he realised he could not live on so little money, so he wrote to an old Fairbridge mate, Alan Scotti, who was working on a sheep farm nearly 600 kilometres south-west of Sydney. According to Derek, Scotti sent him a one-line reply that read 'Catch the next train to Hay,' and included in the envelope was a £5 note.

The following Thursday night Derek caught the overnight mail train to Junee and then connected on the branch line service, reaching Hay after 3 p.m. the following afternoon, on a journey that had taken more than seventeen hours. Derek said he was the only passenger to get off the train at Hay, where the local railway station attendant pointed him in the direction of the town centre. It was a stinking hot day, well over 100 degrees. Derek was dressed in his best clothes: 'Blue long trousers, white shirt and tie, black leather shoes and carrying a suitcase similar to what we had arrived with at Fairbridge,' which had been almost nine years earlier. He said:

> Having only gone about a hundred yards or so a taxi pulled up alongside me and the driver, dressed in a singlet, shorts and thongs, asked if I was going to a wedding and needed a lift. I told him I had no money except enough for a small packet of Capstan cigarettes. He said, 'No charge, mate, too hot to be walking – jump in,' which I did.

With nowhere to go in town, Derek 'walked up and down the main street' and eventually went to sleep on the taxi rank bench.

A copper woke me around midnight and when I told him I was waiting for a mate who would be in town in the morning, he said, 'That's fine but you can't sleep here – you'll have to go and sleep on the banks of the river [the Murrumbidgee],' which is straight across the road and about two hundred yards further on. It would have to have been the longest night of my life to this point, with a massive invasion of mosquitos making sleep impossible.

Scotti arrived in town around eleven that morning and found Derek, who was still walking up and down the main street. A few days later Derek was told that Jack Carver, Scotti's boss and the manager of Toogimbie Station, would be in town the following weekend and was looking for hands. Toogimbie Station, about 40 kilometres outside of Hay, spanned around 46 square kilometres. It had more than 50,000 sheep and 20,000 head of cattle and a workforce of about thirty men. All the stock-mustering was done on horseback in those days, long before the motor bikes, four-wheel drives and helicopters used today.

Derek said he was almost sick with anxiety about meeting Carver, but he got the job:

I never forgot that first job interview. It was an extremely frightening experience – and would be every time I went looking for work over the years. Lots of other Fairbridge kids went through exactly the same thing. We had all been found jobs when we left Fairbridge and none of us had been given any guidance on how to apply for, or get a job on our own.

A number of Fairbridge children ended up in prison as adults. Ian Bayliff, who worked for many years as a prison warder in a number of the state's jails, including Goulburn and Grafton, said he was saddened but not surprised at coming across many of the people he had been with at the farm school:

> Most of them had achieved very little. They were mainly sentenced for thieving. Typically, they had no family and had drifted around a lot. They had no educational or professional qualifications and had only ever worked as unskilled labourers. It was tragic how many of them had already been to jail.

Many Fairbridgians feel that the absence of parental love when they were young left them with less knowledge about nurturing their own children. Gwen Miller feels that Fairbridge not only robbed her and her brothers and sisters of their childhood, but also meant:

> my children missed out on the most important thing in a child's life. I didn't know how to show them that I loved them, apart from when they were babies. I didn't kiss them and cuddle them enough as they were growing up. I didn't show any real emotion . . . I don't think they ever saw me cry. I wish I had been able to tell them they were the most important thing in my life. I don't know, maybe it was that I didn't trust or get too close because it makes one vulnerable, then you must get hurt. [At Fairbridge] no one ever put their arm around you or touched your arm or your hand. The word love was never mentioned . . . you don't show any emotion and you never let anyone know you were upset about anything . . . I don't recall hearing anyone ever say to a child, 'You did very well. That was very good what you did.'

Bob Stephens believes the lack of affection he experienced has been a big issue throughout his adult life:

> A huge factor. Particularly later in life. I mean, in my case . . . I never had it as a child, affection of a parent, having been in an orphanage from day one . . . I never knew how to cuddle; I never knew how to love someone, or things like that. Now, that had huge implications down the track . . . there was an incredible lack of affection . . . there was just a theme right through the place: you were a sook if emotions came into it.

Billy King never experienced any family life before he arrived in Australia and says:

> I had lots of problems with my kids. It's only now the kids are grown up I give them a cuddle when they come over. But it took me years to be able to do it . . . all the years I was at Fairbridge . . . there was no one to turn to [who would] put their arms around me and give me a bloody cuddle and say, 'It will be all right, Billy. It will be all right.' . . . There was no love in the place at all. It was just absolutely stone cold. I had a lot of trouble when I left Fairbridge, like as a matter of fact I was under a psychiatrist for quite a while, and I remember him saying to me, 'Look, Bill, the problem is, if you have never been shown love, how the hell do you give it? These things have to be taught.'

Janet Ellis was seven when she came to Fairbridge in 1954 with her two brothers, eight-year-old Paul and ten-year-old Mickey, and spent ten years at the school. She says of the personal and physical guidance there:

I didn't know anything. Absolutely nothing. I remember the first time I got my periods and I thought, oh god. I'm bleeding to death. And I went to bed. The cottage mother came in and I said, 'I can't get out of bed. I'm bleeding to death.' And then one day the cottage mother threw this huge old lady's bra at me. I didn't know what it was. It was as big as a tent and I was told I had to wear it.

After leaving Fairbridge, Janet, like so many other girls, was sent to work as a domestic servant on a remote farm out in the west of New South Wales, where she was lonely and embarrassed by her lack of any social skills:

Every time a visitor came I used to run and hide somewhere. We had never socialised with anyone at Fairbridge. We were unimportant. My biggest fear was fear.

She married but that did not work out well:

I think it was just escape, actually. I think it was the worst thing I ever did. So violent, it was unbelievable. I ended up escaping through the bathroom window. He used to flog the hell out of me. I spent so much time in counselling and I tried to commit suicide and I lost babies. I suddenly woke up after so many years and thought, if you commit suicide, you're giving into the bastards. And it's not my fault. It's not my fault.

Janet was typical of most Fairbridge kids in that she looked forward to getting out of Fairbridge but had little knowledge of what to expect when she did. Perhaps because the future was so lacking in prospects, we rarely talked about life after the farm, or what adulthood might have to offer.

I was always aware that my brothers and I were more fortunate. Before we left England we knew Mum would follow us out and we would get back together as a family; what we didn't know was how long it would take, or how tough life would be when we were eventually free of the place.

8

REUNITING

Speaking generally, it is better to have parents of our children not employed anywhere near Fairbridge as they usually become a nuisance after a time.

Very few Fairbridge children ever reunited with their parents. For most of the existence of the farm school the policy of Fairbridge – supported by the British Government – was to prevent parents reuniting with their children. Before a child was accepted by the Fairbridge Scheme and allowed to emigrate, his or her parent or guardian had to sign over legal guardianship. The form they were required to sign read:

I, being the father, mother, guardian having actual custody of the child named _____ hereby declare that I consent to his or her migration . . . through the Fairbridge Society and I further authorize the said Society and the Officers to exercise . . . all the functions as guardians.

Being largely undereducated, few parents were aware that in signing away their guardianship they relinquished all rights to their children and would find it practically impossible ever to get them back, even when the children were dreadfully unhappy at Fairbridge and their parents made every effort to get them home. As a British government report into child migration in 1953 noted:

> There have been a few cases in which the parents have followed their children out to Australia, but this is not encouraged as the child scheme is primarily for those children who have been deprived of a normal home life. The Child Immigration Officer in London and the voluntary organisations have therefore been asked to do their utmost to select children whose parents are not likely to follow them.[1]

Fairbridge took a dim view of parents who tried to later reunite with their children. At one stage, in a letter to the British government seeking further support, the director of Fairbridge, W. B. Vaughan, argued that because the farm school offered fresh opportunities to children, it was undesirable for the children to ever return home to their families, where they could be exploited:

> We feel that such opportunities should be given to more children who need a fresh start in life away from an unhappy environment in Britain – apart from the risk of many children drifting back to their former surroundings by undesirable parents claiming them when they are old enough to work.[2]

Three brothers, Syd, Graham, Stewart Lee, and their half-brother Ian Bayliff, learned almost forty years later how their parents had fought in vain to have the family reunited.[3]

The boys came from a very poor family in Stretford, Manchester, where their father, Sydney, was a labourer who struggled to support the family. When the family made inquiries to Australia House about migrating they were given a lot of brochures, including some about Fairbridge.

The boys' mother, Dora, later wrote that she believed her four boys (though eventually the Lees would have eight children) would get 'a good chance in life' by taking up the Fairbridge offer.[4] Ian says his parents agreed to the scheme believing that they would be able to get back together as a family:

> My parents would not have let us go if they knew they wouldn't be able to get us back. They were encouraged by Fairbridge to believe they would be able to eventually follow us out to Australia . . . but also that if we wanted to, we could come home after two years.

Within months of the boys arriving in Australia, and after Dora had received letters describing how unhappy they were, she wrote to them telling them she would endeavour to reunite the family: 'Well, boys, what do you think, shall we all come over to Australia to live or would you like to come to Stretford? . . . write and let us know.'[5]

Fairbridge, which intercepted all the children's incoming and outgoing mail, moved to stop the parents undertaking either option. Principal Woods wrote to the director of the UK Fairbridge Society, W. B. Vaughan, to tell him about the children's letters to their parents: 'I hope you will be able to explain to the parents that notions of going back again to England are both impractical and injurious to the children's emotional wellbeing.'[6]

Vaughan in turn wrote to Miss E. M. Knight, the regional secretary for Fairbridge in Manchester, who had recruited the Lee children to Fairbridge, to instruct her to disabuse Dora and Sydney of any notion of their children being returned.

Knight went round to the Lees' home and told them they were not getting their children back, reminding them they had given up their rights when they signed over guardianship of the boys to Fairbridge. In a subsequent letter to Vaughan, Knight said:

> I am quite furious at the very suggestion of bringing them home. I have replied to Mr Lee's letter reminding him of the statement he signed when the boys went, in which he agreed to leave them in the care of Fairbridge.

Meanwhile, the parents continued, unsuccessfully, to have their children returned. Nearly four years later and after many failed attempts, the Lees applied to migrate to Australia. But as Australia House advised the UK Fairbridge Society, their application was rejected:

> This office has recently received application forms from Mr Sydney Lee of 25 Conniston Road, Stretford, Lancs, who states that he wishes to travel to Australia with his wife and four children in order to join the four children who are already at the Fairbridge Farm School at Molong. You will recall that in 1957 Mr Lee requested the return of the boys to this country but in view of the cost involved no action was taken at this time. We have indicated that it is not possible to assist him under a group nomination at present, but that it would be helpful if he could obtain a personal nomination for himself or his family.[7]

Lee tried again the following year to migrate to Australia but was told even more firmly that he would not be accepted:

> This office has advised Mr Lee that he would not be considered under a suitable group nomination at present and that the prospect of considering him in this way in future is not very good. Mr Lee has been further advised that he will not be eligible for consideration as a Commonwealth nomine after his 50th birthday on 6/7/59.[8]

It was more than forty years before Ian learned that his parents had fought for years to get him and his brothers back.

> For all those years I thought they had abandoned us. I felt terrible. I went to see my mother in 1997 in England and told her I now had my Fairbridge records and asked her why she hadn't told us that she'd tried for years to get us back She turned around and said, 'I thought you wouldn't believe me'. And you know what? I probably wouldn't, but now I know it was true.

By the late 1950s, and with more criticism of child migration from child welfare professionals in the UK, child migrant recruitment numbers began to fall. To counter its declining numbers, in late 1957 Fairbridge announced a change to its rules to allow a single parent to follow their children out, which is how, about eighteen months later, I travelled with my two brothers to Australia.

By then, parents such as my mum were being told that once they arrived in Australia they would be encouraged to make regular visits to their children. A brochure explaining the scheme stated that the parents 'will follow the children out to Australia at a later date. The parents will be found employment and accommodation in the same state, so that they may keep in touch with the children and visit them.'[9]

But Mum complained that from the time she arrived in late 1959 Fairbridge provided her with neither assistance nor guidance in finding a home or a job. At one point she applied for a job as a cook on a farm, Gamboola, which was owned by the Glasson family and only a few kilometres from Fairbridge. Mum was at the farm school visiting us and was to be picked up after eight o'clock that evening by Mrs Glasson, who proposed to drive her over to Gamboola, show her around, interview her for the job and then drop her off at Molong station in time to catch the overnight Forbes mail train back to Sydney.

Nearly fifty years later, a file note, signed by Woods, was discovered in a miscellaneous collection of papers in the Fairbridge Foundation offices in Sydney:

> Phone message from Mrs Glasson. She has seen Mrs Hill but cannot engage her now as she already has someone coming to work here tomorrow. She has however arranged to fetch Mrs Hill tonight at 8.20 and will take her to Gamboola and then on to the train, so that Mrs Hill can see the place and the job in case she might take the job there later.
>
> The Glassons however do not usually keep anyone very long.
>
> Speaking generally, it is better to have parents of our children not employed anywhere near Fairbridge as they usually become a nuisance after a time – Mrs Hill is the least likely to become so, but proximity might make a change for the worse in her.

The difficulty for Woods and the authorities was that when parents were able to visit the farm school, they tended to be very disturbed by what they saw. In some cases, parents were so upset they wanted to remove their children immediately, even before they themselves had found any employment or accommodation. One example involved two parents who were visiting their children for the first time. After a two-day stay, one of the fathers said the children 'were treated far more badly than he himself had been treated as a prisoner of war'.[10] The Fairbridge after-care officer Bill Phillips reported that at lunch on the day these parents were leaving, the father said very loudly, 'I wouldn't leave my kids here for anything if I had somewhere else to leave them.' When Phillips suggested the father take the children when he left, the father responded that he had already checked with the migrant hostel manager in Sydney where he was heading and been told they could not take the children.[11]

On another occasion, a mother who had sent her children under the One Parent Scheme lodged a complaint with the New South Wales Child Welfare Department when she first visited Fairbridge. Mrs Jeanette Bradfield, who had sent out thirteen-year-old daughter Clair and ten-year-old-son William first visited Fairbridge in 1963 and was upset with what she described as the ill-treatment of the children. While many of her allegations were not substantiated, an investigation found that others were, including the use by a cottage mother of a riding crop to whip small children.[12]

I can still recall when my mother first came to Fairbridge and saw the conditions in which we were living. She was horrified. On her arrival, she was put in one of the two guest houses for visitors at the back of the village – simple accommodation with two single beds in each room, and a communal bathroom and a toilet at the end of the verandah. The guest accommodation had a common room with an electric jug so my brothers and I were allowed at certain times during her visit to go up and have a cup of tea with her. The joy of us all being together again was completely overwhelmed by the obvious distress she felt about Fairbridge.

On her first morning she was shaken by the scene in Nuffield Hall. She was obliged to sit up on the stage with staff, where visitors were served a full cooked breakfast. Looking down, she would have seen us being marched in with nearly 200 other children who were mostly barefoot and dressed in rough clothing, with terrible haircuts. Then she would have seen us all sitting on the wooden benches at a lino-topped table eating our bread and porridge from steel bowls and plates.

Mum was so distressed after breakfast that Dudley, Richard and I had to console her as she mumbled words to the effect of 'What have I done?' and 'It's like something out of *Oliver Twist*.' She wanted to remove us immediately. But she was unable to support us, so we were pretty well locked in to the farm and this situation till we each reached minimum school-leaving age and were able to get jobs to help pay our way.

For the next two years or so, after following us out from England, Mum visited us at Fairbridge every few months, usually between jobs. She worked variously as a nursing aide, café waitress and on one occasion as the shearers' cook on a remote sheep station in the state's north-west at Pokataroo on the Queensland border. One Christmas we were allowed to join her and camped in a tent in the backyard of Mum's sister, Auntie Effie, who lived in a tiny two-bedroom fibro house with her husband, our uncle Harold, and their daughters, Jan and Ann, in the suburb of Panania in Sydney's south-west.

*

In 1961 I turned fifteen, and in the normal course of events I would have been expected to become a trainee working on the farm for the next two years. But because Mum was in Australia and I'd completed my Intermediate Certificate, I was able to leave the farm school to go and get a job and live with her.

When I told Woods at the end of the school year that this was my intention, initially he refused me permission to leave, saying that having finished school I was expected to work on the farm full-time as a trainee for the next two years like everyone else. The following Saturday, when I intended catching the train to Sydney, he overruled my plan by announcing at village breakfast that I was to captain the under-fifteens cricket team, which was to play that morning against a team from Molong. I was filled with dread at the thought of not being allowed to leave and of spending the next two years at Fairbridge as a trainee. During the cricket game I hit a ball to the boundary through mid-wicket and heard Woods, who was umpiring the game sitting on an upturned oil can, shout, 'Ho, ho, Hill leaves Fairbridge victorious,' which signalled to me that he was not going to stand in my way after all. Mum had booked me a train ticket from Molong to Sydney, so, with little time to spare and having got the approval, I hurried down to my cottage to pack my belongings into a small cardboard suitcase. It struck me how sad it was that after nearly three years at the farm school I had so little to take away with me. I had just enough time to say goodbye to my brothers, who intended to stay on at Orange High School – they were getting on there better than I had but would also leave a few months later. In my haste to catch the daylight train I didn't have enough time to say goodbye to any of my friends, Woods, my cottage mother, or her vile husband Ted Roach.

It was by then too late to catch the daylight train to Sydney at Molong as it would already have passed through, but Paddy O'Brien had his driver's licence and was driving a Fairbridge truck into Orange to pick up supplies. He was happy to give me a lift, once I assured him I wasn't absconding and he wouldn't get into trouble with Woods. We were able to reach Orange with a few minutes to spare, as it had taken over an hour for the train to get there on the steep railway line from Molong through Amaroo and Borenore.

On the long and exhausting 300-kilometre trip to Sydney, I thought about my years at Fairbridge and contemplated what life now held in store. The train was crowded. I was sitting next to a man who worked as a piano tuner, travelling around the country-side for weeks on end, going home to his family for a few days every month. It sounded like an unappealing way to spend a life and I remember hoping that fortune would smile more kindly on me.

I arrived in Sydney around nine that night, tired and hungry, having spent the last of my money some hours before on a bread roll from the train buffet. Mum was at Central Station to meet me. It had been almost three years since she waved us goodbye from the house at Knockholt in Kent. Now she was excited and relieved that we were back together; but she would not be totally relaxed until my brothers joined us a few months later.

She and I caught a suburban train through the city's underground and over the Harbour Bridge to North Sydney. I sat wide-eyed on the window seat, marvelling at the harbour and seeing the bright lights of a big city for the first time. We walked down from North Sydney station to the tiny downstairs bed-sitter Mum had found for herself, which was in a terrace house at 96 Union Street that had been split into five flats, all occupied by migrants from Europe. We all had to share one bathroom and one toilet, which were upstairs. Mum's bedsitter had two small rooms. In one was a single bed, a bedside table, a tiny wardrobe, a small table pushed up against the wall under the window and three chairs. There wasn't room for a fourth chair. The other room was even smaller; it had enough room for a stove, a sink and in the corner a camp stretcher for me. The flat had no phone, no refrigerator, no TV and only a small transistor radio.

The day after I arrived was a beautiful summer Sunday and I spent it walking with Mum around the foreshore parks of North Sydney. While relieved to be out of Fairbridge I felt little optimism or enthusiasm about my new circumstances. Mum was working as a waitress, we had between us no savings to speak of and I didn't have a job. At the time all we owned was in her tiny rented bedsit – a few bits of furniture that she had bought and was still paying off, and some pieces of clothing that would have barely filled a suitcase.

I also thought about what a struggle life had been for my mum. She had started work as a fourteen-year-old domestic servant, had brought up four children on her own and now was having to start out all over again. Australia was to provide terrific opportunities for us boys, but it was much harder for a forty-five-year-old single mother with no qualifications. I am very grateful that she lived long enough to see all her boys do well in life, which I'm sure would have made her feel all the sacrifices she made were worthwhile.

When I arrived in Sydney Mum was working in the Coles cafeteria in Pitt Street in the city. She wasn't earning a great deal and it was expected that I would immediately find a job and start paying my way. On the first Monday morning when she went to work I caught the bus outside North Sydney station to Crows Nest, where Mum told me I would find the government unemployment office. There, I filled out a form and it was not long before I was called in for an interview. A nice man opened a draw in a wooden filing cabinet marked 'Male 15–16 year old', which was full of cards recording available jobs. In those days Australia was experiencing 'over full' employment, meaning that the number of jobs outstripped the number of people looking for work. For the next few years jobs were so plentiful that I drifted from one to another and could boast I was never unemployed for more than a day. Certainly, we weren't especially badly off – most migrants to Australia in those postwar years lived as we did until they had saved enough for a deposit on their own home, which in most cases took many years of hard work and a lot of overtime.

Of all the work at the unemployment office that was open to unskilled, inexperienced fifteen-year-olds, I applied to Ismays hardware shop on Willoughby Road, Crows Nest, because it was close to Mum's little flat. The Ismays were looking for a junior and paying the award rate of £5, four shillings and sixpence a week (the basic full adult wage was around £12 a week).

Somehow they knew about Fairbridge and were very tolerant and understanding, even though I was dumbstruck standing at the counter of the shop when a customer asked for the most basic item and I had no idea what they were talking about. It was even worse when the shop was busy and someone would yell out for me to answer the phone. I had never used a telephone before and didn't know I had to say something when I picked up the handset.

I knew no one in Sydney except for Auntie Effie, Mum's sister. Sometimes at the weekends, and with nowhere else to go, on Saturday afternoons I'd watch a rugby league match at the

Sydney Cricket Ground. On other occasions I would catch the train out to Penrith in the west of Sydney and stay with Mary O'Brien, who had left Fairbridge at about the same time as me and was living in a small flat with her mum.

Like most of the children, I experienced terrible loneliness after leaving Fairbridge. And I was one of the lucky ones – I was living with my mother. Things got better when Richard and Dudley joined us in Sydney, and we managed to rent a slightly bigger flat.

Mary felt deeply for those children who had nowhere to go and no one to take them after they left Fairbridge. She says:

> I remember arriving in Sydney and being with my mum. And a sense of freedom. Somebody that I loved was there for me, and I really feel sorry for those who never had that: to walk out of Fairbridge and have their mums to go to. My mum was poor and she was sick. But she was my mum. And she took me away from there. And that was everything.

After my first job at the hardware store, I drifted over the next few years, working as a messenger boy, mail order clerk, builder's labourer, printer's assistant, waiter, barman, pub bouncer, garbage collector, sandwich maker and driver of a dry-cleaning van.

In the year after I left Fairbridge I applied to become a police cadet but I failed the fairly simple spelling and arithmetic test when I sat the entrance exam at the Bourke Street Police Centre, which was a clear indication of how far I had fallen scholastically at Fairbridge. After a few years of this drifting, I was driven – largely by boredom – to do something else. I enrolled in a one-year, full-time matriculation course at East Sydney Technical College. Because I still had to pay Mum for my board, I worked as a waiter in a pub at night and at weekends, and skipped the odd day at college to work as a builder's labourer.

At the end I was surprised and delighted to matriculate with my first strong academic results; in fact, I won a scholarship to Sydney University to study economics, which I enjoyed and discovered I was very good at. I loved being at university and threw myself into so much extra-curricular activity, including debating, university sport (I was awarded a Blue in rugby league), student politics and the anti-Vietnam War movement, which was a big issue at the time. In 1970 I was elected leader of a delegation invited on what was a controversial goodwill visit to Hanoi, in North Vietnam. After completing my degree, I was offered a job on the academic staff as a tutor by two professors, who didn't like each other but both invited me to teach courses each of them ran. I completed a Master's in Economics two years later.

I am one of only a few Fairbridge children ever to go to university. But I strongly reject the suggestion that because I made it to tertiary education I am a good example of what Fairbridge kids have been able to achieve. Of the nearly one thousand children who went through the Molong school, probably only about a dozen of us graduated from university, and all but one or two were like me: we left Fairbridge to rejoin a parent, or family member, and then went back to study. Our experience is in spite of the Fairbridge Farm School and not at all typical or representative of the multitude of far less fortunate experiences of most who went there.

9

COVER-UPS

*The reputation in which the Fairbridge organisation has been held . . .
may, we recognise, remove from the sphere of practical politics the
possibility of putting the farms schools of Pinjarra and Molong on your
'black list', although well-informed opinion would condemn them from
the point of view of accepted principles of child care.*

For decades the British and Australian authorities were aware of the serious failures of the Fairbridge scheme but kept these problems hidden.

The first of many scandals at the farm school in Molong, which is documented in the Fairbridge files in both Australia and the UK, involved the dismissal of the first principal, Richard 'Dickie' Beauchamp, for his failure to prevent 'immoral and perverted practices that have been indulged in on a serious scale' at Fairbridge.[1] The incidents, which occurred in 1940, less than two years after the Molong school opened, were kept quiet.

Beauchamp, a retired naval officer, was appointed principal shortly before the first party of boys arrived in Molong in March

1938. Len Cowne, who was in that first party of boys, remembers him as a 'dapper little Englishman of the old school, who met us with his wife Molly when [we] arrived in Sydney by ship'.

The London Fairbridge Society, which had hired Beauchamp, regarded him as a successful appointment, but after only two years in the job he was suspended by the Sydney Fairbridge Council and was offered the opportunity to resign. According to the chairman of the council, Beauchamp had 'failed in his duty' to prevent 'perverted practices'. It seemed there had been some nocturnal liaisons between boys and girls, in the cottages and the principal's house, which included the suggestion of homosexual activity. Beauchamp was ordered to leave the property in twelve hours. Cowne recalls rumours circulating that the principal had been 'fondling some senior girls', before leaving 'for New Zealand in what appeared to be indecent haste'.[2]

Beauchamp was replaced in 1940 by Edward 'Ted' Heath, who had been the farm supervisor for the previous two years. Heath left in 1943 to join the Red Cross. When he resigned he wrote a special report highlighting the failure of the Fairbridge trainee scheme, which he said placed too much emphasis on the use of children as farm labour and provided too little training and learning:

> After nearly five years at the Fairbridge Farm, Molong, and before relinquishing control of the School, there are several matters that I wish to bring before the notice of the Council. During my association with Fairbridge, its failures as well as its virtues have become apparent to me and I offer these suggestions briefly but frankly in the hope that they may be of some use to the Council in future planning.[3]

In the report, which was never made public, he wrote that more adult supervisors needed to be employed:

Too much stress has been and is being laid on the ratio of staff to children and a wrong but general feeling seems to be that all or most of the work should be done by the children. They do it now to the detriment of their training. So much time is spent doing routine work and there are few instructions that there is little time in which to learn. This applies to the farm as well as the village as there the stress is laid on the amount we produce rather than the course of training we give.[4]

No changes were introduced as a result of Heath's report.

Heath was replaced by Frederick Woods, who was confirmed as principal by the London society in 1945 and ran the farm school at Molong until he retired twenty-one years later, in 1966.

Woods' reign got off to a rocky start. When he was given the top job in 1945 the Fairbridge Society was unaware that he was under investigation by child welfare authorities in Australia for sexually abusing a Fairbridge girl. The allegations, which became public only on the publication of *The Forgotten Children* in 2007, were made by sixteen-year-old Joy Watt, who was working at the time as a trainee on domestic duties in Woods' house. Six months after London appointed him, Sir Claude Hill Reading, the chairman of the Fairbridge Council, wrote to Sir Charles Hambro, the chairman of the London society:

> One of the Fairbridge girls had made very serious allegations against Woods, of sexual misbehaviour towards her, which were brought to the attention of the Child Welfare Department by a local parson who heard of the alleged incidents.[5]

Reading went on to explain that a report recently received from the Child Welfare Department completely exonerated Woods and that 'the allegations made by the girl can only be put down to the sexual stirrings of an hysterical adolescent'.

In December 1945 Ruth Woods, in defence of her husband, wrote to a friend, a Miss Hart in the London Fairbridge office:

> I don't think we could have worked harder with or with more care than we did for the Watt twins [Joy and her sister June], they have been the most difficult children here, highly strung and temperamental. I couldn't count the number of nights I have spent sitting on Joy's bed till she fell asleep – she seemed a child that needed parental care more than most.

She said that a few days before, they had been confronted by a private detective inquiring about the accusations of indecent behaviour Joy had made against Ruth's husband:

> They questioned the children and us very closely and are perfectly satisfied that it is the imagination of a distorted mind . . . it is usually rather heartbreaking at times, I was so fond of Joy and always stoutly denied to others that she had lied.[6]

Two months later, Ruth wrote again to Miss Hart, saying that Joy Watt had been upset with Woods, whom Joy blamed for the suicide of fifteen-year-old Fairbridge boy Peter Johnson. The death of Johnson upset a number of Fairbridge children and remained an unhappy memory in their lives for years to come. Ruth wrote of Joy:

> She has a warped mind, we know from a series of notes, dealing with unpleasant sex matters, which were discovered at school some time ago written by an external student, but aided by Joy.[7]

There the matter rested – but Joy Watt never wavered in her claim that Woods had abused her. Sixty years later, in 2006, when she was in a nursing home near Camden, south-west of Sydney, Ian Bayliff visited her as part of him helping me research *The Forgotten Children*. According to Bayliff, when he asked about Woods, Joy, who was then seventy-five, said Woods was 'the most evil person I have known'. She claimed her recollections were clear and she remained adamant her allegations were true.

In 1948 Woods was again under investigation for sexual and other abuse. A number of serious allegations had been made by the newly appointed bursar to Fairbridge. Lieutenant Commander Philipp Oliver Laelius Owen was a naval officer on the HMAS *Perth* at the time it was sunk during the Battle of the Sunda Strait in 1942, and was made a Japanese prisoner-of-war. As a captive and on the way to Japan his ship was sunk by an American submarine and Owen was one of the few survivors. After being demobilised in 1947 he took the job of bursar at Fairbridge.

The first the London Fairbridge Society knew of Owen's allegations against Woods was when William Hudson, in his capacity as the newly appointed chairman of the Fairbridge Council, wrote to Sir Charles Hambro to tell him:

> It was felt that the charges were so serious that they required an immediate independent investigation. As the Director of Child Welfare [in New South Wales] is the legal guardian of the children, he was asked to conduct the inquiry. He delegated the investigation to the superintendent . . . and it was done with care and a minimum of publicity. So far there has been no publicity in the papers here and I do not think there will be.[8]

The investigation, without any reference to the police, was quickly completed by a Mr V. A. Heffernan of the Child Welfare Department, who concluded: 'It was not considered that any of the charges made against Mr Woods have been substantiated.'[9]

The report of the investigation listed six allegations made by Lieutenant Commander Owen: that the children were not sufficiently and properly fed; that Woods had employed a cook in the tertiary stages of syphilis; that Woods was a 'sexual pervert'; that Woods knocked down and kicked a boy until his eyes bled; that Woods beat and injured boys with a hockey stick; and 'other matters too dreadful to mention'.

Heffernan did not accept the children were improperly fed, and reported that Owen could not provide specific details of the matters 'too dreadful to mention'. He found that Woods had allowed the cook with syphilis to stay on upon receiving medical advice that she posed no threat of infection to the children. He also dismissed the allegations that Woods was a sexual pervert, because he was satisfied with Woods' explanation for his possession of sex books.

The inquiry did find that Woods had knocked over a boy in the kitchen and kneed him, and that the boy's eyes were 'bloodshot' after the incident. While it was noted that Woods was 'unwise' to use such a method of punishment, it was 'not considered that this action amounted to excessive punishment or serious assault'. The inquiry revealed that Woods had used the hockey stick to beat the boys, which was illegal at the time, but it said 'he had not used it since he was instructed by the chairman [of Fairbridge]'.[10]

Other incidents of abuse of the children remained hidden in the files of Fairbridge in Australia and in the UK for decades. One case involved the investigation of the notoriously abusive cottage mother Kathleen Johnstone by the New South Wales Child Welfare Department. The investigation followed complaints by Mrs Jeanette Bradfield in 1964. Her children, thirteen-year-old Clair and ten-year-old William, went out to Fairbridge and she followed them under the One Parent Scheme, just as my mum did. When she reached Australia and visited Fairbridge, Bradfield was alarmed at the treatment she witnessed at the farm school. Her complaints were not substantiated by the inquiry, but many of the other children's allegations of cruelty were.

The results of the inquiry were communicated in a letter from the under-secretary of Child Welfare, A. C. Thomas, to the Fairbridge Council, and a copy was sent to the Fairbridge Society in the UK. There were some disturbing allegations in the report:

> In the presence of Woods, Johnstone admitted that on one occasion she had put Vivian Bingham's head down the toilet with the object of correcting the child's habit of bedwetting. Mrs Johnstone claimed that this method had been successfully applied by a previous cottage mother. She agreed in the instance in which she was involved the child's habit had not been corrected. She argued however, in favour of this method taking the view that the end justified the means.[11]

The investigation reported incidents that we at Fairbridge had known about for years:

> There were also complaints concerning Mrs Johnstone caning the children. Mr Woods [stated that] cottage mothers have the right to resort to 'domestic punishment', which was interpreted as allowing them to give children a slap with a stick. Mrs Johnstone did produce a small plastic cane, which she said she used in punishing the children.

She claimed that she just gave them a tap about the legs or on the buttocks but denied that she had done anything more than leave a temporary red mark. In the course of complaints made earlier to Mr Sheriff [the investigator] it had been stated that a whip had been kept by Mrs Johnstone for the punishing of the children ... Mrs Johnstone then produced the handle of a riding crop from this position. She stated, however, that the children had played with this stick and denied having used it to beat them. Here again Mr Sheriff was left with the impression that punishment by Mrs Johnstone may have been more severe and frequent than she was prepared to admit.[12]

Both the Fairbridge Council and the Fairbridge Society saw the report, but no action was ever taken by the Child Welfare Department, or by Fairbridge, other than to tell Johnstone to stop whipping the children. There is no record of her ever being told to stop putting children's heads down the toilet. She continued working at Fairbridge for several more years.

In December 1958, two fifteen-year-old boys, Nobby Stemp and Fred Southern, ran away from Fairbridge when they were taken with a group of children to Orange to do their Christmas shopping. Hitchhiking and sleeping in parks, they made their way to the Pyrmont wharves in Sydney, where the S.S. *Strathmore* was berthed and preparing for a return voyage to England. The boys introduced themselves to a drummer in the ship's band and told him they were unhappy and wanted to either stow away or work for their passage back to England. The drummer wouldn't help them get aboard and suggested they go and talk to the British consul, whose office was in the Prudential Building in Martin Place. The boys went over there and met with a Mr Condon of the UK Information Service, who contacted the Child Welfare Department.

Fairbridge was also notified and the boys were that evening put on the overnight Forbes mail train back to Molong. Before the train left, they were interviewed at Sydney's Central Station by a child welfare officer. The boys made a number of serious complaints, including several about their cottage mother, Lilias Da Freitas, who regularly whipped the small boys in her cottage. They also complained about the excessive hours of hard work the children at Fairbridge were obliged to undertake as trainees on the farm.

Two weeks later, the secretary of the Child Welfare Department, R. H. Hicks, wrote to William Hudson to say, 'I am particularly concerned as to the reasons which prompted the absconding.' Hicks told Hudson that a number of issues needed to be investigated, including the suitability of Da Freitas to have care of the children; which punishments were authorised and administered at Fairbridge; whether a proper log of them was kept; and the working hours of the children. Most importantly, he asked, 'Are the children free to complain on injustices to the principal or other authority and is every complaint properly investigated?'[13]

Hudson took two months to reply to Hicks, in a letter that dismissed his concerns and stressed that Hudson was satisfied the children were well treated: 'The cottage mothers discipline their children by giving them small penalty chores, sometimes a hand slap, or, on very rare occasions, a light caning,' he wrote, 'but the principal is always advised.' Hudson went on to give Da Freitas a glowing reference.[14]

Da Freitas was cottage mother to Ian Bayliff, and he recalls that she owned a number of sheep and earned a bit of extra money from the fleece. She kept the flock in a paddock behind Blue Cottage:

She used to bring sixteen to twenty sheep into the kitchen when it rained and she would make the children keep the cooking stove going at night so the sheep would stay warm and dry. We kids were down in the dormitory with all the windows kept permanently open and no heating. Next morning there would be sheep droppings and urine all over the kitchen floor and we would be made to clean it up.

The chairman of Fairbridge thought this was acceptable. In his response to Hicks, Hudson said:

Now I come to my own personal opinion of Mrs Da Freitas. Her children are well turned out, they are fond of her, they appreciate her interest in their various activities but she may be a little inclined to place too much importance on the junior farmer aspect of the work, but she only does this at the children's urging. I think that it is possible that her interest in animals, particularly sheep, may result in her cottage not being as clean as some others, but I am not at all sure that what she does is not in the best interests of the children.[15]

The British government was also made officially aware of an early investigation by the officer of the British High Commission in Canberra that highlighted failings of Fairbridge. In October 1944, W. J. Garnett, official secretary to the British high commissioner to Australia, wrote a comprehensive forty-page report titled 'Report on Farm Schools in Australia'. Garnett wrote that the pause in child migration caused by the Second World War provided a good opportunity to reassess the farm school system:

The date when the migration of children can be resumed is still uncertain and the time is therefore opportune to review the purpose and results of the schemes and to consider what, if any, changes are desirable when they are in a position to resume operations.[16]

Garnett studied the Fairbridge farm schools at Molong and Pinjarra, the Northcote School in Bacchus Marsh, Victoria, which was based on the Fairbridge model, and the Barnardo's school at Picton, New South Wales. The report was given to Fairbridge but never made public. Garnett said there was 'conclusive proof' that the Fairbridge model was failing in its basic aim of converting child migrants into successful farmers. He believed that the organisation was out of date and fundamental changes needed to be made to the future operation of the scheme. He identified the central objective of boys owning their own farms as largely unachievable, noting that in Western Australia, where Fairbridge had operated for more than thirty years, 'only a handful' of boys had succeeded as farmers:

At the time Kingsley Fairbridge commenced work in Western Australia [in 1912] farming conditions were such as to justify the hope that a boy properly trained and placed in employment as a farm worker would, if industrious and thrifty and after gaining practicable experience, have a reasonable prospect of becoming a farmer on his own account . . . this hope has not been realised and only a handful of boys have succeeded in establishing themselves on their own account.[17]

Garnett argued that the fault lay with Fairbridge for not providing better education and training to equip the children with a wider range of career choices, and that 'the scheme should be modified so that . . . it should be possible for children to exercise some choice of occupation and for boys and girls who show themselves to be specifically qualified to follow the other occupations, to receive the necessary training.'[18]

The report also dealt with the recurring problem of staff who were unfit to work at Fairbridge: 'They do not appear to have made sufficient allowance for the classes of children with whom they are dealing, amongst whom a number of cases requiring patient and sympathetic treatment are bound to arise.'[19] Finally, Garnett highlighted the problems of isolation and loneliness experienced by Fairbridge children, which arose from their being part of 'segregated and isolated communities'.

In a comprehensive response to the report written in August 1945, the secretary of the Fairbridge Society in London, Mr Gordon Green, agreed with most of the points made by Garnett and painted an even bleaker picture of Fairbridge's record. Green agreed that not only did Fairbridge children rarely manage to become farmers, but that its children were destined to be left to a life on the fringes of society: 'For the boys, attainment of an economic status which would warrant marriage and a family, was extremely difficult . . . They have remained the underprivileged class.'[20]

Much of Green's understanding of the farm school came from discussions he'd had with former Fairbridgians who had joined the armed forces and were serving in Europe during the Second World War. A number of them had visited the Fairbridge Society offices while they were in London and had complained to Green that they 'found themselves despised as outcasts from Britain', working for lower wages than Australians doing similar work.

According to Green, the UK society was not responsible for the failures of Fairbridge; the fault lay with the local governing bodies in Western Australia and New South Wales. Green argued that the interests of the children would have been best served had 'no such surrender of right of direction' of the farm schools in Australia 'been made by the London society'.

However, despite acknowledging the deep flaws in the scheme, Green rejected the need for a fundamental rethink, as advocated by Garnett. He reiterated that the basic principles ought to remain those established by Kingsley Fairbridge:

> Certain children are by misfortune denied the security and foster-ing of a normal family life. They need care and protection. The illegitimate child and the child of lawful but irresponsible parents have much to expect from Fairbridge if by the transfer to Australia or Canada it can be free of its disabilities.[21]

The next serious challenge to Fairbridge came in the postwar years with the ground-breaking Curtis Report of 1946 and the Children Act in 1948. Together, these caused a fundamental shift in child care away from institutions and towards foster care, and from benevolent volunteer organisations to trained professionals taking responsibility for the welfare of children.

The Curtis Report was radical in a number of respects. It was chaired by a woman, Myra Curtis, and nine of the sixteen members of her committee were women. Curtis was sixty-two years old in 1946. She came from a working-class family in Sunderland. Her father was a telegraphist at the post office and her mother a teacher. After a career in the civil service she became the principal of Newnham College at Cambridge in 1942 and was made a dame of the British Empire in 1949.

Her report recommended that children who could not be properly cared for by their natural parents should be placed in environments that resembled homes, and that they should be given the 'security of affection' that was not provided in large institutions.[22] Fairbridge had never considered the emotional or developmental needs of the children and was modelled on the provision of discipline, a roof over your head, hard work and basic food. The Curtis Report stated the days of large, impersonal children's institutions should cease; the future demanded that children be afforded affection and understanding. The British government was demanding that volunteer organisations and the churches restructure their children's homes. Childcare professionals, who were replacing the volunteer amateurs, became increasingly opposed to child migration.

The Curtis Report stipulated that future child migration should transform; that child migrants should be given the same care overseas as they would have received had they stayed in Britain. It also argued that 'children should not be cared for in the type of large institutions' like Fairbridge but in 'cottage homes' with a 'surrogate mother' who was suitably trained.[23]

While the Curtis recommendations were accepted by the British government and the Home Office, none were implemented by the Fairbridge Society, which continued to operate for another three decades almost exactly as it had previously.[24]

In April 1948, while the new Children Act was being drafted to reflect the reforms to child care, sixteen British welfare organisations protested at the continuation of Fairbridge and other child migrant institutions. The British Federation of Social Workers sent a letter to *The Times* in March 1948 'expressing concern about the care provided child migrants' and calling for an inquiry into the conditions faced by these young migrants.[25] The federation, which represented sixteen national child welfare associations, was concerned that the new life promised to these children was worse than the one they left behind. The *Daily Mail* quoted an official spokesperson for the group of welfare organisations:

> Our members have heard disturbing reports about the children who have emigrated through voluntary organisations. Some will get nothing better than elementary education and, whatever mental ability they show, will have little chance of raising themselves above the standard of domestic service servants and agricultural labourers. Our greatest fear is that the population needs of the Dominions are being put before the welfare of these children. The children must be safeguarded.[26]

The paper reported that the associations wanted an official inquiry to investigate 'the conditions under which these British children were selected for migration; what happened to the children overseas; what safeguards there are for their well-being; how they can be protected from "blind alley" jobs'.[27] The federation also wanted child migrants to be selected more carefully, and offered to participate in the process. The Fairbridge Society dismissed the offer. In a letter to Lord Scarbrough, its acting general secretary reported:

> It requires an almost inordinate amount of self-esteem not to say 'effrontery' to suggest that the mere participation of their members in the selection of children constitutes the first attempt in this

country to create a systematic method of selection and to gain the confidence and goodwill of the child.[28]

The awareness in official circles of the problems of Fairbridge may have been the reason for a royal rejection of a proposal to rename the Molong farm school after Princess (later Queen) Elizabeth. In 1948 the princess donated £2000 to start a fund to help former Fairbridgians establish themselves in life. A very grateful Fairbridge Society proposed the Molong farm school become the 'Princess Elizabeth Fairbridge Farm School'. After all, the Prince of Wales (later King Edward VIII) had allowed his name to be used for the 'Prince of Wales Fairbridge Farm School' opened in Canada in 1938. However, the princess declined the request with a diplomatic 'deferral' of a decision, as noted in the society's minutes:

> The chairman reported correspondence he had with Her Royal Highness the Princess Elizabeth with regard to using her name for the Molong Fairbridge farm school. The Comptroller has advised Sir Charles that the Princess wished to defer granting the request until such time as she herself might visit Australia.[29]

The school was never renamed. When the Queen visited Australia in 1954, Her Royal Highness declined an invitation to come to the school as part of her tour of the west of New South Wales.

Meanwhile, the criticisms of child migration from professionals continued. In 1950 the Australian immigration minister (and later prime minister) Harold Holt was forced in Parliament to defend child migration schemes in the face of continuing criticism from child welfare professionals:

Replying to allegations . . . that child migration from the United Kingdom had been exploited as cheap labour, Mr Holt, Immigration Minister, said in the House of Representatives today that there were no grounds for such allegations against Australia. No child migration organization could bring children to Australia until the United Kingdom, the Commonwealth and the State Governments were sure that it was suitable in all aspects. Accommodation facilities and conditions under which the children could be brought up, had been investigated and there was complete government supervision from the time they reached Australia until they attained majority.[30]

In 1951 John Moss, a retired Kent County welfare officer, reported on child migrant centres while privately visiting Australia. Although overall he made fairly positive observations, his report was critical of the physical conditions in some of the institutions, the lack of trained staff, and the isolation of some of the institutions, which made engagement of the children with local communities more difficult. He also said the institutions were too big and lacked adequate after-care support when those leaving were looking for work.[31]

The most serious official cover-up, however, was still to come. It occurred when a British government inquiry that categorically found Fairbridge and other child migrant centres were 'unfit for children' was deliberately ignored.

The British government had been funding Fairbridge and other similar schemes under the Empire Settlement acts since 1922. The funding agreements were due to end in May 1957, and in 1956 the government was in the process of considering the appropriate levels of future funding. As part of its policy review it proposed to send what it called a fact-finding mission to Australia to investigate the child migrant institutions. In July 1955 the Overseas Migration Board (the OMB, an advisory panel to the Commonwealth Relations Office) had told the British government it did not have enough information to decide future support for child migration: 'The information presently available about child migrants was not sufficient on which to base long term decisions on Government assistance.'[32]

In agreeing to send this mission to Australia, the British government warned that 'continued government funding should be conditional on child migrant organisations adopting more enlightened child care practices, including a shift from institutional care to foster care'. It continued:

> Approval for increased grants for societies concerned with the migration of children and the extension of the existing schemes beyond 1957 should be dependent upon their acceptance of the new doctrine that the selection of children for unaccompanied migration needs to be carefully done, from the psychological as well as other points of view, and the aim should be that such children are placed in family homes and not in institutions.[33]

The British government made the Australian government aware that its authorities were determined to change the practices of the child migrant schemes:

> Australia House and presumably therefore also the department concerned at Canberra are aware of the difficulties of child migration as a result of the softening-up process on which we have been

engaged for some time and that they would probably welcome any mission which might lead to results which could be helpful from their point of view.[34]

Three people were sent out to Australia: John Ross, who was designated chair of the mission, William Garnett, and Miss Gwyneth Wansbrough-Jones. John Ross had, until retiring at the end of 1955, been assistant undersecretary at the Home Office, in charge of the Children's Department, and had a strong record of advocating for the principles of the Curtis Report and the reforms of the 1948 Children Act. William Garnett was of course familiar with child migration to Australia, having more than ten years before, when he was secretary to the British High Commissioner in Canberra, written a report claiming the Fairbridge scheme had 'failed'. Wansbrough-Jones was considered to be the child-care expert in the party, having worked as a children's officer with Essex County Council. The secretary of the committee was Mr R. H. Johnson of the Commonwealth Relations Office.

The mission arrived in Australia in February 1956 and met with federal and state government officials before inspecting twenty-six child migrant centres in all six Australian states. They said they were 'received everywhere with kindness and consideration' and 'given every facility' to 'acquaint ourselves with the arrangements for the care of the children'.[35]

Prior to the arrival of the party to inspect Fairbridge at Molong, William Hudson wrote to Principal Woods outlining the arrangements for the inspection. The party, Woods was told, would include the three members of the fact-finding mission and other government officials. They were scheduled to arrive at

Bathurst Airport at 8.45 am on 15 February and then drive the 90 kilometres to Fairbridge for lunch and be shown around the village and school in the afternoon. Hudson wrote: 'I would like all seven of them to have their tea separately with the children in their cottages. Breakfast with the children in the morning and then go over the farm.' He added that the children should be instructed to wear shoes for the duration of the inspection:

> I have a feeling that barefooted children would have a very adverse effect on the visitors and suggest that if you agree it would be advisable to see they wore their shoes and socks.[36]

At the end of the tour the mission delivered a highly critical report based on what they had seen. At its heart was the claim that the child migrant centres were out of date and operating fundamentally at odds with acceptable standards of child care that had been progressively introduced into Britain since the passing of the Children Act. The mission found that the Australian organisations wanted to retain the large impersonal institutions and would not give 'serious thought' to the more modern approach of 'boarding out' or foster care. The report argued that child migrants deserved special sensitivity that was largely lacking in Australia:

> We think it will be agreed generally that the desirability of enabling children deprived of a normal home life to be brought up in circumstances as approaching as nearly as possible those of a child living in his own home applies with particular force to migrant children, who, in addition to the basic need of children for the understanding and affection that lead to security, have experienced disturbance arising from the transfer to new and unfamiliar surroundings.[37]

The sensitivity to the emotional needs of children was a totally alien concept to the ethos of Fairbridge. Indeed, the entire thrust of Ross's report was fundamentally at odds with the Fairbridge model. While the farm schools provided institutional accommodation to hundreds of children, the mission recommended child migrants be fostered out to Australian families. The implementation of this recommendation would have required a repudiation of the Fairbridge philosophy and a total reconstitution of the scheme.

The mission was made aware of the scheme's difficulty in attracting suitable cottage mothers, and found there was 'no specialist scheme of training in Australasia for child care work'. Ross, Garnett and Wansbrough-Jones were especially critical of the children's 'segregation in large from the life of the [local Australian] community', lack of 'homely atmosphere', lack of 'personal privacy', which resulted in the children's difficulty in adjusting to normal life when they left the institution and were found a job.

The report struck at the heart of the Fairbridge model by recommending that children not be kept to run the farm for two years after they reached minimum school-leaving age before being found employment. In a clear reference to Fairbridge, which used the children to run the farm, they found:

> We gathered at one place that the work done in this way by the boys was essential to the running of the farm. It seemed to us that these arrangements were unsuitable for boys and girls who did not intend to follow farm and domestic work . . .
>
> Children should not ordinarily remain in an establishment between leaving school and entering outside employment, except

for the purpose of receiving training for the occupation they intend to enter.[38]

Finally, Garnett and his co-writers dropped a bombshell by recommending that in future the consent of the home secretary should be required for any child to migrate. The implications were clear: if Fairbridge did not fall into line with recommended modern practices, it would not receive authorisation to send more children to Australia.

The report of the Ross fact-finding mission caused quite a stir in government circles in London. The OMB, which had initiated the mission in the first place, was embarrassed by the findings and recommendations, and moved quickly to distance itself from the report. In his own report to the government's Commonwealth Relations Office in May 1956, M. K. Ewans of the OMB observed:

The Overseas Migration Board yesterday discussed the report of the Child Migration Mission. It was quite a stormy meeting and it is clear the Board are now rather sorry that the mission was sent at all.[39]

The board indicated that some of its members wanted the report hushed up. Sir Colin Anderson, a member of the OMB and a director of the Orient Line, whose ships carried many child migrants to Australia, was among those who were opposed to its release. His rather original argument was that the Australian child migrant organisations were likely 'to close ranks to resist criticism; hence publishing the report may in fact defeat efforts to get organisations to raise their standards'.[40]

While a number of the OMB urged that the report should not be published, it was eventually agreed that its dissemination was inevitable in view of the certainty of leakage in one form or another. However, if it were to be made public, the board wanted to have the opportunity to say that they viewed the report with 'extreme disfavour'. Cyril Costley-White, who was then the head of Communication Department at the Commonwealth Relations Office, alerted his superiors as to the problem this would cause the government:

> The Overseas Migration Board would like the preface [of the report] altered so that they can escape responsibility for being instrumental in the appointment of the mission whose report they do not approve . . . they wish to put their own independent comments on the report.[41]

The government was happy for the OMB to criticise the mission's report but was concerned it would then be forced into declaring an opinion.[42] The assistant undersecretary of state in the Commonwealth Relations Office, G. E. B. Shannon, suggested a way the government could play for time after the report was published would be 'by saying that we are consulting the government about the action to be taken in the report, without saying whether we agree or disagree with it'.[43]

While this drama was being played out in Whitehall, there was more controversy in the findings of Ross's mission that were not in the official report. Separately, in secret addenda, he and his colleagues had provided assessments of each of the twenty-six centres they had inspected in Australia and some of these were highly critical, particularly of Fairbridge. The addenda were a bombshell.

On 9 June 1956, Costley-White sent the complete report, including the highly sensitive addenda, to R. J. Whittick of the

Home Office. Costley-White made it clear the addenda were to be kept quiet, even from the OMB and the Australian government, and that:

> It is not our intention to publish them at the time that the report is published; we are not intending to give them to the Australian Government, to the Overseas Migration Board, or the Voluntary Societies. You will understand that it is therefore important that they should not be quoted or referred to in dealing with outside persons or organisations.

Keeping the addenda secret was one thing, but the government had to make a decision about whether to continue to allow the migration of children to Fairbridge and the other institutions that had attracted critical comment from the mission. Costley-White acknowledged in his letter to Whittick that it would be difficult for the government 'to approve children going to institutions that have been criticised by the fact-finding mission', but, he said, 'rather than make a complete closure on all child migration it may be considered wiser to adopt a middle course of allowing institutions provided they have not been adversely criticised'.

The Home Office then used the addenda to draw up a 'blacklist' of institutions 'unfit for children'. On 22 June 1956 Whittick wrote to Shannon, his boss, to advise him of how this list had been compiled:

> Establishments in category 'A' are those that we think are not fit to receive more migrants, for the present at least. Category 'C' are establishments that pass muster. Category 'B' contains those about which we do not know enough to say whether they ought to be

placed in 'A' or 'C'. Some of the establishments in category 'A' are so wrong in the principles on which they run that they would need a complete metamorphosis to bring them in to category 'C'. Organisations on the 'black list' would be told that their establishments had been criticised by the Mission, would be shown the reports, or parts of them, or given the gist of the criticism and would be asked to put matters right before you approved any more children being sent to their establishments.[44]

The Fairbridge school at Molong was in category A. A passage in the secret addenda described why:

Furnishing and equipment: the cottages have the minimum of furniture and little comfort. The beds consist of wire mesh, which tend to sag, on a steel frame, with very poor mattresses. There is no other furniture in the dormitories and the floors are bare wood.

A typical playroom contains one large table, with plain wooden chairs, and lockers forming seats around the walls. Bathrooms and kitchens are shabby and poorly though adequately equipped. In the dining room the children use plain metal plates and beakers.

Children's Activities: a considerable amount of domestic and other work is done by the older school children, who spend about two hours before morning school and another hour in the evening on their duties in the cottages, kitchen bakery, etc., or at farm or garden work.

General comments: the children at Molong have to work hard and have no luxuries . . . from conversation with a number of children it was clear that at first many of them find life strange and are homesick.[45]

The report pointed out that Fairbridge at Molong was harder for girls than boys: 'Those who leave school at fifteen have little preparation for anything but domestic work and even less opportunity to see much of Australian life.'

Fairbridge at Pinjarra in Western Australia was also in category A. The mission found it 'was complacent, and reluctant to accept new ideas' and 'showed a lack of appreciation of current thought on child care'.

The criticisms of these institutions put on the blacklist were in contrast to other schools that attracted more favourable assessments. Of the Clarendon Church of England Home at Kingston Park, Tasmania, the mission reported:

> In this home there are good material conditions, and the children appear to receive individual affection and understanding. The home is run on sound principles, and the children seem to have plenty of interests and to be happy and spontaneous. [46]

And the Methodist Home at Burwood in Victoria was described as providing 'good material care and a high standard of comfort, in an attractive setting. The Superintendent is keen, active and enlightened, and has considerable personal knowledge of individual children. These appear to be really good homes of the grouped cottage type.'

Of the twenty-six institutions inspected, those in category A were the Fairbridge Farm Schools at Molong and Pinjarra; St Joseph's Roman Catholic Orphanage, Lane Cove, Sydney; Dhurringile Presbyterian Rural Training Farm, Victoria; St Joseph's Roman Catholic School, near Rockhampton, Queensland; the Salvation Army Training Farm, Riverview, Queensland; the Methodist

Home at Magill, Adelaide; St Vincent's Roman Catholic Orphanage, Castledare, Western Australia; St Joseph's Roman Catholic Farm School at Bindoon, Western Australia; and St John Bosco Roman Catholic Boys Town at Glenorchy in Hobart, Tasmania.[47]

When Whittick drew up the blacklist, he was well aware of Fairbridge's influence in high places in Britain and the political difficulties that would flow from putting the Fairbridge schools on the list, even though they certainly deserved to be there:

> The reputation in which the Fairbridge organisation has been held in this country – and no doubt in Australia as well – may, we recognise, remove from the sphere of practical politics the possibility of putting the farms schools of Pinjarra and Molong on your 'blacklist', although well informed opinion would condemn them from the point of view of accepted principles of child care.[48]

By the end of June and following consultation with John Ross, the Home Office decided that it would suspend further child migration to institutions on the blacklist. At the same time, the secretary to the British high commissioner in Canberra gave the Australian government a copy of the mission's report, but not the addenda.

The Fairbridge Society in London was by now aware of much of what had been happening. With its political influence and contacts in high places, it had been leaked details of the mission's report in the middle of April. By the end of July Fairbridge had a total of sixteen children at its home in Knockholt in Kent being prepared to go to Australia. Ten were destined for Fairbridge in Molong and the other six for Pinjarra.

On Monday 2 July, W. B. Vaughan, the secretary and director of the London Fairbridge Society, telephoned R. E. Armstrong, the chief migration officer at Australia House. According to Armstrong, Vaughan expressed 'deep concern' that formal approval had not been given for the children to go to Australia.[49] Vaughan said the children were being readied in Knockholt, their adult escorts for the voyage had been appointed and the bookings had been made to sail on the S.S. *Fairsea* a little more than three weeks later, on 26 July, from Tilbury. Armstrong suggested Vaughan call into Australia House that day, where Armstrong 'explained the situation arising out of the Fact-Finding Mission Report'.

Vaughan, according to Armstrong, said that the board of the Fairbridge Society was meeting in three days and he wanted the situation resolved before then. There would be a 'first-class row' if he had to report to the board that approval had been denied for the sixteen children to go to Australia. Vaughan, said Armstrong, would apply political pressure: 'He had no doubt that a sudden suspension of child migration would lead to pressure on the Secretary of State and possibly questions in the Commons and the House of Lords.'

Immediately after the meeting, Armstrong reported to R. H. Johnson of the Home Office, who in turn put the details in a memo to Costley-White and Shannon. The following day, 4 July, Costley-White wrote to Shannon describing the political 'dangers' of blocking the Fairbridge children from sailing to Australia:

We would certainly incur the wrath of the voluntary organisations, particularly Fairbridge, both in this country and in Australia. This would in itself be unfortunate and would almost certainly have immediate parliamentary repercussions since Fairbridge has the means of making itself heard here in both Houses of Parliament and to the public at large.[50]

Fairbridge was not short of influential supporters in high places. At the time of the appointment of the fact-finding mission, Douglas Dodds-Parker was the under-secretary of state in the Commonwealth Relations Office. His wife, Aileen, was on the board of Fairbridge, where she worked for more than fifty years, becoming its chair in 1983. Douglas Dodds-Parker was leaked an early copy of the fact-finding mission report and privately lobbied the home secretary, Gwilym Lloyd-George, in favour of Fairbridge against some of the mission's recommendations.[51]

Meanwhile, Costley-White also emphasised that Fairbridge had the additional political 'clout' of His Royal Highness the Duke of Gloucester, who, in addition to being the brother of Edward VIII and George VI, and the uncle of the Queen, was president of Fairbridge.

Costley-White went on to say that it 'was almost impossible' to resolve the matter before the Fairbridge board meeting the following day and he was starting to look at ways to back down on the issue. Having deliberately withheld the addenda from the Australian government, he now used the need for consultation as a possible way out of the impasse. 'To take what would appear to be a somewhat high-handed decision to hold up child migration without consulting the Australian Government would appear to be dangerous.' He ended his memo saying his department within the Home Office would suggest backing down. The recommendation of the department would be that the 'stand still' policy should not, however, be applied to the sixteen children at Knockholt.

G. E. B. Shannon hastily took the lifeline, and, in the first of a series of backdowns, sent a memo to Costley-White on the

morning of 5 July, before the meeting of the Fairbridge Society
that afternoon:

> I have discussed the foregoing with Sir Saville Garner and Commander
> Noble. They agree that the sixteen children for Fairbridge and three
> others for the Northcote Fund should be allowed to go, on the under-
> standing that we cannot guarantee approval of future applications
> pending consideration of the Fact-Finding Mission's report and
> consultation with the Australian authorities about it.[52]

Costley-White had met with Vaughan the previous afternoon,
telling him that the children already booked could go to Australia.

So, as a result of these political machinations, sixteen more
children and hundreds after them – including me and my brothers,
two and a half years later – were dispatched to Australia to spend
the remainder of our childhood in institutions blacklisted by the
British government as unfit for children.

Meanwhile, the Fairbridge Society considered the report. Having
pressured the government to send the children to Australia in July,
it was in no mood to reform. In a letter to the Commonwealth
Relations Office, Vaughan made it clear that Fairbridge disagreed
with the principle thrust of the fact-finding mission – and the
views of most child welfare experts – that the days of institutions
were over. He also said there were not enough homes in Australia
to take foster children. This was at odds with the reality. Many
of the children at Fairbridge were regularly taken into private
homes during school holidays and many of those families wanted
to foster or adopt the children but were thwarted by Fairbridge.

Ian Bayliff remembered as a nine-year-old being taken in for the Christmas holidays by the Allan family, who lived on a small farm on the edge of the town of Cowra, about 100 kilometres south of Fairbridge. He said a number of other Fairbridge kids were taken for holidays by families in the Cowra district. He thought the idea was promoted by the local Apex or Rotary Club. 'Keith Allan was a local school teacher. It was the best Christmas I ever had. The Allans organised heaps of presents. I never had so many presents, many from people I never even knew.'

Bayliff said that towards the end of the holidays Keith Allan asked if he would like to stay and live with them and attend the local school.

I said 'yes please'. When he took me back to Fairbridge he met with Mr Woods in his office, I assume to talk about me going to live with the Allans. I was sent away. I was never told what happened but I never heard from the Allans again, and never went back to their farm at holiday time.

Vivian Bingham has a similar recollection:

Up the [Amaroo] road from Fairbridge a local family . . . wanted to adopt me and by some uncanny thing they were not allowed to . . . Maybe . . . my life would have been a lot better – but it wasn't.

From the age of eight, and for several years, Derek Moriarty and his younger brother Paul were taken every Christmas by Godfrey and Frances Savage, who lived in a grand house at Cheltenham on Sydney's fashionable north shore. Derek remembers the Savages wanted to adopt him but nothing ever came of it, and he thinks Fairbridge blocked the idea.

Tony Stepney was ten years old when he went to Fairbridge. At Christmas and other school holidays he was taken in by Betty and John Bryden, who lived in the country town of Gilgandra, about 180 kilometres north of Fairbridge. 'I absolutely loved it there. They did everything for me. I felt totally at home. I called them Mum and Dad. They bought me clothes, which I left at the home when I had to go back to Fairbridge.' Tony said that the Brydens eventually asked if he wanted to live with them. He said he wanted to very much, so they wrote to Woods, who told them it couldn't be done. 'The next time I saw them, "Mum" said: "I have some news. It's not good, I'm afraid." She said that Fairbridge had told them I could not leave the farm to live with them.'

Tony said it was a similar story with his half-brother and sister, Robbie and Shirley Hillman. The two went for holidays with the Cameron family near Forbes, who wanted to foster them, but Fairbridge again said no.

The London Fairbridge Society was supported by the Sydney Fairbridge Council, which also criticised the fact-finding mission's proposal to foster out migrant children in Australia. In August 1956 William Hudson wrote to his counterpart in London, Sir Charles Hambro, dismissing the idea: 'I am convinced that 90% of the homes to which the children could be boarded out would be a poor substitute for the upbringing we give them at Fairbridge.'[53]

The following year, 1957, the British government was given one more chance to force Fairbridge and the other child migrant schemes to introduce overdue reforms to their operations. The need to renew the agreement that involved the British government providing funding for child migration under the Empire Settlement Act gave the government one more chance to force Fairbridge and the other child migrant schemes to introduce reforms to their operations: as a condition for continued funding, it negotiated an agreement that required the organisation to introduce the reforms identified by the fact-finding mission.

The new agreement, between the Secretary of State for Commonwealth Relations and the Fairbridge Society, was signed by Vaughan on behalf of Fairbridge. In it, the organisation agreed to adopt the reforms recommended by the fact-finding mission. It accepted that its future staffing 'shall be as far as possible persons with knowledge and experience of child care methods'; that there would be 'an adequate standard of comfort and amenity' for the children and 'the opportunity for children to be assimilated to Australian life'. Specifically, it agreed to actively pursue the fostering out of children:

> The practice of arranging for children to spend school holidays together in private homes shall be developed to the full . . . whether possible suitable arrangements shall be made to board children permanently with foster parents.[54]

The agreement included the ultimate sanction for non-compliance. If Fairbridge did not implement the agreed changes, its funding would be stopped:

> Last (but not least) the Secretary of State, if he is not satisfied with the manner in which the said scheme is being administered or

carried out in any respect may . . . at any time, terminate his obligations hereunder.

However, in subsequent years, some of them after my arrival at the Molong farm school, the interests of the organisation were put before the interests of the children and there were no changes to the way Fairbridge operated. There were no improvements to the 'comfort and amenities'. They remained unsuitable and unclean. The ranks of the cottage mothers were still dominated by unqualified women who were at Fairbridge because they had nowhere else to go. We were still isolated from Australian society, and, apart from being taken to secondary school and back, and to church and sports matches, had no social engagement with locals. And over nearly four decades, until the end of the Fairbridge scheme, there is no record of any child ever being fostered or adopted to an Australian family.

10

FIRST STEPS TO JUSTICE

Former child migrants are to begin a landmark class action today over the horrific abuse they allegedly suffered at a farm school in western New South Wales.

The Forgotten Children attracted widespread publicity when it was published in 2007, and the reviews were generally positive. The *Sydney Morning Herald* wrote:

> This book is part memoir, part oral history, part archival study – and a successful hybrid . . . As an Old Fairbridgian, Hill has insights that could only come from an insider and was moreover able to elicit a high degree of confidence and co-operation from other former students. It's ultimately these voices, including Hill's, that make this book memorable. From them we learn of the physical and sexual abuse and emotional and material deprivation.[1]

The book also attracted a lot of interest in the UK media. In a seven-page feature story the *Sunday Times* magazine said the book challenged long-held beliefs that Fairbridge schools 'had been seen as models of a stiff upper lip British education, a little harsh but no worse than a standard English public school':

> Hill's research at Molong revealed a very different picture . . . he heard a recurring story of cruelty and abuse and workhouse labour conditions. He was staggered to discover just how much had been known and effectively hidden, in Britain and Australia . . . of an institution that for decades had subjected children aged between 4 and 15 to sexual abuse, virtual slave labour conditions and daily beatings with straps, canes, electric cords and on occasions a hockey stick.[2]

But the book did attract criticism, including from some former Fairbridge children. The then chairman of the Old Fairbridgians Association John Harris emailed his colleagues on the association board to say that he was 'very annoyed' about the book and the publicity that it had generated: 'I watched in disbelief and disgust at the ABC [TV] report on Tuesday . . . the veiled comments with no hard evidence . . . as what was claimed went unchallenged.'

Harris was one of a number of people who were so upset with the book that they refused to read it. 'It will be everyone's own decision whether to purchase the book and in my case it will not happen and I trust many Old Fairbridgians will opt out accordingly,' he said. One of his OFA board colleagues, John Stocker, emailed back to say he was disappointed with me for 'muckraking and attacking Fairbridge'. John Kennedy, the chairman of the Fairbridge Foundation, said he was not convinced of the abuse. 'I don't know. And that's the problem I've got . . . I've got to rely on what is written by David Hill . . . but I don't know . . . I'd be shocked [if the abuse was as described].[3]

The book caused such consternation around Fairbridge that a planned launch in Molong was cancelled. The *Australian* newspaper reported that the event, which was organised by the local *Molong Express*, had been called off at short notice, with the newspaper's owners using its front page to cite 'the strength of feelings expressed by a wide cross-section of the community against the anti-Fairbridge publicity'. It seems many people in the district were hearing about the allegations of abuse for the first time – and simply did not want to believe it.

The *Australian* also reported that much of the opposition to the book came from local people who had not even read it:

> Des Sullivan, 76, admitted he had yet to read the book but accused the author of profiting from the suffering of others. 'Does David Hill say anything in the book that is good about Fairbridge? All he is doing is exploiting the things that happened,' said Mr Sullivan.[4]

As the *Australian* reported, we went ahead with the Molong launch of the book anyway:

> [David Hill] defied a decision to cancel a book-signing for *The Forgotten Children* to be held in Molong, 300 km northwest of Sydney, where the school was based, after protests from residents ... He threw a table, chair and a stack of books into a ute and set himself up in the carpark outside Molong's railway station. 'I'm very grateful for the ... cancelling because we attracted more people due to the publicity they gave it. But I'm sad for what this says about Molong,' said Mr Hill, whose three years at Fairbridge started in 1959, aged 12.[5]

*

Some weeks after publication I was phoned by former Fairbridge kid Bob Stephens, who told me he had contacted leading law firm Slater & Gordon about the possibility of Fairbridgians taking legal action for the abuse they had suffered at Fairbridge.

Bob had arrived at the farm school as an eight-year-old and was there for nine years. He had already done five years when I arrived. He told me now that he had phoned a senior lawyer named Bill Madden at Slater & Gordon's Sydney Parramatta office, who asked Bob how many people would be interested in exploring legal action. Bob said he thought I would have a better idea and suggested he would get me to call.

So I phoned Madden and told him I could find out how many Fairbridgians might be interested. I also said that I thought few of them had much money and my guess was that they would only consider legal action if Slater & Gordon could agree to take the case as 'no win, no fee'. When Madden said he would consider proceeding on that basis I told him I would bring in some of the Fairbridgians to his offices.

At this stage I had never contemplated any of us taking legal action. Even though I had no doubt many had a strong case to prosecute, I knew that civil litigation could become protracted and costly, and often had an uncertain outcome. We might be looking at years in the courts, running up huge legal bills and with no guarantee that we would win in the end.

A few weeks later, I helped organise about twenty-five of us to meet in Slater & Gordon's Sydney offices, and a couple of weeks later about fifteen other Fairbridgians turned up for a similar meeting in Orange, hosted by the legal firm. There, Madden confirmed that Slater & Gordon was prepared to represent us in a claim against the Fairbridge Foundation, which still functioned out of an office in King Street, Sydney, and still owned assets valued at millions of dollars.

After child migration had ended and Molong closed in 1974, the Fairbridge Foundation sold off the farm and invested the money. From the profits and dividends it earned, it continued to operate by offering educational scholarships to rural families and making financial grants to children's charities. However, it rejected calls that some of the profits from the proceeds of the farm be paid to help needy former Fairbridge children and their families.

Derek Moriarty recalls trying to reach out to Fairbridge for help. His brother Paul's wife had died when she was thirty-seven, and later Paul also passed away – of renal failure at the relatively young age of forty-seven – leaving their four children orphaned. At the time, in the early nineties, Fairbridge was providing scholarships to children of Australian farming families to send their children to the exclusive private Kinross Wolaroi School in Orange. Derek applied on behalf of Paul's son Graham for one of the scholarships, but was told by Fairbridge that as he was not from a farming family he did not qualify. Derek was upset, 'I was absolutely appalled,' he said. 'Many of the children given scholarships were from wealthy pastoral families. They even gave money to the Molong Baby Health Centre and the Molong Hospital. It seems just about everyone could qualify for Fairbridge money, except Fairbridge kids.'

Bob Stephens was also angry with the Fairbridge Foundation regarding the money it had earned from the farm sale:

The Fairbridge farm is worth millions and millions. The reason why it sold for so much is that it was a very good farm. But who did it? It was child labour, unpaid child labour that created the value . . . I believe they have the right to benefit from the proceeds of the farm.[6]

Despite the protests of many Fairbridgians, the board remained resolutely against giving financial support to any former Fairbridge children. Almost forty years after the closure of the farm school, chairman John Kennedy said:

> The objective of the Fairbridge Foundation is to use its assets widely and prudently, and to distribute the proceeds to other charities who have as their primary objectives the assisting of children in need, or are disadvantaged . . . we have the objective of helping today's children and future children . . . we don't want to be distracted from the needs of now and the future by what happened in the past.[7]

This lack of empathy from the foundation did not come as a surprise. Since its board was established in 1937, its men (there has never been a woman on the board) were invariably from the opposite end of the social spectrum to those who were at the farm school. Typically, they were products of Sydney's exclusive private boys' schools, and university educated. Many, like Kingsley Fairbridge, were Rhodes Scholars. For some years they invited former Fairbridgian Dennis Silver to sit on their board – but most of us saw Dennis as an apologist for the place and unlikely to ever rock the boat. He had made it clear to me when I started exploring the Fairbridge story that he felt uncomfortable about the public airing of complaints about what had happened there. However, when I visited him in Springwood Hospital shortly before he died in 2019, he told me that he now supported what I was doing, and shortly before his death made a generous donation towards the funding of the Fairbridge children's memorial park that we were building.

In 2006, when I was still researching the Fairbridge story and was coming to terms with the large number of accounts of abuse being given to me, I asked John Kennedy to meet me for coffee one afternoon near the Fairbridge city office. Kennedy had been on the board of Fairbridge for more than thirty years, including for a time when it was still operating as a child migrant farm school. I tried to tell him that the story emerging from my research and from interviews with Fairbridge kids was extremely confronting, but Kennedy just didn't want to know.

I then approached one of his board colleagues, David Calver, who was younger than Kennedy and would eventually succeed him as the Fairbridge Foundation chairman. I hoped Calver would be more receptive but I found him intransigent: I recall him telling me that he thought the Fairbridge children who were complaining about abuse were 'ungrateful'.

The Fairbridgians decided to pursue a civil action. After the initial briefings, Slater & Gordon had gathered about forty clients. By the time the case ended eight years later the number had steadily grown to more than two hundred. I decided at the outset not to be a claimant, though I would have been eligible. I'd had my share of physical abuse at Fairbridge, and I'd been subject to what might be called 'sexual molestation', but from what I had learned from my interviews, what I'd endured was nothing compared with what had happened to many others. Besides, the role I wanted to play, the one in which I saw myself as most effective, was as an advocate and supporter of the other former Fairbridge kids.

And I knew I'd be far better in that role if I were not also seeking compensation for myself.

Once Slater & Gordon had begun proceedings, we discovered that the wheels of justice indeed move slowly. I don't think any of us thought that the legal process would drag on for anything like as long as it did, and that it would only finally be resolved by forces brought to bear outside our own case.

The law firm first approached the Fairbridge Foundation in September 2007 with a proposal for an out-of-court settlement scheme, which would be set up to pay damages to those who had been physically and sexually abused while they were at Fairbridge.

In January 2008 Fairbridge agreed to consider this proposal, but they wanted 'specific and substantive details of individuals who are claiming reparation'. Our lawyers spent about a year gathering evidence, including thirty-seven statutory declarations and a large amount of other information about what had happened to the children sent to the farm school. Much of the evidence that was used in the case came from revelations I had included in *The Forgotten Children*. The material collected was handed over to the Fairbridge Foundation.

In September 2009 the foundation said it would not agree to set up an out-of-court settlement scheme. While the decision angered me, I was not the least bit surprised: the Fairbridge Foundation had never accepted any of the claims that wrongdoing or abuse had taken place, even though some of the evidence they were presented with consisted of copies we had made of paperwork that was sitting in cardboard boxes in their Sydney office at the time.

In addition to discussions with Fairbridge, Slater & Gordon also had preliminary discussions about an out-of-court settlement scheme with the New South Wales government, whose department of child welfare had been responsible for oversighting the operations of Fairbridge. These talks also proved fruitless.

Having failed to reach a negotiated settlement, Slater & Gordon launched legal proceedings in the New South Wales Supreme Court in December 2009. At the same time as taking the matter to court, the firm broadened the claim to include both the federal government and the New South Wales state government as defendants, along with the Fairbridge Foundation. The rationale for including the federal government was that when we had become child migrants to Australia the federal minister for immigration became our legal guardian and therefore responsible for our welfare. The New South Wales government was included because, the lawyers argued, the state government's child welfare department had been delegated the responsibility for day-to-day operations of Fairbridge. I thought enjoining the two governments was a good idea as there was plenty of evidence to show that both had failed in their responsibility to adequately protect the children, even in cases where they were aware the children were not being properly cared for.

I have no doubt that Slater & Gordon decided to sue the governments because they had already spent two years on the case and the Fairbridge Foundation had assets of only around six to eight million dollars. If Fairbridge was the sole party paying compensation, there would be little left, after the deduction of several years of legal costs, to pay the victims of abuse.

But commencing proceedings against two governments was not easy. Governments generally play it hard when prosecuted so as to discourage others from considering doing the same. That said, we had no idea quite how hard the two governments would play it; that it would take six years of battling it out in the Supreme Court, involving twenty-one appearances and the presentation of 50,000 pages of documents.

I attended almost all of the hearings with other Fairbridgians, including Derek Moriarty, who was now the chairman of the Old Fairbridgians Association, and Ian 'Smiley' Bayliff, who had been a great help to me in researching the Fairbridge story over many years. The hours we spent in the public gallery of the Supreme Court building in Sydney's Phillip Street were frustrating and tedious.

To us laypeople it was clear the defendants were stringing out proceedings with technical legal arguments, including complaints to the court that our side wanted them to hand over unreasonable amounts of information ('discovery' as it's described in legal parlance) to support the prosecution of our case. At one point, the New South Wales government's barrister made the absurd claim that the search to find what Slater & Gordon needed to know would cost more than $100 million – to dig out all the relevant information from different government files.

In all these six years, the case never got to trial. We spent not a single day debating abuse or hearing any evidence from any witnesses. The entire time was taken arguing technicalities raised by the defendants, including an attempt to have the case thrown out because we had exceeded the statutory time, or 'limitations' period.[8]

They also argued against our fundamental manner of proceeding. Slater & Gordon had sought to have the case heard as a class action, which would allow for all the plaintiffs to be represented by one or two lead plaintiffs who had experienced the same or similar levels of physical and sexual abuse. Without a class action, each and every one of the former Fairbridge children would have had to launch individual legal proceedings, which would have meant years of court time as each case would have to be heard separately. Yet it took three years before the court even ruled we *could* proceed as a class action.

In late 2011 the case was again delayed, this time by the court. The assigned judge, Justice Clifton Hoeben, was double-booked and the scheduled hearing for November was adjourned till June the following year. When we resumed in June 2012 we were told Hoeben had left the Supreme Court and for the rest of the case we would have a new judge, Justice Peter Garling.

The frustration of these drawn-out proceedings was made worse by the fact that the health of a growing number of the older Fairbridgians was failing. By the end of the case the Old Fairbridgians Association membership record showed that between 2008 and 2015, fifty-seven former Fairbridge kids out of a total of 220 had died. Almost all of them would have been eligible to mount a claim for compensation.

Among those who died was Malcolm 'Flossie' Field, who was the first of a number of boys who claimed to me that he had been sexually abused at Fairbridge by the then governor-general of Australia Sir William Slim. Flossie died in 2012. Another was Roger Smith, who was a close friend of mine at Fairbridge and someone with whom I had remained in contact for many years after we'd left. Roger, who died in 2015, had hated the farm school and often complained about the abuse he'd suffered there. He had *genu valgum*, otherwise known as 'knocked knees', which made it more difficult for him to run. He never forgot and never forgave Woods, who would chase after him on the sports field whipping him with a cane on the back of the legs to make him run faster.

Meanwhile, in 2012 the federal and state governments were ordered by the court to file their defences. The two defences were similar. Each denied it had a duty of care for the Fairbridge children and denied responsibility for the claimed abuse. The Fairbridge Foundation's defence was quite different, however. It said it had not run the Molong Fairbridge school but merely owned the property, and that the responsibility for the management rested with the UK Fairbridge Society in London. This evidence was the exact opposite of what the Fairbridge Foundation chairman John Kennedy had told an Australian Senate inquiry a decade earlier in 1998 when he explained that, unlike the Fairbridge Farm School in Pinjarra in Western Australia, the Molong school in New South Wales was 'independent' of Fairbridge in the UK:

> It is also important to say that the situation in New South Wales is different from the situation in Western Australia, in that Pinjarra was directly controlled, if you like, by the London office of Fairbridge. We were not. We were an independent group affiliated with London and used the name, but essentially we were an independent group in New South Wales. So there is that difference between Pinjarra and Molong.[9]

In July 2013 and now having been in court five years, Slater & Gordon again proposed a formal settlement scheme, but all the defendants argued it was premature because they were still seeking 'further particulars' about the claims from our side. At the same time, the defendants issued thirty subpoenas to various doctors who had treated some of the abused Fairbridge children for the lasting effects of their abuse, seeking yet more information.

By this stage a number of those accusing Fairbridge and its staff of abuse were feeling under increasing stress and talked to me about withdrawing from the case. Many of them felt they were still not believed. We were lucky that for most of the time the leading solicitor handling the case at Slater & Gordon was Roop Sandhu. Roop was quietly spoken, empathetic and reassuring. The Fairbridge kids trusted him and without him I don't think many of them would have stayed the distance.

Finally, in February 2014 we had something of a breakthrough when Justice Garling finally determined the case could proceed as a class action. The court also rejected the defence proposal to knock out the case on limitations grounds, saying that the defence could mount arguments about limitations as part of the trial.

The media claimed it was a big victory for the Fairbridge kids:

> Former child migrants are to begin a landmark class action today over the horrific abuse they allegedly suffered at a farm school in western New South Wales. After years of technical legal arguments, the state's Supreme Court has granted 65 plaintiffs the right to sue the NSW Government, as well as the Commonwealth [Government] and the Fairbridge Foundation.[10]

After finally obtaining more information by way of 'discovery', our lawyers handed their evidence to the defence. The two lead plaintiffs were Vivian Bingham and Geraldine Whinn (they were named in documents related to the case by their married names – Vivian Drady and Geraldine Giles). Our case consisted of a vast amount of material, including lengthy affidavits, psychiatrists' reports, six lever-arch folders of historic information and a further fifty-nine statements of group members intended to substantiate the abuse. Geraldine was seven years old when she arrived at Fairbridge and Vivian was five. Both were sexually and physically abused from an early age.

On 11 December 2014 – and now five years after us starting proceedings – Justice Garling fixed the date for trial in the Supreme Court: it would take place over an eight-week period from 24 August 2015. It had taken seven years in total to reach this point and the future of our case was littered with great uncertainty. The defendants had not admitted any wrongdoing and obviously would contest our claims. We faced the risk of further delays and the possibility of further adjournments. Even if we won, the defendants could appeal. We were nervous the case could still go on for many more years.

And while I did not relish proceeding to court, which I knew might not yield a positive result, Slater & Gordon had agreed to go ahead on a 'no-win, no-fee' basis, so the Fairbridge kids had little to lose.

11

THE FIRST BIG WIN

Fairbridge accepts that you suffered physical abuse or sexual abuse or both during your childhood which was perpetrated by staff at the Farm School and other persons.

At the same time as our case was bogged down in the Supreme Court, a number of other factors were raising awareness in Australia and overseas of what had befallen Fairbridge children and the hundreds of thousands of others who were in similar institutions in this country and around the world.

In the early days of our case, the ABC broadcast *The Long Journey Home*. When it had agreed to show the documentary, it planned to put it to air in 2010, but the date was brought forward to November 2009 to coincide with the apology from Labor Prime Minister Kevin Rudd to Australians who had been institutionalised as children.

More than a year earlier, Rudd had publicly apologised to the Stolen Generation of Indigenous children – the tens of thousands who for more than a century had been forcibly removed from their families. This inhumane policy of successive Australian governments was shaped by the belief that these children would be better off brought up by white families to be trained largely as domestic servants and eventually become assimilated into white society.

In November 2009 Rudd issued a second apology – to several hundred thousand child migrants and wards of the state, the so-called 'lost innocents and forgotten Australians'.[1] Like the earlier apology, this came after more than a decade of formal inquiries and at least five national and state investigations into the past treatment of these young migrants, and as the result of agitation by concerned groups, including the highly effective Care Leavers Australia Network (CLAN).

Several thousand former institutionalised children and child migrants converged on the Great Hall in Canberra's Parliament House on 16 November 2009, where both Rudd and the then leader of the federal opposition Malcolm Turnbull read apologies:

We come together today to offer our nation's apology. To say to you, the Forgotten Australians, and those who were sent to our shores as children without your consent, that we are sorry. Sorry – that as children you were taken from your families and placed in institutions where so often you were abused.

Sorry – for the physical suffering, the emotional starvation and the cold absence of love, of tenderness, of care.

Sorry – for the tragedy, the absolute tragedy, of childhoods lost, – childhoods spent instead in austere and authoritarian places, where names were replaced by numbers, spontaneous play by regimented routine, the joy of learning by the repetitive drudgery of menial work.

We Fairbridge kids were well represented, though child migrants were less than ten per cent of the total number of children who had spent all or part of their childhoods in Australian institutions.

The apology was carefully drafted so as not to provide a basis for survivors of child sexual abuse to legally challenge the government, but it was well received and, we all felt, long overdue. I remember sitting in the vast hall of Parliament House with a few dozen other former Fairbridge kids, in the middle of thousands of others who had spent all or part of their childhood in institutions, and how most of them were crying, so hungry and grateful for something as basic as a few words of apology. For all of us it was a very moving and unforgettable experience.

Afterwards, we all spilt out into the sunshine and onto the lawns in front of Parliament House, where an almost festive air had replaced the sorrow of earlier in the day. I was asked by an ABC radio interviewer what I thought of the event, and whether an apology could, as Rudd had said, begin to heal our pain.

'Not on its own, no,' I said, emphasising, however, that I didn't want to be negative about the apology. 'It is a step forward and it does bring a lot of comfort to a lot of people who have never been believed and [for whom] nobody appeared to care.' I agreed it was the beginning of a process 'that's appreciated by a lot of those poor bloody kids that suffered so much'.

Three months later, British Prime Minister Gordon Brown made a similar apology in the House of Commons to British child migrants. A number of us were invited to the residences of the British consuls in Sydney and Melbourne to hear Brown read his government's apology:

To all those former child migrants and their families . . . we are truly sorry. They were let down. We are sorry they were allowed to be sent away at the time when they were most vulnerable. We are sorry that instead of caring for them, this country turned its back. And we are sorry that the voices of these children were not always heard, their cries for help not always heeded. And we are sorry that it has taken so long for this important day to come and for the full and unconditional apology that is justly deserved.

We thought that the apology to child migrants had been Rudd's idea and that Brown was now catching up. However, in his statement to the House of Commons Brown made it clear that it had been his initiative and hinted that Rudd had jumped the gun by apologising first:

When I was first made aware of this wholly unacceptable practice, I wrote to the Prime Minister of Australia to urge that together we do more to acknowledge the experiences of former child migrants and see what we could achieve. It is right that today we recognise the human cost associated with this shameful episode of history and this failure in the first duty of a nation, which is to protect its children.[2]

In 2011, after our court case had been running for more than two years, I approached the relevant Commonwealth government minister, the minister for immigration, Chris Bowen, and the New South Wales state government minister for child welfare, Pru Goward, asking them to consider introducing an appropriate redress scheme as an alternative to the protracted and costly civil litigation. At least Bowen agreed to see us and I went to meet him in his Sydney office with the Old Fairbridgians Association president Derek Moriarty and vice president Jan Barby. While Bowen gave us a fair hearing we later received a letter saying the federal government proposed to continue with the civil litigation.

Pru Goward did not even reply to my letter, let alone agree to meet us. I subsequently received a letter on her behalf from Bruce Cantrill of the state Crown Solicitor's Office that Sir Humphrey Appleby would have been proud of. Cantrill said the minister would not see us, that the government intended continuing with civil litigation, that future communication should be with the Crown Solicitor and not the minister, and that the Crown Solicitor would not discuss the matter with me anyway:

> I am instructed to advise that whilst the above claims remain unresolved, the Minister will be unable to meet with you to discuss matters that might impinge on or otherwise relate to the litigation. It will be appreciated if future correspondence in connection with the claims (including these proceedings) should be addressed to my office, and not the Minister's office, so that I can obtain instructions and respond. Please note that I cannot agree to any meeting with yourself or others concerning these proceedings, and any issues relating to these proceedings.

Awareness of the abuse of children in institutions was given another boost with the establishment of the Royal Commission into Institutional Responses to Child Sexual Abuse in Australia announced by Prime Minister Julia Gillard in November 2012. This followed growing calls for a national inquiry into explosive allegations of the widespread abuse of children in an increasing number of institutions, including, most prominently, claims that the Catholic Church had over a period of decades covered up evidence of abuse involving paedophile priests.

When the Royal Commission started in May 2013, I wrote an article for the *Sydney Morning Herald* and the Melbourne *Age* saying how I warmly welcomed it. However, I pointed out, while the prime minister said it was now 'time to stare some very uncomfortable truths in the face', the federal government was itself a defendant in a major sex abuse case that had for years been bogged down in the courts:

The [Fairbridge] case has returned to the NSW Supreme Court 11 times in the past three years, and lawyers for the Federal and NSW governments have been arguing on a raft of procedural issues, which has resulted in the substance of the claims not even being heard yet. It is anybody's guess how many millions of dollars this has already cost the taxpayer or how many more years it will run.[3]

Nevertheless, the Royal Commission went on to do a very good job of dragging a huge amount of ugly evidence out of the darkness and into the public spotlight. In the four and a half years it ran, it received over 40,000 phone calls, more than 25,000 letters and emails, and held more than 8000 private counselling sessions, which included some with former Fairbridge children. It referred 2575 matters to police or other authorities, held 57 public hearings and heard from more than 1200 witnesses in over four hundred days of hearings.

I made two written submissions to the commission about the failure of civil litigation to satisfactorily deal with our claims of abuse, and argued that a redress scheme would be a much more sensible way of dealing with the issue. In my first submission in April 2014, I pointed out that our case had already been in the Supreme Court for five years, during which time only procedural matters had been dealt with, 'including arguments relating to further and better particulars, strike out applications, discovery, limitations, whether the matter can proceed as a class action, applications for the determination of separate questions, and the scheduling of all these matters . . . I am advised that the matter could take another five years, or even longer, depending on whether issues are appealed during the process. It is unlikely we will get a trial date until mid-2015 at the earliest, if the court proceedings go as planned and without further procedural disputes.'[4]

I explained that a number of the original claimants had died and that many others were getting very old with declining health. I said that ten years to resolve such matters was unacceptable, and that the process was extremely costly for both the plaintiffs and the defence.

My second submission was in January 2015. In it I repeated my assertion that civil litigation was not working, that more of the original claimants had died, and we needed to establish an alternative settlement scheme process. I argued again that Australia should, as an alternative, establish a national redress scheme.

My representations appeared to have little impact on the tortuously protracted process in the court, where there was no sign the Fairbridge case was progressing. The whole affair was becoming more and more frustrating, with all of us involved wondering if we would ever get a result. But what I did not know was that at the same time I was making my submissions, the Royal Commission was conducting a case study into a parallel and similar case to Fairbridge involving the inmates of another children's institution – the Bethcar Children's Home: 'Case Study Number 19' of the Royal Commission – which would ultimately provide the breakthrough in the Fairbridge case.

*

Bethcar was a small children's home in western New South Wales in the town of Brewarrina, which is more than 450 kilometres north-west of Fairbridge. It began operating as the Bethcar Aboriginal Children's Home in 1969 when Burt and Edith Gordon took a five-year lease on the old Brewarrina mission homestead and, with support from the Department of Aboriginal Affairs, took a number of children into their care. Over the next fifteen years, and with state and federal government funding, the Gordons operated the home, which was licensed to accommodate up to twenty children. Around 1984 they moved Bethcar to new premises in Orange, from where it operated until it was closed down in 1989.

The case study of Bethcar was given to one of the Royal Commission's six commissioners, Robert Fitzgerald, who had decades of experience working in the disadvantaged and disability sectors. Fitzgerald's study started with an account of the abuse of the children at Bethcar. The inquiry found that the state's management of Bethcar had many similarities to the way the Fairbridge case had been handled. The inquiry heard that police and the Child Welfare Department were aware of allegations of abuse at Bethcar around 1980, when some of the girls complained about Burt Gordon and his son-in-law, Colin Gibson, sexually abusing them. There are surviving police and Child Welfare Department records of the allegations of abuse occurring between 1980 and 1984, but no action was taken.

Fitzgerald heard that the abuse was inflicted regularly and over many years on the children, from the age of five years old, and included digital penetration, fondling, molestation, oral sex and vaginal intercourse, some causing vaginal bleeding.[5] He also heard of the devastating long-term effect the sexual abuse had on the lives of the children, including alcohol and drug abuse, mental health problems, problems with intimacy, violent domestic relationships, and difficulty caring for children.[6]

Fitzgerald found that, from the outset, the inquiries were not conducted properly. After the first complaints of abuse at the Bethcar home were recorded by police, Burt Gordon was allowed to sit in on the interview with the girls and afterwards take them back to the home. Subsequently, no further action was taken.

Twelve years later, in 1999, one of the former residents lodged a formal complaint of sexual abuse while she was at Bethcar. In the investigation that followed, police also examined earlier complaints. Colin Gibson was finally convicted on multiple child sex charges in 2006 and was sentenced to a minimum of twelve and a maximum of eighteen years in prison. At the same time, a decision was taken by the police not to charge Gordon, based on a lack of corroboration and the fact that he was elderly and in poor health, and was unlikely to live to see the matters progress to trial. (He died in 2006.)

In noticing how long the process had taken, Fitzgerald found that both the police and the Child Welfare Department had repeatedly failed to follow proper procedures going back more than a quarter of a century to 1980.

In May 2008 – twenty-eight years after the first complaints of sexual abuse – two former residents of Bethcar commenced proceedings against the New South Wales government in the state District Court, making allegations that they were abused while at Bethcar and that the department was liable for their abuse.[7] The Royal Commission was highly critical of the way in which the New South Wales Crown Solicitor had run the case. It found that the Crown Solicitor had spent time in court 'seeking information from the plaintiffs that the state already knew or had available to it'.[8] It also found the Crown Solicitor sought from the plaintiffs 'information known to the Department, in circumstances where it was likely that the plaintiffs would not have that information'.[9] And Fitzgerald found it 'inappropriate for the Department to ask the plaintiffs for information the Department could have found out for itself', which caused 'delay in the conduct of the proceedings' and that the state misled the court by not admitting it was aware of available witnesses.[10]

At one point in the inquiry, senior Crown Solicitor Helen Allison admitted her office had still been seeking proof of sexual abuse from the abuse victims after the perpetrator had pleaded guilty, been tried and convicted and was at the time serving a twelve-year jail sentence:

> Can I ask this question, Ms Allison? If it were the position that it was known within the Crown Solicitor's Office at the time the defences were filed that there had been convictions of Mr Gibson in respect of the sexual abuse that was the subject of the allegations in the litigation . . . there is, it might appear, a rank hypocrisy where the State has indicted and convicted a person in respect of allegations of sexual abuse for the State to later, in civil proceedings, put the plaintiffs to proof in respect of those same matters; would you comment on that?
>
> HA: I agree that if that was known, it should have been admitted.[11]

The Bethcar court case began the year before ours. Coincidentally, also in 2008 the New South Wales government announced a new policy aimed to make these sorts of cases easier, quicker and less costly. The New South Wales Department of Justice announced that the Model Litigant Policy 'is designed to provide guidelines for best practice for government agencies in civil litigation matters' and would be 'founded upon the concepts of behaving ethically, fairly and honestly to model best practice in litigation'. Specifically it stipulated that government agencies were required 'to deal with claims promptly', 'not take advantage of a claimant who lacks the resources to litigate a legitimate claim', 'not require the other party to prove a matter which the State or an agency knows to be true', 'pay legitimate claims', 'avoid litigation', not cause 'unnecessary delay', and, most importantly for 'disempowered, disadvantaged people' who had few resources – like the Bethcar kids and the Fairbridge kids – 'keep costs to a minimum'.[12]

In addition to finding that the police and the Child Welfare Department had failed for nearly thirty years to properly deal with the claims of sexual abuse at Bethcar, Fitzgerald's study found the New South Wales government and Crown Solicitor's Office were also in serious breach of its own Model Litigant Policy.

Ian Knight was head of the Crown Solicitor's Office for twenty years and he confessed to all these breaches when called to give evidence to Fitzgerald's inquiry. Knight had spent his entire forty-five-year legal career working in government, having started as an articled clerk in the early 1970s. After a stint as ombudsman in the Northern Territory he returned to the New South Wales Crown Solicitor's Office, where he was eventually appointed Crown Solicitor.

In the witness box Knight acknowledged that under his management the Crown Solicitor's Office had breached its own policies in a number of key respects. He admitted that the office needed to have better trained people managing sensitive child sex abuse cases. He accepted that the office had challenged victims' claims even after the perpetrator had been jailed. And he agreed 'absolutely' that the culture of the office needed to change, and that the government should have agreed much earlier to mediation rather than engage in protracted litigation. Towards the end of his evidence, Knight was forced to apologise: 'I think that was a breach of the Model Litigant Policy and I apologise to the plaintiffs that the Crown Solicitor's Office – to the extent the Crown Solicitor's Office contributed to that breach, I apologise.'[13]

Some months later he retired.

After the controversy of the Bethcar case, the New South Wales government would have been well aware of the potential embarrassment the much bigger Fairbridge case could cause, having now dragged on for years largely due to the stalling in court by the defendants.

Our case was scheduled for trial in August 2015. However, following the Royal Commission's hearings into Bethcar (and even before it published its damning report) the state government finally agreed to mediate the Fairbridge matter, which meant the other defendants in the case, the Fairbridge Foundation and the federal government, had little choice but to go along with the decision.

Within the New South Wales government, it was the Department of Family and Children's Services that drove the decision to mediate our case in order to try to reach a settlement, rather than continue the civil litigation. Michael Coutts-Trotter, the head of the department at the time, also gave evidence to the Royal Commission and made no secret of the fact that he thought the policies pursued in the Bethcar case were wrong:

I have reflected significantly, both personally and with those that assist me, on the conduct of the Bethcar proceedings and how the conduct of the proceedings might affect victims of abuse . . . I acknowledge that some of the processes of civil litigation ultimately, in this case, added to the time taken for the proceedings to reach their conclusion. While I understand that civil litigation processes are complicated and that those processes and procedures are designed to place parties in the best position possible to understand the case they have to answer at a trial, I regret that the Bethcar proceedings took 5 years to reach a resolution.[14]

Coutts-Trotter was asked if the government would deal with such cases in a different way in future and he replied:

If circumstances similar to those in the Bethcar proceedings arose today, my expectation would be that the Department would take what steps it could to ensure the matter progressed as quickly as it could. Applying hindsight and our present policies, my expectation would be that my Department would do all they could to arrange for a mediation to be held earlier in the proceedings. In this regard, we are currently examining our current Department policies and procedures in relation to where we can do things better or in a different way.[15]

Coutts-Trotter was true to his word. The Royal Commission took evidence about Bethcar in October and November 2014. By the end of October, and before the hearings were completed, the government announced that it had agreed to mediation in the Bethcar proceedings and had agreed to pay the victims substantial compensation.

The mediation of the Fairbridge class action was accepted only a few months later, in February 2015, and took place about ten weeks later on 23 and 24 May. It took only two days. I was angry. Six years, we had been bogged down with legal manoeuvrings in the court and still no trial, and after only two days at mediation the defendants had agreed to pay compensation to the complainants of $24 million – a record payout – and to apologise to each of the victims.

The mediation was run by Ian Callinan, a Queensland QC and former justice of the High Court of Australia. It took place in the Slater & Gordon offices in Sydney's CBD, where the lawyers for the three defendants were each provided a room, the major discussions taking place in the main conference room.

I still remember the shock when our lawyers and the defendants' barrister, Peter Semmler QC, told us of the $24 million settlement proposal. I cast my mind back to 2007 when Slater & Gordon had proposed to our complainants a settlement package of $6.5 million dollars. And now this was a record-breaking settlement. By the time it was offered, there were more than 200 claimants and even allowing for Slater & Gordon's fees, the average payout – of above $90,000 for each of the Fairbridge claimants – was still substantially more than most experts had expected, and far beyond our expectations.

The result was widely reported. The *Sydney Morning Herald* summed up the outcome. 'Adults who were physically and sexually assaulted as children at the notorious Fairbridge Farm School in central-western NSW have been awarded $24 million in the largest compensation payment for survivors of institutional child abuse in Australian legal history.'[16]

Most of the Fairbridge kids were elated. Not just because of the compensation but because at last their suffering had been acknowledged and at last they were believed. After decades of denial and cover-up and claims to a Senate inquiry that nothing 'illegal or improper' had happened to them, the victims of abuse were pleased to receive a written apology from the Fairbridge Foundation as part of the settlement:

> This apology is offered on behalf of the Fairbridge Foundation in relation to the Fairbridge Farm School operated at Molong from 1938 to 1974. Fairbridge accepts that you suffered physical abuse or sexual abuse or both during your childhood which was perpetrated by staff at the Farm School and other persons. Fairbridge recognises that this abuse has caused you distress, hurt and grief, and understands that it has had, and will continue to have, a serious effect on the rest of your life. Fairbridge acknowledges that what you experienced at the Farm School should not have happened and that stronger measures should have been in place to protect you from being abused. Fairbridge unreservedly apologises to you for the abuse that you suffered at the Farm School and sincerely regrets its ongoing effects on your life.

As reporters acknowledged, I thought it was a good result, but I was critical that it had taken so long. It still sticks in my craw that both governments' lawyers could run up millions of dollars of costs that were both unnecessary and in breach of their own policies, and paid by taxpayers, and hardly anyone was called to account. The *Central Western Daily* wrote in June of that year:

> Former Fairbridge Farm resident David Hill expressed relief that the settlement would save abuse survivors the trauma of a trial but criticised the defendants for dragging out legal action at an

estimated cost of $10 million to the taxpayer. 'This is a terrific acknowledgement after decades of denial and resistance from the Fairbridge Foundation, from the State Government and from the Federal Government, of the great wrongs which were done to so many of these kids,' he said. 'It's outrageous that it has been bogged down by the defendants in the Supreme Court for years. [Many] of our friends have died in the process, waiting for justice.'

After the settlement was announced, the New South Wales state government invited me to bring in some of the Fairbridge kids who had been victims of abuse to hear the government's apology, which would be read by the deputy secretary of the Department of Family and Community Services, Deidre Mulkerin. I duly arranged for about half a dozen of the Fairbridgians who'd been involved in the case to join me and we met in a large boardroom in the Crown Solicitor's Office. Mulkerin's apology was heartfelt and genuine. She began to cry. We were all deeply affected and moved to tears. I don't think any of us expected to be moved in that way, but looking back it wasn't really surprising that we were. It was the pinnacle of not just the long legal battle, but a struggle to expose the truth of what happened, which had started many years before.

At the end of the little ceremony I took a deep breath and said that while the apology was very much appreciated, I wanted each and every one of the men and women who'd suffered so much as children at the farm school to receive the apology from the premier himself. I meant a letter containing an apology and signed by Premier Mike Baird. To my surprise, however, a couple of weeks later his office asked me to bring a party of Fairbridgians to Parliament House to meet him so he could talk to them and apologise in person.

I organised for about twenty-five former Fairbridge kids to come to the state Parliament, in Sydney's Macquarie Street. On 29 October 2015 we were ushered into the grand Jubilee Room, which is located between the Parliament's Lower House chamber (Legislative Assembly) and Upper House chamber (Legislative Council). It was the first time I'd met Baird, and in truth I expected a rather guarded, well-orchestrated event. Yet to my surprise he arrived with only one staff member and shook hands with everyone before we sat down. I opened proceedings and asked each of my party to introduce themselves and tell the premier at what age they'd arrived at Fairbridge and how many years they were there.

Ron Simpson, who was sodomised at Fairbridge and had his back broken when beaten by Woods, later said how impressed he was by Baird:

> He listened to [a number of] us who were ill-treated. I was the first one to say my bad experiences at Fairbridge Farm . . . He was showing signs of sadness as I spoke . . . and as the others told their story . . . his reply was: 'How did this go on for so long?' He again showed signs of sadness, choking up two or three times. After . . . we had a group photograph taken . . . he touched me on the shoulder and said, 'Have a photo with me.'

Baird then stayed with us in the Jubilee Room, where we were given a fine buffet lunch before being invited into the public gallery. At 2 p.m. Premier Baird read out the government's apology:

Today I want to place on record the apology I have made to each and every one of the former residents of Fairbridge Farm on behalf of the people of New South Wales. It is something we cannot really put into words. It is something which tears our hearts apart. We want to tell those former residents of Fairbridge Farm just how sorry we are . . . I thank each and every one of the former residents of Fairbridge Farm who have come to Parliament House today. I know that they have endured suffering we cannot imagine and I know that coming here today would have taken a special kind of strength. I want to thank them for their courage and for sharing their stories.

On behalf of the State of New South Wales, I want to recognise all former child migrants who attended Fairbridge Farm in Molong, New South Wales. They arrived here as vulnerable and trusting children whose parents wanted nothing more than a better life than the one they could offer. They were not given the future they were promised or the childhood they deserved. They were betrayed by the people whose job it was to protect them; and they were betrayed by this State, which did not ensure their safety. I recognise these wrongs knowing that it will not bring back the childhood they were robbed of.

I acknowledge the harm and the lifelong effects Fairbridge Farm has had on former residents and their families. I acknowledge the burden many of them carry each and every day as a result of their experiences. I am, and we all are, deeply, deeply sorry . . . I want to pay particular tribute to the immense strength and courage Ms [Geraldine] Giles and Ms [Vivian] Drady showed in bringing this claim on behalf of others. It has taken too long and the State should have managed the civil litigation process so much better. Thank you for having the courage to share your stories; they have touched me, and they have touched all of us, very deeply. I can promise that we will not forget any of you. Again, we are deeply, deeply sorry; and I want to assure you that institutions like Fairbridge Farm will never happen again.

At the end of the Fairbridge case I wrote to Senior Counsel Campbell Bridge, who had for years been the barrister representing the New South Wales government in the Supreme Court hearings, to ask for an interview about the lengthy court case. I said I was particularly interested in why we had been bogged down on procedural matters for more than seven years before the matter was finally, and quickly, resolved by mediation in 2015. I pointed out that Ian Knight had told the Royal Commission that often in the relationship dynamic involving a client such as a government department, the views of senior counsel prevailed when deciding on legal tactics. I asked him if that is what had happened in the Fairbridge case. Bridge declined to answer and responded by saying that it would 'be entirely inappropriate to comment about any aspect of the Fairbridge litigation which is not on the public record'.

12

THE BRITISH INQUIRY

Child migration was a bad and, in human terms, costly mistake.
Mr David Hill . . . remarked to us during our visit to Australia that
irreversible, irrevocable damage had been done by the schemes.

For many years the British government and the UK Fairbridge Society successfully defended child migration and denied there were any serious problems with their schemes.

The first British parliamentary inquiry into child migration – the Inquiry into the Welfare of Former British Child Migrants – was opened in 1997 by the House of Commons Health Committee. It came about after the election of Tony Blair's Labour government that same year, and was driven by Labour MP David Hinchliffe, who for many years had agitated for an investigation into British child migration.

At the start of the inquiry the British government's Department of Health provided the committee with a background paper, which it described as 'the government's current position'.

The paper made no criticisms of child migration and emphasised its positive achievements, observing that:

> Child migration as a policy was, in a social climate very different from that of today, a well-intended response to the needs of deprived children. At the time this was seen to be in the best interests of the children concerned, providing them with a fresh start in countries which potentially offered them greater opportunities. There were many success stories. The migration schemes were run by respected national voluntary bodies. The schemes were sanctioned by laws passed in both the UK Parliament, and in the colonies, dominions and countries receiving children. There was much public debate, including discussion between the governments concerned, official reports and visits.[1]

The government went on to praise the organisations that had operated the migrant schemes – for saving children from a raft of social ills, including disease, prostitution and death:

> A strong driving factor in child migration was the British philan-thropic, religious and benevolent organisations, who were rescuing children from poverty, destitution, vagrancy, criminality or neglect and saw better opportunities for such children in the expanding colonies and Empire. At the time the choice was seen to be between begging, thieving, disease, prostitution and early death in the British Isles; or learning farming or domestic skills.[2]

In preparing its background paper for the committee, the government referred to the Ross Report of 1956 and other documents in the Public Records Office at Kew. It did not acknowledge the

Home Office's blacklisting of Fairbridge and other child migrant schemes to Australia, which were also in those files.

Nigel Haynes, the director of Fairbridge in the UK at the time, gave evidence to the inquiry. He insisted that after 1938 when Richard Beauchamp was dismissed as principal at Fairbridge in Molong,[3] there were no other records of physical or sexual abuse:

> Turning to sexual and physical abuse, we have got cases in the records of a case of neglect, it was called, and physical abuse in 1938 in a farm school called Molong. These complaints were received in London, investigated and the staff were dismissed immediately. Molong then became semi-autonomous from 1948, although accepted funds from London. Apart from that, we have no cases of complaint or abuse on record as far as Fairbridge is concerned, other than – and I hate to go back to it – the context of disciplines relevant at that time against what was happening in this country as well.[4]

Fortunately, the House of Commons committee was not persuaded by the misinformation provided by the government and the UK Fairbridge Society – and made it clear that it was never okay to abuse children. In its final report it said its inquiry participants 'had met many former child migrants' in Australia, 'who continue to suffer from emotional and psychological problems arising directly from this misguided social policy'.

The report included comments I made when I met the committee at the British High Commission in Canberra during their visit to Australia:

> Child migration was a bad and, in human terms, costly mistake. Mr David Hill, a successful ex-Fairbridge Resident . . . remarked to

us during our visit to Australia that irreversible, irrevocable damage had been done by the schemes.[5]

The committee also heard some terrible stories of sexual abuse in child migrant boys' homes in Western Australia:

> The worst cases of criminal abuse in Australia appear to have occurred in institutions run by agencies of the Catholic Church, in particular the Christian Brothers (especially the 'Boys' Town' at Bindoon, north of Perth, although we heard grim stories about Clontarf, Tardun and Castledare as well) and the Sisters of Mercy (especially the orphanage at Neerkol in Queensland, and also Goodwood Orphanage in South Australia). The Sisters of Mercy were frequently described to us as the 'Sisters without mercy', just as the Christian Brothers were often described as the 'Christian buggers'.[6]

The committee recommended the British government establish a database so that child migrants could access all the available information and histories of their families, which many had lost; that the government establish and pay for a travel fund so that child migrants could return to Britain to restore lost contact with their families; and that migrants be offered therapy and counselling, and legal aid to allow the pursuit of 'redress for past criminal abuse'. Finally, it recommended that, when all this had been done, the government apologise to the child migrants.

In December 1998 Blair's government accepted the committee's findings that child migration had been 'misguided' and agreed with its report's main recommendations, including the call for the government to apologise. This recommendation was not taken up by Prime Minister Blair, but was by Gordon Brown more than a decade later in 2011, some four years after the publication of *The Forgotten Children*.

The House of Commons inquiry in 1997 was followed by an Australian Senate inquiry in 2001. Led by the Labor Party and supported by the Australian Democrats, a Senate committee investigated 'whether any unsafe, improper, or unlawful care or treatment' occurred in child migrant institutions.

The committee received ninety-nine confidential submissions and 153 public submissions, 'with most coming from former child migrants who wished to have their stories placed in an official record'.[7] It also heard evidence from more than eighty witnesses. Among them was William Hoyles, director of youth services and aftercare at Barnardos, which had operated a child migrant centre in Australia from 1921 till 1965. Hoyles was unequivocal in his condemnation of the scheme: 'We have no hesitation in saying it was a shameful practice and it was completely against any practice that we currently uphold.'[8]

When giving evidence before the inquiry, long-standing chairman of the Fairbridge Foundation John Kennedy was asked if he agreed with Hoyles. Kennedy replied: 'I believe our view would not agree with Barnardos.'[9] In its written submission to the inquiry and in contradiction of information contained in Fairbridge's own files, Fairbridge maintained that nothing seriously wrong happened at the farm school in Molong:

> The Fairbridge Foundation is unaware of any unsafe, improper or unlawful treatment occurring at the Fairbridge Farm School in Molong. It is also unaware of any serious breach of any statutory obligations occurring there.[10]

The Australian Senate was more generous to the child migrant operators than the UK House of Commons inquiry had been, but acknowledged there was no avoiding the failures of the policies in practice:

> The Committee believes that the Commonwealth Government's policy of child migration in the post-war period reflected the values of the time and was well-intentioned. However, this policy is now regarded to have been seriously flawed. The policy had obvious serious and long-lasting deleterious impacts on the lives of many former child migrants.[11]

It recognised the appalling extent of the abuse:

> Evidence to the Committee indicated the disturbing extent of physical, sexual and psychological abuse that was inflicted upon child migrants over a number of years . . . Many of the stories of abuse recounted to the Committee were graphic and horrendous in detail. Abuse took many forms including excessive beatings as punishment and other indiscriminate physical assaults using specially made weapons, sexual abuse including sodomy and rape, psychological and other forms of emotional abuse including depersonalisation, arduous and exploitative work regimes, limited educational opportunity, inadequate food and clothing, and poor after care.[12]

And it registered the long-term harm caused by such abuse of children:

> The lack of identity, and lack of confidence and self-esteem resulting from years of physical and mental abuse, have led to a diversity of

problems including an inability to establish and maintain personal relationships, marital difficulties, depression and anxiety, and alcohol and other drug abuse. The Committee believes that, based on the anecdotal evidence it received, an especially tragic outcome of these problems has been a suicide rate of child migrants well above the Australian average.[13]

The Liberal government gave the Labor/Democrat-dominated Senate committee report little more than token support. It said it welcomed the report as a 'sensitive, comprehensive and insightful appraisal of the child migration schemes and child migrants' experiences in Australia' and that it gave former child migrants an opportunity to 'tell their story'. It added that it concurred 'with the committee in its hope that this will contribute to the healing process for those who have conflicting or painful memories of the schemes'.[14] But it avoided engaging with much of what was recommended by stating that what the committee wanted was 'clearly directed to state governments or sending and receiving agencies', which together should 'respond in spirit and in practice to the Committee's recommendations'.[15] Apart from making available a relatively small amount of money to allow some child migrants to travel to the UK to restore contact with their families, the Australian government did not take any further tangible steps.

Apologies and inquiries notwithstanding, until 2017 the British government and the UK Fairbridge Society had – incredibly – managed to avoid serious scrutiny for its betrayal and abuse of British child migrants. But all that changed following the exposure of paedophile entertainer Jimmy Savile.

Jimmy Savile was a highly successful and popular TV entertainer in Britain for almost half a century. For twenty years from 1964 he was the top-rating presenter of BBC TV's *Top of the Pops*. From 1974 till 1994 he hosted another hugely popular BBC show, *Jim'll Fix It*, in which he would realise the wishes of children who wrote into the program, some of whom were very unwell. Savile was a huge star, and a significant part of his career involved him visiting schools and hospital wards, where he came into regular contact with young children. He was given a papal knighthood in 1990, as well as numerous other honours, before his death in October 2011 at the age of eighty-four.

Around a year after his death, reports of his sexual abuse of children in Britain began to come to light. By late 2012 British police were investigating what had become a flood of claims that Savile had abused hundreds of children, from prepubescent boys and girls to older children, stretching over a period of more than forty years. In October 2012 London's Metropolitan Police described the alleged abuse as being on an unprecedented scale, and said it was pursuing over 400 lines of inquiry, based on the claims of 200 witnesses, via fourteen police forces across the UK.

Following a tidal wave of further claims against Savile, and other prominent British figures, the home secretary Theresa May established the Independent Inquiry into Child Sexual Abuse (IICSA) to examine the failure of British institutions to adequately protect children.

The IICSA got off to a tumultuous start when its first appointed chair, High Court judge Baroness Butler-Sloss, was forced to resign after only six days, admitting to a family conflict of interest. Her late brother, Baron Havers, had been attorney-general in the 1980s and was being accused by some victims' groups and opposition

MPs of having prevented the airing of claims in the House of Commons that members of the British establishment had been involved in child sexual abuse. Havers had also been criticised for not prosecuting diplomat Sir Peter Hayman for being involved in the distribution of child pornographic material. Opposition MP Simon Danczuk, among others, claimed the family connection made the baroness ill-suited to investigate allegations about how the government and institutions handled alleged paedophiles:

> She is a very intelligent woman with some knowledge of the subject, but she is far too much an establishment figure. It's astonishing the government didn't realise that they were appointing the sister of someone who had tried to deter the prosecution of a significant paedophile in the 1980s.

The replacement chair was Dame Fiona Woolf, a prominent lawyer and a former president of the UK Law Society and lord mayor of London. She was appointed in September 2014 but was also forced to resign only a month later – again for appearing compromised by connections with disfavoured members of the British establishment. Woolf lost the support of victims' groups and the parliamentary opposition when it was revealed she was a neighbour and friend of former Conservative home secretary Leon Brittan. Lord Brittan had dealt with allegations of child abuse in the 1980s, as a result of which he was now facing claims of wrong-doing, including that a dossier he had been given, containing accusations about paedophiles in Westminster, had gone missing from his department when it should have been handed to police.

Four months after the departure of Woolf, Home Secretary Theresa May announced the appointment of the IICSA's third chair. This time it was to be someone as far away from the British establishment as possible – a New Zealand High Court judge, Dame Lowell Goddard. Announcing Goddard's appointment, Theresa May described her as an outstanding candidate who had experience in challenging authority, having led an inquiry in New Zealand into child abuse cases.

Goddard was the first woman of Maori heritage to sit as a judge on the New Zealand High Court. Her salary as chair of the UK inquiry of more than £350,000, plus generous entitlements and benefits, took the package above £500,000, which was believed to be the highest of any British civil servant and twice as much paid to the British prime minister.

In the eighteen controversial months Goddard was at the helm, the IICSA showed little progress. But on 27 November 2015 she announced the IICSA would conduct twelve separate inquiries. They would include investigations of the Anglican and Catholic churches, online child sexual abuse, child abuse in residential schools and a number of specific investigations into abuse in various county councils. Also on the list, a surprise to many, was an investigation into 'the protection of children outside the United Kingdom'. I recall thinking to myself at the time that such an inquiry couldn't do any harm, but I had no inkling that it would become such an important part of the Fairbridge story, or that I would be such a big part of it.

It was not immediately clear how an investigation of British children 'outside the UK' had crept on to the list – it was perhaps a personal pick of Goddard; certainly it was not prompted by anything done by Jimmy Savile, who had no known connections with children overseas. It also appeared, from the detailed statement issued by Goddard, to apply to British children currently, or more recently, overseas, rather than British child migrations schemes, the last of which had ceased to operate almost forty years earlier in 1980. Goddard said:

> We will investigate the extent to which organisations in England and Wales have satisfied their duty to protect children abroad. In recent years, grave allegations have emerged regarding child sexual abuse by individuals working for British institutions and organisations abroad. Our investigation will look at institutions based in England and Wales which recruit people to work abroad, including the Armed Forces, the Foreign and Commonwealth Office, the British Council and private companies and voluntary organisations. It will examine the extent to which such institutions have failed adequately to protect children abroad by, for example, employing individuals who should not work with children. We will investigate how effectively the United Kingdom justice system is equipped to address the potential for abuse abroad by those known to authorities in England and Wales as posing a risk to children. And we will consider the adequacy of Whitehall responses to reports of institutional failures to protect children from sexual abuse in overseas territories.[16]

Intended or not, this was the basis on which the IICSA launched an inquiry into historic British child migrant schemes the following year. On 26 July 2016 it announced the details of the public hearings to be held on British child migration. It said it wanted to investigate the extent of sexual abuse of child migrants; the extent to which institutions took sufficient care to protect these children; and the extent to which they knew, or should have known, of the abuse that took place.

When Goddard resigned, having chaired the IICSA for only eighteen months, the inquiry was once again left in disarray. It seemed that much of the pressure for Goddard to go had come from within the organisation and included opposition from some of her panel colleagues. Allegations against her included claims that she had made derogatory racist remarks about Britain's ethnic mix, which she strongly denied. In her resignation statement Goddard said the job of chair of the IICSA had been 'an incredibly difficult step to take' as it meant relinquishing her career in New Zealand and leaving behind her family. She added that by now the inquiry was beset by a legacy of failure and problems with its sheer scale and size.

After her departure, one of the IICSA panellists, social worker and academic Professor Alexis Jay, became the organisation's fourth chair. Immediately there were calls for the struggling inquiry to scale back its enormous agenda, but Jay rejected these calls. She said that with a staff of more than 150 people, no public hearings would be cancelled and all the investigations would be retained, starting with the inquiry into British child migration, which would open early the following year.

By now there was widespread scepticism about the entire inquiry. It had made very little progress under three different chairs, and after operating for more than two years had embarked on no public investigations. It was somewhat a puzzle as to why British child migration – which was the least talked about issue of all – should be chosen for the first public hearings. The IICSA later said that a factor was that most of the surviving British child migrants were very elderly – even then only a minority were alive to give evidence to the inquiry.

However, when I arrived in London in February 2017 for the first hearings, British journalists privately advised me of another reason. They said that the IICSA, having begun its preliminary research into the history of child migration, was becoming aware of the amount of evidence of abuse, which was likely to attract widespread media interest, which in turn would bolster public support for the ongoing work of the inquiry. I hadn't been sure how much attention our evidence at the inquiry would attract, but I quickly realised that its impact would be far more explosive than I'd anticipated.

13

THE LONDON HEARINGS

This [is] . . . probably the biggest national sexual abuse scandal . . . bigger than what people have said about [Jimmy] Savile, bigger than what people have alleged about individual children's homes, bigger in scale, bigger in geographic spread, bigger in length of time it went undetected.

When the IICSA announced in mid-2016 it wanted to take evidence from former British child migrants, I wrote expressing my interest in making a submission. I was pleased when the inquiry's lawyers responded by saying they would like, in the first instance, to talk to me by phone. When they called me in Sydney they made it clear they knew who I was, telling me, for example, that they and other key members of the inquiry were familiar with my book *The Forgotten Children*.

At the inquiry's request, over the course of the next few months, I submitted a total of five written witness statements, mostly to address particular issues or questions asked of me. Much of what was in my witness statements was shaped by specific questions

I was emailed by the inquiry's lawyers. In addition to supplying personal details, I laid out the time I had spent in children's institutions in England before going to Molong, as well as evidence of sexual and other abuse I and others had suffered at Fairbridge. I was asked to explain the process of researching and writing *The Forgotten Children*; how I became aware of the sexual abuse of the other children at Fairbridge; and what I had learned from these children about the effects on them of the sexual abuse.

I identified the institutions that had been responsible for the abuse. I pointed out that in Australia three institutions (the federal government, the state government and the Fairbridge Foundation) had all been responsible for the failings at the farm school in Molong, had finally admitted these failings and by now had paid out the full $24 million in compensation. But, I said, the British government and the UK Fairbridge Society had also failed to protect the children.

After I'd submitted my initial statement, the inquiry invited me to give evidence in person at the public hearings that were scheduled to start in February 2017. I was also invited to apply to become what the inquiry called a Core Participant. The status of a Core Participant is granted to organisations or individuals who have a special interest in the inquiry and are therefore given special rights. This standing gave me some considerable advantages. I was given access to all the documents and evidence collected by the inquiry, the right to suggest lines of questioning to put to other witnesses, and was allowed to make opening and closing statements at the public hearings.

For the two hearings, the first in February 2017 and the second five months later in July, each of which lasted for a fortnight, I was flown with my wife, Stergitsa, to London, where we stayed in a little one-bedroom flat in Doughty Street, in the heart of London's legal district. Coincidentally, the flat was across the road from the Doughty Street law offices, where prominent Australian barrister Geoffrey Robertson is head of chambers. Robertson is an old friend of mine from Sydney University. He is very familiar with the Fairbridge story and launched *The Forgotten Children* when it was released in the UK. (Quite aside from the child migration issue, Geoffrey and I have for many years worked together on the campaign to persuade the British Museum to give back the classical sculptures of the Athenian Parthenon that were taken in the early nineteenth century by Lord Elgin.)

Most of the London IICSA hearings were held in the International Dispute Resolution Centre at 70 Fleet Street, a few hundred metres down the hill from the Old Bailey and Australia House. For a few days when the centre was not available the hearings were shifted to a similar facility at Hatton Garden in Holborn.

The inquiry was set up like a large court room. At the end of the chamber was an elevated bench where the panel of four members sat: the chair, Professor Jay, with her more than thirty years' experience in child welfare; Ivor Frank, a barrister with a background in child protection, human rights and family law; Professor Malcolm Evans, an expert on international law and human rights; and Drusilla Sharpling, a crown prosecutor. It was a very impressive panel, which produced a very good report, but during the hearings its members said little and asked very few questions. Most of the questioning and proceedings were left to the lawyers assisting the inquiry, led by Henrietta Hill, QC, who coincidentally hailed from Robertson's Doughty Street Chambers. Although small in stature, Hill had a commanding presence in the court room. She was very sharp, kept the proceedings relevant and was forthright without trying to dominate the witnesses. In the two long sessions I spent in the witness box giving evidence to the inquiry I found her questions insightful and easy to follow. I think she should take much of the credit for the inquiry being able to uncover so much evidence over a relatively short period of time.

There was a well-attended public galley and a witness box in which we each gave our testimony and were questioned.

In the centre of the hearing room there were about twelve tables for participating Core Participants and their legal representatives. All the Core Participants were institutions, except for me and Oliver Cosgrove and his legal representatives. Oliver Cosgrove was a child migrant who had suffered physical and sexual abuse at the Castledare Christian Brothers Boys' Home, outside Perth in Western Australia. I had a table to myself, at which I sat throughout the proceedings with my wife, because I was the only participant who had decided to appear without legal representation. It had been offered to me by the inquiry and I'd been advised to take up the offer, but I wanted to feel unrestrained, and not have a cautious lawyer telling me what I ought and ought not say. At the end of it all I felt it had been quite the right decision. In the inquiry's final report I was mentioned more times than any other witness, and I was pleased that the inquiry addressed every important issue I had raised.

Outside the hearing room there was another large room for the media and the overflow from the public gallery, who could watch proceedings on a video link that was delayed by thirty seconds. This was a device that allowed the inquiry to halt proceedings if sensitive material needed to be deleted (redacted) before being shown to the press and made public.

Despite the often unfavourable press coverage the inquiry had received, it was well run. It had conducted extensive inquiries that had yielded vast numbers of files, many of which I had been prevented from seeing during my research for *The Forgotten Children*, but which were now all made available to me as a Core Participant. The inquiry was advised on the history of British child migration by two eminent academics who specialised in British migration studies, professors Stephen Constantine and Gordon Lynch.

On the first day of the hearings I was invited to give an opening address, which proved to be highly emotional – much more so than I'd expected. I have many years' experience at making public speeches and presentations but was not prepared for how this turned out.

I started by telling the inquiry that I thought the perpetrators of the sexual abuse of the children should be named:

We will never be able to undo the wrongdoing to these children. But what is important to survivors of sexual abuse is, where the inquiry is satisfied with the evidence, to name the villains. Many of them are beyond the grave, but it would bring a great deal of comfort to the people who as children were their victims if they were named and shamed.[1]

I found myself becoming more emotional when I was outlining outlined my hopes that the inquiry would provide a better understanding of the suffering of many of the youngest child migrants:

The typical Fairbridge kid was only eight or nine, and some were as young as four, when they were to sail out to Fairbridge Farm

School at Molong, never to see their parents again, and to endure an entirely loveless childhood . . . These younger children were to be the most vulnerable, and the most abused.

As I was describing the long-term consequences of sexual abuse on young children, many of whom I'd interviewed and become close to, it was obvious to television audiences across the UK and Australia that I was feeling the emotional strain: 'Many never recover,' I said, 'and are permanently affected with guilt, shame, diminished self-confidence, low self-esteem, fear and trauma.'[2]

The BBC and other media reported that I broke down when I was at this stage of the statement. I was later amazed how many people had seen the segment on TV or heard it on radio, both in the UK and Australia, and while I realised that everyone understood, I nevertheless felt clumsy and awkward. But I think perhaps it was only then that I fully realised the impact this story had had, and continued to have, on me, it having been part of my life for more than a decade by that time. And it was a story that became more confronting, not less so, with the passage of years.

I'd thought the pressure of facing this inquiry and the exposure to the British and international media would be easy to manage. I had been the head of a number of large public organisations, and was familiar with being exposed to the regular glare of public and media scrutiny. I prided myself on handling heated situations well and never felt under any great pressure dealing with them. But this was very different. I found that day immensely confronting and there was no way of deflecting it. For once I felt every bit as emotionally vulnerable as the next person – and probably even more so.

*

It was a relief to have that first week behind me, and to have ridden the wave of emotion that had overtaken me. I now felt an even greater responsibility to the Fairbridge kids and was emboldened by the messages of support from my brothers and friends in Australia and the UK.

In the second week of the first session, on 8 March 2017, I was first taken through the evidence in my witness statemen by Henrietta Hill, who was primarily concerned with the extent and nature of the sexual abuse of the child migrants. She began by pointing out that I was not only appearing to talk about my own experience as a child migrant but also as someone who had 'undertaken a significant amount of research', as she put it, having written *The Forgotten Children* and been involved in the documentary *The Long Journey Home*.

Hill began her questioning by going through my family background – how I was illegitimate, from a very poor family and how my brothers and I had spent some time in children's homes in England before we came to hear about Fairbridge. I was asked to describe going to stay at the Fairbridge mansion in Kent and being outfitted in a wardrobe of new clothes before the luxury voyage out to Australia, and our reaching Molong.

I was then asked to outline the physical harshness of Fairbridge, including beatings, public thrashings and the terror of sadistic cottage mothers who whipped young children with ironing cords and riding crops.

Much of my testimony dealt with the sexual abuse of the Fairbridge children:

For a short time at Fairbridge I was subject to what might be described as 'sexual molestation'. I did not report the abuse at the time. Compared with what I have learned, it was nothing like what happened to many of the other children. I would place this at the lower end of the scale of seriousness and I would not have made a witness statement to the Inquiry on the basis of this experience alone . . . Ted Roach, the vegetable garden supervisor, would approach us boys (usually between the age of about 12 and 14), half turn his back and say 'look at the lump on my shoulder', before grabbing our genitals. We all saw it as a sick joke that made us feel dirty and uncomfortable.[3]

I was asked about what I had learned of the sexual abuse of the other Fairbridge children. I explained that when I was researching the book, while the majority had talked about being physically abused, only a few had mentioned being sexually abused:

HH: Can you tell us, please, about the way in which many of the former child migrants discussed their experiences with you? . . . Is this right, that when you first interviewed them, many, the majority, I think you have said, talked about being physically abused?
DH: Yes.
HH: But only a few described being sexually abused?
DH: I think when I did those original forty interviews, there were three or four that talked about sexual abuse. When we did the—
HH: Just pause there. Is this right, that in those original oral interviews you . . . you didn't ask people directly if they had been sexually abused? . . . What you said was, 'What are your best and worst memories of Fairbridge?', and in response to that question, three or four talked about being sexually abused?
DH: Yes.

. . .

HH: They all said, is this right, that was the first time they had told anybody about that?

DH: In every case.

HH: After completing those interviews, another four or five told you about being sexually abused at Fairbridge but did not want anything on the record; is that right?

DH: That's right.

. . .

HH: Is this right, that, as you say, some of them had never previously spoken about this and, when you asked them why they had spoken about it now, they said they had previously thought it had only happened to them but now understood it had happened to lots of the other children?

DH: Yes . . .

HH: You have also said then that further children from Fairbridge spoke to you about being sexually abused after the book was published in 2007 and after your documentary was broadcast in 2009. Is that right?

DH: Yes. And . . . it's since then that the largest number have told me . . . Most of it not formal interviews, just privately. Some have phoned me, some have seen me at reunions and said – just indicated or intimated, 'It happened to me too.'[4]

The inquiry was particularly interested in how I had concluded that as many as 60 per cent of the children had been sexually abused, a figure that most people – including the members of the inquiry – would have found shockingly high.

HH: Doing the best you can . . . what percentage of those do you believe have either told you or intimated to you that they were sexually abused while at Molong?

DH: Based on my own discussions with Fairbridge kids, and other data, I think about 60 per cent of the Fairbridge kids were abused at Fairbridge, and—

HH: Were sexually abused?

DH: I think well over 90 per cent will say that they were at some stage abused physically or emotionally or sexually, but the figure of, I would say, 60 per cent of the kids that went to Fairbridge Farm School, Molong, were sexually abused.

HH: Just helping the chair and panel understand how you reach that figure a little bit more, is this right that of the 100 or so that you spoke to, you would say around half reported sexual abuse, but you have also been provided with information arising from the Slater & Gordon class action that has helped you reach that figure?

DH: Yes.

HH: Is this right, that there were 239 surviving Fairbridge Farm School inmates, you have described them as, when you began? Of those, you understand 215 received compensation. And your understanding is that of those 215, Slater & Gordon have indicated to you that 129, or 60 per cent, suffered sexual abuse. So that is roughly how you get to your prediction of around 60 per cent; is that right?

DH: Yes.

HH: You have also referred to a report from I think it is the University of New South Wales, December 2016 report, about the long-term outcomes for children growing up in care in Australia . . .

DH: Yes, it is a study into the long-term consequences of institutionalisation of children. I was on the oversighting board, the Critical Reference Group, for the study . . . They did a survey of about 700 former institutionalised children, but they extrapolated these figures for me for child migrants. It is the same consistent figure, around 60 per cent. 50, 60, 70 per cent is turning up in all of the data.[5]

I told the inquiry that in a UNSW survey, the university noted that women were far less willing to talk about the sexual abuse than men, which led Henrietta Hill to ask if this meant the actual figure might be higher than 60 per cent:

> HH: You believe, do you, that this might be an under-figure, if you like, a lower figure than the real figure, because there are still some who did experience sexual abuse who don't want to talk about it?
> DH: Absolutely, absolutely.

Hill then took me through the nature of the sexual abuse of children. Unpleasant though that was, I felt it was important the inquiry had as clear as possible an understanding of what had taken place. I still feel upset and traumatised about giving this evidence.

> HH: Just turning, finally, to some of the details of the sorts of sexual abuse that you have described hearing about from other former child migrants, is this right, that although some former child migrants talked to you about being abused, they were more comfortable telling you where, geographically, the abuse took place, so in the gardener's shed or in the staff quarters, for example, rather than who the perpetrator was or the details of it? . . . You have, though, putting aside those difficulties, been able to elicit some details from people?
> DH: Yes.
> HH: Is this right that girls, female former child migrants, have told you that they have experienced abuse from as young as five years of age through to their teenage years?
> DH: Yes.

HH: And, as with the boys, they were often embarrassed about giving you details of the sexual abuse, but is this right, that a few have admitted that they were raped—

DH: Yes.

HH: involving penile penetration?

DH: Yes.

HH: Many have claimed that they were forced to strip, were fondled, rubbed, spanked and digitally penetrated?

DH: Yes.

HH: Some have said they were forced to kiss and masturbate the perpetrator. In a case involving one adult male member of staff, a number of girls said they were regularly forced to strip naked and perform exercises in front of the staff member?

DH: We can now name him. It was Phillips.

HH: I see. Thank you. That's Mr Phillips. I think the aftercare officer; is that right?

DH: Yes.

HH: Is this right, though, that your understanding is that because at the time the girls didn't understand very much about sex education and what sex was, that many were very confused by what they were being asked to do and didn't understand it?

DH: In the research, those that told me said they were confused about sex. Most of them didn't know what menstruation was. I remember a number of girls saying they thought they were going to bleed to death with the onset of menstruation because there was nobody there to guide them. Again, all of this stuff they thought was the norm. They had no other reference point.[6]

Hill asked me to confirm that a number of the girls who had described sexual abuse to me had named the same perpetrators. I responded that, yes, the same names would keep coming up:

DH: So many of the girls talked about [Jack] Newberry. Phillips. Of course, there were the allegations about [the principal] Woods, who was investigated and cleared, but there were a number of suggestions about Woods going over a very long period of time. But, yes – bear in mind, there were very few male staff at Fairbridge. There were . . . three farm supervisor staff, a gardening supervisor, a dairy manager, the principal, the aftercare officer and the bursar . . . and sometimes a maintenance man. Because all the work on the farm was done by the kids.

HH: Is this right, though, that as well as those adult male staff members, in some cases, female former child migrants have reported abuse by older boys?

DH: Yes.

HH: And in one case, by an older half-brother?

DH: Yes.

HH: The boys, the male former child migrants who have described sexual abuse to you have talked about most of the cases involving genital fondling or the victim being forced to strip and masturbate in front of the perpetrator or forced to masturbate the perpetrator or perform oral sex; is that right?

DH: Yes.

HH: In three or four cases, people have reported anal penetration to you?

DH: Yes.

HH: In most of the cases, the perpetrator was described as being an adult male member of staff or an adult male visiting the school?

DH: Correct.[7]

I was relieved when I finished giving my first evidence. By then I was becoming increasingly aware that I was in a fairly unique situation. The inquiry's witnesses included academics who specialised in the research of child migration, and separately it took evidence from some of the child migrants. But I was both, and much of the research I had provided had not been known beforehand, including material from internal Fairbridge archives in Australia and the UK, which verified many of the claims of abuse by the Fairbridge children.

Over several days, the inquiry took evidence from, or read the witness statements of, eleven other child migrants who were abused. They included not only Fairbridgians but also those from the other child migrant schemes, including those who had been sent to the notorious Catholic Christian Brothers homes in Western Australia, where the incidence of sexual abuse was probably higher than at the other schools. I met some wonderful, brave men and women, who often struggled when recounting stories of the abuse they had suffered as children. Encountering these people, often in tears as they gave their testimony, I appreciated why so many others still keep their own sexual abuse a secret— it is just so hard to talk about it, even decades later.

Michael O'Donaghue was born in Aldershot in Hampshire and was sent as an eleven year old to the Clontarf Christian Brothers home in Western Australia, where he said he was severely beaten and raped. Oliver Cosgrove told how he was sent to another Catholic home at Castledare, Western Australia, which one former inmate described as being run as a 'legal paedophile ring'.[8] Cosgrove said that he was regularly sexually abused, which included Brother Murphy coming 'to my bed and forced me to give him oral sex'.[9]

My next appearance in the witness box was at the second IICSA hearings five months after the first, in July 2017. Having examined the extent and scope of abuse of child migrants, the inquiry now wanted to focus on the institutions that were responsible.

Early on in these hearings I was asked if the institutional failure was in Britain or Australia.[10] I told the inquiry:

> In relation to the institutions in Australia, the Fairbridge Foundation of New South Wales, the New South Wales State Government . . . and the Australian Federal Government . . . all three were institutions that were responsible for the welfare of the children . . . I also think that the British Government and the UK Fairbridge Society . . . are both responsible for failing to take sufficient care to protect the children of Fairbridge.

I went through the details of how, in 'one of the really great betrayals', the British government did not protect child migrants, even when they had decided the institutions were 'unfit for children' and had drawn up the blacklist of institutions deemed unfit for children. Yet, in the end, the blacklist was of course quietly torn up and hundreds more children, including me, were sent over to organisations that had been condemned as unsuitable to care for them.

I was then taken through a number of files that confirmed the British government was aware Fairbridge operated 'below the modern standards'. The inquiry also questioned me about ongoing British government funding of Fairbridge, even after it was aware that the farm schools had not introduced reforms as agreed with the government. In fact, around 1960, the funding was increased to record levels.

One of the biggest reforms sought by the British government was for Fairbridge to foster out children in Australia. But I was able to tell the inquiry that, despite the opportunity to do so, and though this was absolutely central to the reforms the British wanted, not one Fairbridge child, to my knowledge, was fostered out in the entire history of the scheme, even though that was the single most prominent reform sought by the British government.

During the second hearings the inquiry called the former director of the UK Fairbridge Society, Nigel Haynes, to give evidence. The UK Fairbridge Society was the biggest British child migrant operator. It had been the first to open a child migrant centre in Western Australia, in 1912, and the last to close one, in 1980. During its operations it had attracted widespread support from the royal family and the upper echelons of British society. Edward, Prince of Wales (later King Edward VIII) and Queen Elizabeth II both made personal financial donations to the society. The Queen's uncle, the Duke of Gloucester, became the society's president. Both the Queen Mother and Prince Charles had paid visits to the Fairbridge Farm School at Pinjarra in Western Australia.

After ending child migration in 1980 the Fairbridge Society continued to operate as a charity in the UK, providing assistance to young people in Britain who were experiencing homelessness, unemployment exclusion, antisocial behaviour, substance abuse and mental health issues. Operating sixteen centres in most major cities, including London, Liverpool, Manchester, Newcastle, Birmingham, Edinburgh, Glasgow and Swansea, Fairbridge helped troubled youths back into education, training and employment.

However, the organisation's ability to raise public funding became more difficult after 2007 with the widespread press coverage of *The Forgotten Children*, and particularly after the allegation that British war hero Lord Slim had sexually molested Fairbridge children when he was the governor-general of Australia in the 1950s. It began struggling financially and in 2010 it merged with the larger Prince's Trust.

Nigel Haynes had been the director of the UK Fairbridge Society from 1993 to 2008. Throughout its long life as a child migrant operator and in the years that followed, including after it merged with the Prince's Trust, the Fairbridge Society continued to deny any wrongdoing or abuse of children.

Haynes had already provided two written witness statements in response to questions sent to him by the inquiry. He had been asked about the 'neglect/physical abuse' that occurred at Fairbridge and what knowledge the UK Fairbridge Society had of the abuse. In his first written response Haynes repeatedly said he had no knowledge of any incidents any allegations regarding sexual abuse at Fairbridge, had no detailed knowledge of the governance, protocols and procedures of Fairbridge, and as director had been too busy 'to become involved in the historic affairs of the Fairbridge Society'. In the second of his written responses to the inquiry he said, 'I have had a look at the further questions and am unable to add anything of fact, substance or indeed evidence that is anything other than hearsay.'

Clearly unimpressed, the inquiry called Haynes into the witness box on 19 July to answer some additional questions. The inquiry was aware that Haynes had told a House of Commons committee a decade before that Fairbridge had 'no cases of complaint or abuse on record' and gave him a torrid time about what he knew, or should have known. Again, Henrietta Hill did the questioning.[11]

HH: Mr Haynes . . . in his book David Hill had made allegations of sexual abuse of a range of children at the Molong school. You are aware that that is part of what's in David Hill's book, aren't you?

NH: I have not read David Hill's book, but I have been made aware of it, yes.

HH: So you do know, don't you, that at least from that one source there are allegations of sexual abuse that have been made?

NH: Yes.

HH: Is that right, so help us then, please, with how it is you can say in paragraph 3 [of your witness statement]: 'I have no knowledge of any . . . allegations regarding sexual abuse in the former Fairbridge Society'? Because you do know about what David Hill's book alleges, don't you?

NH: They were alleged, yes.

HH: Can I ask you, please, to look [at] a Q&A sheet . . . This is a document that is prepared, as it says at the top, 'in response to an article that appeared in the *Sunday Times* on Sunday 29 July 2007 which featured David Hill' and I think it was a precursor or publicity article about his book . . . This is an internal document, I think, prepared within Fairbridge 'if queries from the media arose'. Is that right?

NH: As far as my recollection is concerned, yes.

HH: Do you see, please: 'Hill interviewed 40 ex-pupils of Molong, some of whom made allegations of cruelty, sexual abuse and work-house labour conditions' . . . But then over the page, there is a question as if this might come from a member of the press, do you see it? It says: 'Does the Fairbridge archive contain any cases of abuse?' Do you see that? Then the prepared answer that Fairbridge would give it if they were asked that by a journalist was: 'The Fairbridge UK archive – held at the University Library – does not contain any cases of child abuse at Molong or any other services in Australia'. Do you see that?

NH: Yes.

Haynes then protested that the brief had been produced by his company secretary at the time, John Anderson, and that he couldn't remember the construction of it.

HH: But you were the director of Fairbridge at the time – correct?
NH: I was.
HH: So presumably you would be concerned to make sure that public statements to the media were accurate?
NH: As I have said in my original statements, at that stage I was fully employed with my core business and articles and beneficiaries. I had delegated to my company secretary . . . if it was an error, then it was an error, as you have said.

While Haynes was in the witness box we also learned that he ordered Anderson to go to Liverpool University in August 2007 'to acquaint himself with the records' only a week after the *Sunday Times* report about *The Forgotten Children*. In his report back to Haynes, Anderson said he had found a file confirming that a six-year-old girl had had her head put down the toilet by a staff member to cure her of bed wetting and other small children were regularly whipped by a cottage mother with a riding crop. It also contained information about Fairbridge principal Beauchamp being dismissed for 'immoral and perverted practices'.

Asked if he recalled the documents referred to in Anderson's ten-page report, Haynes said, 'I may have seen them, but I have no recollection of their content.' He was then asked what he'd done with the document once he'd received it. He said he couldn't remember.

HH: Do you think it would have been appropriate, as the director of Fairbridge, for you to have familiarised yourself, Mr Haynes, with the details of the report?

NH: If I had the time, yes, but again, I return to my core work, my core responsibilities, and at that particular time I was preparing to select and hand over the job to my successor.

In fact, as it turned out, this had taken place in August 2007 and Haynes was director until the following year.

He was asked why Fairbridge had not corrected its media Q&A:

HH: Mr Haynes, this Q&A sheet has been prepared in immediate response to an article [in the *Sunday Times*] around 29 July 2007, that Mr Anderson then goes and inspects the archives and provides a report in mid-August 2007. But at no point does it appear, from what we have, that Fairbridge sees fit to revise its Q&A sheet to say, for example, 'Mr Anderson has now looked at the archive and we can see that there are some cases of abuse in it'.

NH: I had delegated all responsibilities concerning the Fairbridge Society to [company secretary] Mr Woods initially and then to Mr Anderson. I had to rely on their good judgement.[12]

At the end of her questions and before dismissing Haynes, Henrietta Hill walked over to my little legal table and asked me quietly if there was anything further I wanted her to put to him. I said that she might ask what he thought now that all the facts of abuse had been laid bare. And she did just that, with an additional question:

HH. Pulling all these threads together, if you like, and seeing all the issues that I have now put to you . . . is there anything else that you wish to say to former child migrants about the fact, it seems, that Fairbridge has not offered any apology until what you have said today?

NH: . . . if any abuse, sexual abuse, be proven, then I am deeply sorry. I am not Fairbridge now. I am Nigel Haynes. And I cannot speak on behalf of Fairbridge. But I would be the first to apologise personally should this be the case.[13]

At the end of his testimony I swelled with rage. In it, Haynes had expressed no sign of regret or responsibility for the failings of Fairbridge, or for its failing to recognise the widespread abuse of children while they were there. He continued his denials of any personal knowledge of mistreatment of the Fairbridge children, which had begun twenty years before when he told a House of Commons committee back in 1997 that Fairbridge had 'no cases on record' of abuse, when of course it did. In his evidence he seemed to want us to believe that as director of Fairbridge he knew nothing of the plot by Fairbridge management to lie about what was in *The Forgotten Children* and to pretend they hadn't read it. And all this in the face of the terrible suffering endured by the Fairbridge children.

Subsequently, the inquiry heard from two former British prime ministers, John Major and Gordon Brown, about the child migration policies of their governments. Major did not appear as a witness, but, at the request of the inquiry, provided a written witness statement. Brown appeared in person to give evidence.

Major, who was prime minister between 1990 and 1997, said he had only a limited recollection of any dealings with child migration, which had been more than twenty years ago. He went on to say: 'As is evident from my original and supplementary state-ments, very little information on this issue was referred to me, personally, during my time as prime minister. I therefore have no informed opinion or knowledge to offer.'

He said that the files showed 'the earliest reference to the child migrant programmes in which I was involved is a written answer by me on 14 July 1993 to the question of David Hinchliffe MP . . . In it, I confirmed that I was aware that there were allega-tions of physical and sexual abuse of a number of child migrants some years ago in Australia, but that any such allegations would be a matter for the Australian authorities.'[14]

He added that his belief at the time was there were 'no allega-tions of physical and sexual abuse involving the British authorities'. And he made it clear that in his eyes the British government could wash its hands of any responsibility for British children who were abused, once they'd been sent overseas: 'The position of the British government remained . . . that any concerns relating to the treat-ment of children in another country is a matter for that country.'

Gordon Brown struck a more sympathetic stance. He reminded the inquiry that as prime minister he had publicly apologised to child migrants in 2010, and said he had only recently learned of the extent of the abuse – and particularly the sexual abuse. He accepted that the British government was to blame for what he described as 'a modern form of government-induced [human] trafficking'. He acknowledged that as prime minister he was 'only partially aware of the magnitude of the abuse. It was only in these . . . later years, that I came to be told of the scale of the problem . . . the huge violation of human rights, and we are dealing here with the loss of identity, the loss of family, the loss of a sense of belonging.'[15] He characterised child migration as:

probably the biggest national sexual abuse scandal . . . bigger than what people have said about [Jimmy] Savile, bigger than what people have alleged about individual children's homes, bigger in scale, bigger in geographic spread, bigger in length of time it went undetected. I am shocked at the information I have seen, but it is information I have seen, sadly, since 2010 and not before it.

He admitted that what he had subsequently learned of the plight of British child migrants was far worse than he knew at the time of his apology:

I am shocked that we are here now in a position in 2017 where we now know that the apology was only half the story, and we have yet to do something to remedy and to deal with the consequences of what is the other part of the story, which is as significant, perhaps more brutal: the abuse of so many hundreds and perhaps thousands of children, something that – children who have been forgotten, children who have, even as adults, seemed invisible for most of these years . . .

He told the inquiry that the abuses were 'so serious that we have a duty to offer some form of redress'. He went on to argue that given the failure of duty of care, a flat-rate payment should be made to all child migrants still alive.

He was asked why the government was unaware in 2010 of the files in Kew's National Archives Office that contained evidence of the poor treatment of children, many of which I had used when writing *The Forgotten Children*. Henrietta Hill put it to him that:

a lot of the information that set out the reality of the conditions in which children were kept in institutions in Australia is in the national archives and has been there for many years, so it could be said that that was all material that could have been accessed by government prior to your apology.

Brown agreed that some people must have been aware of that material, and that the inquiry should investigate why:

I think you should look at what happened and I think you should decide whether there was a failure, or how it happened. Clearly, I was not made aware of this material. Clearly, other ministers were not aware of this material. But clearly, there were people within the machinery who must have known more than we did, and perhaps should have drawn it to our attention ... I think if you understand why the issues of sexual abuse were not raised with me in any meaningful way, then you will understand, perhaps, why we need to do more to rectify or remedy the abuse that was experienced by so many of the child migrants ... there was a failure, and that failure leads to where we are today.

14

THE BRITISH GOVERNMENT AGREES TO PAY COMPENSATION

As the person who established the IICSA we want to thank you. But now as Prime Minister we want you to ensure the IICSA Inquiry into child migration is not just another worthy report that will gather dust with all the others.

The UK IICSA published its final report into sexual abuse in child migration schemes in March 2018. The report was unequivocal in its criticism of the programs:

Many witnesses described 'care' regimes which included physical abuse, emotional abuse and neglect, as well as sexual abuse, in the various settings to which they were sent. Some described constant hunger, medical neglect and poor education, the latter of which had, in several instances, lifelong consequences. By any standards of child care, then or at the present time, all of this was wrong.[1]

Notwithstanding the earlier admissions of the Australian government, the New South Wales government and the Fairbridge Foundation in Australia that they had all failed to protect the children, the IICSA report concluded:

> the institution primarily to blame for the continued existence of the child migration programmes after the Second World War was Her Majesty's Government (HMG). This was a deeply flawed policy, as HMG now accepts. It . . . was allowed by successive British governments to remain in place, despite a catalogue of evidence which showed that children were suffering ill treatment and abuse, including sexual abuse.
>
> The policy in itself was indefensible and HMG could have decided to bring it to an end, or mitigated some of its effects in practice by taking action at certain key points, but it did not do so.[2]

The inquiry came to the same reasons for these failures as I had – 'the politics of the day, which were consistently prioritised over the welfare of children'.

It went on to acknowledge that successive British governments had been reluctant 'to jeopardise relations with the Australian government by withdrawing from the scheme, and also to upset philanthropic organisations such as Barnardos and the Fairbridge Society. Many such organisations enjoyed patronage from persons of influence and position, and it is clear that in some cases the avoidance of embarrassment and reputational risk was more important than the institutions' responsibilities towards migrated children.'[3]

The inquiry found evidence of widespread 'physical abuse, emotional abuse, as well as sexual abuse . . . hunger, medical neglect and poor education', and reported children not being able to report abuse for 'fear of being disbelieved, or beaten', or further 'threatened . . . by their abusers'.[4]

It also found that when the British government was faced with critical evidence of the cruelty taking place at Fairbridge and other institutions, it still failed to act:

Many reports on child migration were available to HMG during the 1950s . . . The reports on many of these places were extremely critical. The conditions at several of them were judged to be so bad that they were put on a 'blacklist' and regarded as not fit to receive any more child migrants. Still, HMG did nothing effective to protect the children.[5]

The inquiry was equally critical of the Fairbridge Society of the UK, which it said was aware of abuse at its farm schools going back as far as the 1930s. The report said Fairbridge did not 'take sufficient care of the children' and 'remained wedded to its migration ethos, even in the wake of outside criticism and post war changes to child care'.[6]

The report noted a series of serious problems at the Molong farm school over three decades: the sacking of the disgraced Richard Beauchamp in 1940; W. J. Garnett's critical report about Fairbridge in 1944; the investigation into the principal F. K. S Woods following allegations of sexual misbehaviour against him in 1945 and 1946; further allegations against Woods involving abuse of the children in 1948; Ross's investigation that led to the British government's blacklist of institutions in 1956; correspondence from the head of the New South Wales Child Welfare Department in 1958 that Fairbridge was behind on modern child welfare standards; concern in 1964 about the rundown nature of the farm school and its standard of child care; the departure of Bill Phillips in 1962 amid rumours of the sexual abuse of children; a letter in 1969 from the New South Wales Child Welfare Department that Fairbridge failed to comply with the department's standards of child care; Jack Newberry being forced to leave Molong in 1969 due to allegations of sexually abusing children.

A litany of red flags – all ignored by layers of administrators, governments and organisations.

The IISCA report was generally welcomed by child migrants; however, Oliver Cosgrove surely summing up the feelings of many when he said:

> Whilst I welcome apologies and compensation which is way overdue, I deserve more; those who suffered sexual abuse deserve more. It is not enough to acknowledge and apologise for what happened in the past – we need to learn from the obvious failures to ensure that no child suffers as I did. Because sexual abuse is still taking place in our society.[7]

The inquiry made a series of recommendations, including that an apology be made, counselling offered and compensation paid – all three things I had sought in my submission. With regard to the compensation, the report said the panel's recommendation was for 'a Redress Scheme for surviving former child migrants, providing for an equal award to every applicant. This is on the basis that they were all exposed to the risk of sexual abuse'.[8]

The inquiry was well aware that the health of many surviving child migrants was ailing, and that increasing numbers were dying, so it urged the British government 'to establish the Scheme without delay' and to commence the payments 'within

12 months'.[9] The inquiry recommended compensation of equal amounts to each surviving child migrant but left the amount to be determined by the government.

The report was widely reported in the British media, including the BBC:

Thousands of British people who as children were forcibly sent abroad, where many suffered abuse, should be compensated, an inquiry says. They were sent to Australia and parts of the British Empire from 1945–1970 by charities and the Catholic Church. The Independent Inquiry into Child Sexual Abuse (IICSA) said the government should pay all 2,000 former migrants still alive within 12 months. The Australian and UK governments apologised in 2009 and 2010. About 4,000 children, mainly from deprived backgrounds, were sent to Australia, New Zealand, Canada and Southern Rhodesia, now Zimbabwe, between 1945 and 1970, to give them better lives and strengthen the British population abroad. The inquiry heard from various former migrants who claimed they and others suffered sexual and physical abuse at the hands of those running the schools and orphanages they were sent to.[10]

In the face of the pressing nature of getting these payments moving, we waited anxiously for a response from the British government. I wrote to Prime Minister Theresa May that March to complain about the delay, enclosing a copy of *The Forgotten Children*:

Dear Prime Minister,
I am a former British child migrant sent to Australia as a twelve-year-old with my two brothers in 1959. A decade ago I wrote a book *The Forgotten Children* about the experiences of child

migrants and last year appeared as a witness before the IICSA inquiry into Child Migration programs.

As I am sure you are aware the inquiry has found HMG was the institution 'primarily responsible' for child migration and 'had failed to respond appropriately' to ensure the protection of the children. The Inquiry has recommended HMG establish a redress scheme that involves payment of compensation to surviving child migrants. This is a just and fair recommendation. Without it there is little of tangible value in the report for the many child migrants who were victims of abuse.

The Inquiry has made the very sensible observation that this should be done soon since most of the child migrants have already died and many of the approximately two thousand survivors are in variable health. I pointed out to the inquiry in its July hearings last year that in the decade since I wrote *The Forgotten Children* 25% of the former Fairbridge children had died . . .

As the person who established the IICSA we want to thank you. But now as Prime Minister we want you to ensure the IICSA Inquiry into child migration is not just another worthy report that will gather dust with all the others. So, on behalf of the surviving British child migrants I implore you to implement the recommendations of the Child Migrant Program inquiry without delay.

Six months later there had still been no response from the government about when the payments of compensation would come, and my frustrations were reported in the British and Australian media:

In an interview for Radio 4's *Today* Program, former British child migrant David Hill said that the response of the Australian government to survivors of abuse, while far from perfect, is still markedly better than the lack of any British government response to its former child migrants. Hill's comments refer to a report published by the Independent Inquiry into Child Sexual Abuse (IICSA) on March 1, 2018, which recommended that the UK government establish a redress scheme to make reparation payments to all surviving British child migrants. Noting the advanced age of these former child migrants, IICSA stated that this redress scheme should be set up as a matter of urgency.[11]

Professor Gordon Lynch, who had advised the UK inquiry, explained that the delay had been caused partly because of issues around the precedent the compensation scheme might set. But, said Lynch:

It's difficult to understand the government's concern on this point. Redress for anyone exposed to physical or sexual abuse, or for anyone for whom government systems of oversight failed, would undoubtedly extend far beyond the case of British child migrants. But in the case of its child migrants, the government didn't simply fail to implement effective safeguards. It failed to do so knowingly, despite clear recommendations about standards that should be applied.[12]

We were lucky to have the persistent support of Wigan Labour MP Lisa Nandy, who campaigned tirelessly on our behalf. At the beginning of July she raised the matter in Westminster again:

The report of the independent inquiry into child sexual abuse was published four months ago . . . [It] made just three recommendations [including] that adequate financial redress be made to the more than 2000 surviving former child migrants. It also made it clear that this is urgent – many have died and others are dying, and it was unequivocal that the scheme must be up and running within 12 months.[13]

Finally, on 1 February 2019, the British government appeared to have agreed to pay £20,000 (AUS$36,000) compensation to all surviving child migrants, with the *Guardian* reporting that it had seen a letter in which the government said the compensation scheme was open to:

> any former British child migrant who was alive on 1 March 2018, or beneficiaries of any former child migrant who was alive on 1 March 2018 but had since died . . . The Child Migrant Trust would accept applications from 1 March 2019 and the scheme would remain open for two years.[14]

The government acknowledged that more child migrants had died since the publication of the IICSA report almost a year before, so it made sure that anyone alive when the report was published was eligible to receive the payment:

> A number of former child migrants have sadly passed away since the Inquiry published its report, so the Government will accept claims in respect of any former child migrant who was alive on 1 March 2018, when the Inquiry's Child Migration report was published.[15]

In addition to the ex gratia payment, the government agreed to provided more funding to the UK Child Migrant Trust to continue its Family Restoration Scheme. For many years, with financial support from the government, the trust had been helping migrants reunite with families back in the UK.

To its credit, the British government moved quickly and by engaging the services of the trust made the process of claiming the £20,000 easy. Within months practically all had received their money.

15

REDRESS FROM THE FAIRBRIDGE SOCIETY

David Hill has accused a youth charity set up by Prince Charles of 'covering its backside' by denying it had known of serious abuse suffered by child migrants.

So, finally the British government joined the Australian federal government, the New South Wales state government and the Fairbridge Foundation in, first, admitting its failure to protect the children at the farm school at Molong, and then settling on an amount of financial compensation.

That left the fifth and final institution, the UK Fairbridge Society, to offer reparation. The Fairbridge Society was the largest child migrant organisation and responsible for recruiting and sending thousands of British children to its farm schools in Canada, Australia and Rhodesia for almost seventy years between 1911 and 1980.

In my evidence to the Inquiry into Child Sexual Abuse (IICSA) in London in 2017, I clearly stated that Fairbridge UK had failed 'to take sufficient care to protect children' and 'in some cases [was] aware of some allegations of sexual abuse'.[1] In its report, the IICSA reached much the same conclusion, observing that Fairbridge UK 'did not take sufficient care to protect its child migrants . . . from the risk of sexual abuse'.[2] It said, too:

> The responses of Fairbridge UK to the allegations of sexual abuse of child migrants made in the post-migration period have been inadequate. Fairbridge UK denied responsibility, and was at best wilfully blind to the evidence of sexual abuse contained within its own archives. This stance has caused significant distress to child migrants.[3]

The IICSA also found that Fairbridge deliberately tried to misinform the public when *The Forgotten Children* was published by suggesting Fairbridge management give false answers to media inquiries, as had been revealed in the questions to Nigel Haynes during the inquiry. And the report judged that Haynes was wrong in claiming the UK Fairbridge Society was not responsible for what happened at the farm school in Molong.

At the time of the IICSA, the Fairbridge Society had been merged with the UK Prince's Trust for five years. The Prince's Trust is a far bigger charity than Fairbridge. It was founded in 1976 by Prince Charles to help disadvantaged and vulnerable young people get into work, education or training, at a time when youth unemployment in the UK was reaching historically high levels. Nowadays it continues to support eleven- to thirty-year-olds who are unemployed or struggling at school and are at risk of exclusion. Many of those helped by the Trust are in, or leaving, out-of-home care, and facing issues such as homelessness or mental health problems. Some have been in trouble with the law.

In 2013 the Trust opened in Australia. By then the merger with Fairbridge had been completed and according to the Trust's website, since then in Britain, 'Over 22,640 young people have taken part in the Fairbridge programme at the Prince's Trust and the Prince's Trust has spent £43.9m on the Fairbridge programme.' In October 2013, Fairbridge as an independent entity was dissolved.

At the time of the IICSA hearings in 2017 there remained a Fairbridge representative on the Prince's Trust board and some of the Fairbridge programs were still operated by the Trust. However, shortly before the start of the second London hearings, the chief executive of the Trust, Dame Martina Milburn, wrote to Professor Jay to explicitly disassociate the Prince's Trust from Fairbridge in a public statement:

> I wanted to express the horror and sadness I have felt upon hearing the stories of people who experienced abuse on child migrant programs, including those operated by the former Fairbridge Society. I would be grateful if you would share this letter with the visitors and survivors who have courageously shared their experiences through the Independent Inquiry into Child Sexual Abuse . . . As far as I am aware, Fairbridge has never apologised. Now, having seen the evidence you have unearthed, I do not believe that the Fairbridge approach is acceptable.[4]

Eight days later Dame Martina was invited to the inquiry to give further evidence in person, where she elaborated on her criticism of Fairbridge:

> Although the Prince's Trust has never had any involvement in child migration schemes, and whilst the Fairbridge Society no longer

291

exists, as the holder of the archive and the organisation which currently uses the Fairbridge name for one of its programmes, we would like to say sorry. We categorically condemn all forms of child abuse and are deeply sorry for the hurt and suffering experienced by victims and survivors. I would like to thank you for all the important work you are doing to ensure victims and survivors of abuse are finally able to have their voices heard.[5]

Under questioning, Milburn agreed that as part of the merger, the Prince's Trust had inherited the archive held at Liverpool University, which, as she described it, included 'literally millions and millions and millions of documents'.[6] She said that the Prince's Trust had removed restrictions on accessing the archives:

Q. When you inherited the archive, the restrictions were a closed period of 100 years for records relating to Fairbridge clients, 75 years for those relating to staff, and 30 years for the administrative archives. But what in fact I think you are saying is that you have waived – is this right? – all of those restrictions?

MM. Absolutely correct, yes.

Q. Certainly, as far as individual former child migrants are concerned, you have facilitated them in accessing their own case files?

MM. Yes.

Q. And specifically as part of your assistance to this inquiry, have enabled those former child migrants who wished to see unredacted versions of those files to have those?

MM. Yes, and the case notes.[7]

This was certainly a positive move, not least bearing in mind the difficulty I'd had accessing the files when I was originally researching *The Forgotten Children*.

Milburn acknowledged, though, that the Prince's Trust may have been naïve about what it was inheriting along with the Fairbridge name. She admitted that she was aware of adverse publicity about Fairbridge at the time of the merger but claimed the Trust was not told the truth:

> We were aware of the issues. As we went through the due diligence . . . we were reassured that there had been no claims against Fairbridge and there was certainly nothing when we did the legal due diligence that came out. What has emerged, again as a result of this inquiry, certainly over the last few weeks, is it was clear that we weren't told the full truth of what was happening around the child migrants. What wasn't disclosed to us was the amount of queries and things that had come in to Fairbridge as a result. So we were reassured it was all in the past. We were very focused on the programme we were taking over, which was in the United Kingdom, and, perhaps in hindsight, naïvely, we accepted what we were told and there was no evidence that we were able to uncover then that said anything differently.[8]

Welcome though Dame Martina's comments were, I thought it implausible that the Prince's Trust had not known of the allegations of abuse at Fairbridge before the merger, or afterwards when they took possession of the organisation's archives. They'd had plenty of time in the years after the merger to read the material in Fairbridge's archives. It also seemed unlikely the Trust could have been unaware of the serious allegations levelled at Fairbridge in previous years. In 2007 the publication of *The Forgotten Children* had attracted coverage in the UK as well as in Australia, and it made references to much of the evidence of abuse I had seen in the Liverpool University archives.

I said as much to the media during the second hearings in London, as the *Guardian* reported:

> David Hill has accused a youth charity set up by Prince Charles of 'covering its backside' by denying it had known of serious abuse suffered by child migrants . . . He said the Fairbridge files had been with the Prince's Trust for the past six years and contained many references to abuse.[9]

If the Prince's Trust was trying to distance itself from any responsibility for Fairbridge in 2017, I was delighted to see that it moved to make amends in Australia two years later. While the IICSA was still completing its hearings in London, the Australian government was in the process of implementing the recommendations of its Royal Commission into Institutional Responses to Child Sexual Abuse. The royal commission submitted its final report, including more than 400 recommendations, in late 2017. Among those recommendations was one for the establishment of a National Redress Scheme (NRS), to include financial compensation for the victims of child abuse. It was also recommended that 'the institution in which the abuse is alleged or accepted to have occurred should fund the cost of redress'.[10]

The long list of offending institutions identified by the Australian inquiry included the UK Fairbridge Society, which, of course, no longer legally existed. However, the Royal Commission also recommended, and the Australian government agreed, that, 'Where the institution in which the abuse is alleged or accepted to have occurred no longer exists, but the institution was part of a larger group of institutions, or where there is a successor to the institution, the group of institutions or the successor institution should fund the cost of redress.'[11]

Over the next year a number of organisations signed up for the NRS, and in May 2020 the Prince's Trust – to its credit – announced that it would, as Fairbridge's successor organisation, make funds available to the now defunct Fairbridge Society to pay into the redress scheme. A spokesperson from the Trust told the *Canberra Times*: 'The Prince's Trust is providing Fairbridge with funds, to give victims and survivors the opportunity to make claims, and it is also our hope that Fairbridge will sign up to the Australian redress scheme.'[12]

The following day the *Guardian* reported that the Prince's Trust had announced it had created a legal entity called Fairbridge Restored and confirmed the Prince's Trust would provide it with money to be paid as compensation to the former child migrants:

Fairbridge has now been reinstated as an organisation in the UK, under administrators. The Prince's Trust is providing Fairbridge with funds, to give victims and survivors the opportunity to make claims, and it is also our hope that Fairbridge will sign up to the Australian redress scheme . . . We are in proactive and ongoing talks with the Australian authorities and with the administrators of Fairbridge, and we are committed to finding the best way to support the victims and supporters . . . We categorically condemn all forms of child abuse . . . Although the Prince's Trust has never had any involvement in child migration schemes, we once again want to say we are deeply sorry for the hurt and suffering experienced by victims and survivors.[13]

However, what the former Fairbridge kids and I didn't know was that over the next year, negotiations between the Prince's Trust and the Australian government to commit Fairbridge Restored to joining the Australian Redress Scheme would drag on until, finally, they failed.

The first sign that things were not going according to plan was about three months after the Trust's announcement, when on 1 July 2020 Social Services Minister Anne Ruston announced that Fairbridge, along with five other institutions, had failed to sign up with National Redress Scheme: 'It is completely unacceptable that these institutions have failed to meet their moral obligations to join the National Redress Scheme,' Ruston said. 'These are institutions which know they have been named in applications and yet they have chosen to shirk their responsibility to finally do the right thing by these survivors.'[14]

Three months later, Prime Minister Scott Morrison announced in Parliament that two of the six organisations had now agreed to sign up to the NRS but they did not include Fairbridge:

We still have, reprehensibly, four institutions who have been named publicly and who have blatantly refused to join the Redress Scheme. They are: Jehovah's Witnesses, Kenja Communication, Lakes Entrance Pony Club and Fairbridge (Restored) Limited. It is not acceptable.[15]

Morrison went on to threaten sanctions against the organisations:

We are currently finalising the further sanctions, I know that are supported by the Opposition, the Commonwealth will place on institutions who continue to refuse to join the Scheme. Including withdrawal of their charitable status for these offending organisations.[16]

Since the Prince's Trust launch in Australia, it had been granted tax deductible status and the withdrawal of that status would have serious implications for the organisation's fundraising.

The problem was the way Fairbridge Restored had been legally established by the Prince's Trust. As soon as Fairbridge Restored was created, the Trust put it into administration, which is what is done when a company is insolvent. An insolvent company is usually in administration for only twelve months while it pays out as much as possible to creditors before legally being wound up. In the case of Fairbridge Restored the creditors would be the Fairbridge survivors, who would be paid with the money supplied by the Trust.

That Fairbridge Restored was to be wound up after only one year was the major stumbling block. A condition of all organisations signing up to the NRS is that they must do so for ten years – to give all the victims of abuse plenty of time to settle their redress claims. Fairbridge Restored would cease to exist in 2021 and the terms of the NRS demanded it exist till 2028.

It seemed to me the federal government and the Prince's Trust should have been able to sort out this administrative issue, but it wasn't to be.

I'd always thought it was a mistake for the Prince's Trust to establish Fairbridge Restored and then put it straight into administration and I was quick to tell the Trust this – that it should have settled on a structure that would have worked alongside the stipulations of the National Redress Scheme.

I believed that a simpler way of proceeding would have been for the Prince's Trust to pay directly into the NRS on behalf of Fairbridge, but I think the reason the Trust wanted the compensation paid by some other entity was to distance the name and reputation of the Prince's Trust from Fairbridge, with its now sullied reputation. If this was the Trust's strategy, it did not work: the media kept its focus on Fairbridge while noting that it was now under the control of the Trust.[17]

Simon Major, the Prince's Trust group general counsel and company secretary, with whom I corresponded for nearly two years, also insisted to me the Trust had no alternative, that because Fairbridge Restored wasn't trading, no other options were available; its 'sole purpose', Major said, was to pay out claims to Fairbridgians and any other creditors.[18]

Two months after Fairbridge Restored had missed the federal government's deadline, in September 2020 one of its administrators, London insolvency lawyer Chris Laverty, explained to an Australian government joint select committee convened to monitor the implementation of the National Redress Scheme that the legal structure of Fairbridge Restored was incompatible with the legal requirements of the scheme.

The committee had members from both the House of Representatives and the Senate, and from the ranks of the government and opposition. It took a particular interest in the Fairbridge issue, but ultimately failed to have Fairbridge join the NRS.

During Laverty's appearance before the joint select committee, she said that despite the difficulties of joining the scheme, Fairbridge Restored still intended pressing on with payments to victims of abuse. This sounded a little implausible since Fairbridge Restored had by now been established for seven months and was due to be wound up five months later in February 2021.

Two months after Laverty's testimony, Emma Kate McGuirk, the group manager of the NRS, told the select committee that negotiations with the Prince's Trust to include Fairbridge in the scheme had been exhausted and that the NRS could not see that it would be able to join.

The next development came the following year when, in March 2021, the federal government, with the support of a number of relevant state governments, announced it had agreed to step up as 'funders of last resort' and pay into the NRS the money Fairbridge Restored had failed to pay so that the victims of abuse could be compensated:

> Former Fairbridge farm schools will now be covered by the National Redress Scheme allowing survivors of these institutions to have their applications progressed . . . We all have a part to play to help survivors access redress. Survivors of Fairbridge have had to wait too long for the recognition they absolutely deserve. Their wait ends today.[19]

To us Fairbridge kids it was important that the UK Fairbridge Society was seen to be called to account and we were devastated that yet again they appeared to be getting away with it. On hearing the news, I wrote to the government to say that we were very grateful that it had stepped up; however, we were also concerned that Fairbridge was being let off the hook; that Australian taxpayers were now footing the bill; and the Prince's Trust appeared to be turning its back on Fairbridge victims, having pledged to provide compensation funding. I said I thought the Trust and Fairbridge Restored should be approached again to find a way of participating in the NRS. I also asked the government if it intended to sanction the Prince's Trust, as had been threatened by the prime minister the previous year.

I was told in a reply from the NRS office that they would not: 'As Fairbridge is named as the responsible institution, the sanctions cannot be applied to the Prince's Trust,' Emma Kate McGuirk told me in a letter in June.

I had always thought it highly unlikely the government would carry out the threat of sanctions against the Prince's Trust, which had influential friends in Australia. The chair of the Trust here is Julie Bishop, former deputy leader of the Liberal Party and long-serving foreign minister. I was also told that the Australian high commissioner to London, former cabinet minister George Brandis, had placed some calls to Canberra about the issue – although his office would not confirm or deny if he made any representations on behalf of the Prince's Trust.

The previous November I had contacted Simon Major to say I'd hoped the Trust and the government would have found a way to honour the commitment for Fairbridge Restored to sign up to the NRS. In his reply Major complained of a 'lack of engagement' in the negotiations, which included the cancellation by the Australian Government Solicitor of an attempt at mediation. He stated that sadly the inaction of the government had been the cause of the problem.[20] Some months later he also stressed the Trust had been working to provide funds to Fairbridge, even if those funds were separate from the Australian redress scheme. He reiterated that the Trust had hoped Fairbridge could join the NRS 'as one avenue' through which Fairbridgians could seek compensation. He acknowledged that, however, this had not been possible, but said that claimants would still be able to seek compensation directly from Fairbridge.[21]

The Fairbridgians and I thought the creation of a separate compensation scheme was a bad idea, which anyway would come to nothing because Fairbridge Restored was due to wind up in March 2021. However, without any announcement the Prince's

Trust gained more time when it successfully applied to the High Court in London to have the administration extended for eighteen months, until September 2022.

Through the second half of 2021, I made more representations to the joint select committee on the implementation of the National Redress Scheme, appearing as a witness in August and November. On these occasions, I told the committee that it did not make sense for Fairbridge Restored to run a separate scheme, as doing so would add unnecessary complexity and confusion to an already emotionally trying situation:

> Do the Fairbridge kids lodge their application forms with the NRS, do they lodge their applications with Fairbridge Restored, or do they do it to both, and in what sequence? . . . Most of these people are not able to comply with the process. They need help just filling out the forms, because most of them are ill-educated and most of them are very old now. Added to that is the trauma of revisiting the abuse that's inherent in these applications. It's a very difficult, traumatic and trying experience.[22]

My representations did not result in any change in direction and the Prince's Trust and Fairbridge Restored pressed on with a scheme to compensate the Fairbridge victims of abuse, outside and separate from the Australian redress scheme.

Over the next few months both organisations continued to provide me with some but not all of the details of how the separate scheme would work.[23] They told me: '[the] Trust's primary concern was, and still is, to ensure that the former child migrants of Fairbridge receive some redress'. They confirmed the Trust would provide the funding and that Fairbridge Restored would provide the 'process details' and 'advertise' for claimants of abuse to make claims. Fairbridge Restored (who would legally regard the claimants as 'creditors') would assess the claims of abuse and, along with an apology, pay compensation with the money provided by the Prince's Trust – and they said all this could be achieved by September 2022. They did not provide me details of the criteria they would use to assess the claims, how much money would be made available for compensation, or any information as to when the scheme would start.

The solution that has been reached may not be the best outcome, and it has been messy and taken several more years to get here. But if it does work out, at least those who were abused at Fairbridge will finally be compensated by the vestiges of the organisation itself, for the harm and trauma they suffered.

At the end of what has been a long journey I can't help but reflect on what a hard road it has been. Sure, we've chalked up some big wins but I am not naïve enough to think that we have 'changed the system' for the better. Having worked at high levels in the corporate world and government for some decades, I am well aware of the imbalance of power between big institutions on the one hand and individuals on the other. I know how institutions can wriggle out of their responsibilities, how governments can hide behind process and formal inquiries, how the reports of inquiries gather dust and their sensible recommendations are ignored, how politicians avoid issues and accountability, and how the legal system can be used to indefinitely delay progress and ultimately thwart justice.

But in this case we have some cause for celebration. If the Prince's Trust and Fairbridge Restored honour their promise to the Fairbridge abuse survivors, it will mean that all the institutions that were major players in the sad story of Australian child migration, after decades of denials, cover-ups and lies, will have finally acknowledged they failed the many thousands of innocent children who were sent to Australia with a promise of a better life.

16

RECKONING

*But if you are capable of trembling with indignation each time
that an injustice is committed in the world, we are comrades,
and that is more important.*

H as justice been done?
In some respects, justice can never be done. Great wrongs
cannot be righted. Pain, shame, guilt, diminished self-esteem and
trauma are long-lasting. The damage caused by crushing the spirit
of a small child is impossible to repair. It is too easy to say the
Fairbridgian children should find closure as adults and 'move on',
because the wounds inflicted never completely heal.

However, there have been some positive things to come out
of our long quest for recognition and restitution. The abuse and
the suffering are now better understood. The institutions have
acknowledged their wrongdoing and the apologies have brought
some much-needed comfort to many, who have also found
strength and power in the truth being known. And the financial

compensation has given tangible meaning to the apology we finally received.

That said, for a lot of people it is not as straightforward as simply accepting the money. Mary O'Brien, who went to Fairbridge in the same group as me and has remained a close friend, had mixed feelings after receiving financial compensation for the sexual abuse she suffered:

It's taken almost ten years. When I received this cheque, I thought, 'Yah! Finally,' and went straight to the bank. My . . . life should have been different. I was bright enough to finish high school (I didn't) and to go to university (I did this much later in life). [The money] doesn't make up for the twenty-plus years it took me to get my life back on track. I waited a day before reading the 'apologies' [that came with the cheque] and burst into tears halfway through Premier Baird's letter. The pain is only just under the surface – I seldom cry but it is unbelievable so many of us were abused for so long. The perpetrators got away with it, as most of them have died.

Ian Bayliff, who spent eight years at Fairbridge after being sent there as an eight-year-old, also felt some ambivalence:

I am happy that Fairbridge and the governments in Britain and Australia have all now admitted they failed the kids and have apologised, and that they have all agreed to pay compensation. The money doesn't matter much to me personally now, but it means I can give a bit of financial help to my girls and their families in a way that I couldn't before. On the downside, I just feel that those evil people who abused me, and abused the other kids, got away with it. They're all dead now. None of them were charged or convicted of the terrible things they did. Still, at least we have now named the villains.

Lennie Magee, who was at the farm school for more than ten years after arriving when he was six, thinks the apologies and the compensation were of value to some but not to others:

> The apology to all institutionalised children and subsequent reparation were greatly appreciated by many, including myself. To have the government acknowledge the injustice and abuse that we suffered was a significant landmark. However, it did happen. Our lives were broken. Some committed suicide because they had no way of recovery back from the darkness and despair they were forced to endure.

Lennie also feels that for many of the Fairbridge children all of it is much too late:

> What can you give them to elicit a happy and positive response to the word 'Fairbridge'? I don't think the word 'sorry', spoken by a complete stranger who has never even set foot on the farm, and had absolutely nothing to do with the crimes that were inflicted there, will do. It's too late. Much too late. The perpetrators of so much pain are dead. Some went to their graves knowing exactly what they did but not caring. Others, feeling completely justified in what they did, but not knowing. They can't reach out now and proffer an apology. It's too late.[1]

After he left Fairbridge Lennie became deeply religious and he believes his faith has helped him come to terms with the experience, but he's aware many former farm school children are still suffering.

I have been blessed, so blessed. God has healed me in the deepest and most profound way. I have scars, but they don't hurt. I have a hope that is beyond this world's horizon. My once torn and battered heart has been renewed. I am at peace. Sadly, though, there are still many, not all, who are angry and hurting. They are still carrying a truckload of baggage . . . During the times when I've walked through the dilapidated Fairbridge village, as it stands now, I've sensed a silence and sadness that invisibly lurks through its ruins. For me, I have had to dig deep to recall the feelings of loneliness, anger and abuse.

Ron Simpson said he still had nightmares after the abuse he experienced, which included being raped as a boy by the village chef and having his back broken with a hockey stick by Principal Woods, resulting in three years of hospital treatment. He said the final result was a good one that he hoped would stir future governments into more action: 'These kids, they went through hell. Something has to be done about these things . . . It's taken all these years to get a good decision and I hope it wakes the government up.'

Linda Gidman, who arrived in Molong as a five-year-old, said the settlement would 'not keep the demons away'. But she was pleased that the state and federal governments, and Fairbridge itself, had at last been held accountable:

From my point of view, this is justice for the children of Fairbridge who were exposed to sexual predators, exposed to physical and mental abuse at the hands of unskilled workers, and who were sent out into the wide world without social skills. But the years of legal delays took a toll on the victims.

The financial compensation provides some much-needed material comfort to many of the former Fairbridgians, who are not well off. Syd Lee, who has retired, lives with his wife on the Age Pension in a timber house in a small New South Wales country town. When he phoned me to thank me for all I had done, he said that in winter he and his wife had always had trouble paying their heating bills, but now they could put the heater on without worrying about the cost.

Stewart Lee also lives in a modest home in a small rural town. With his compensation payment he bought a very large refrigerator with an enormous freezer at the base. He then went to his butcher and bought $600 worth of the best eye fillet steak and says that it will now be the only meat he eats, having previously found it too expensive to buy regularly.

A former Fairbridge kid who was at the Pinjarra school in Western Australia, and gave evidence to the UK inquiry in 2017, said that if he received any compensation he would use the money to secure a plot in a cemetery so he could be buried there with his mum. He said he had put down a deposit on the plot but needed to pay the balance. 'When I die,' he said, 'I would like to be buried with my mother in Plymouth . . . I want to go in the same grave.'[2]

A number of Fairbridgians paid off their mortgage or bought a new car for the first time with the money they received – often the car they had always dreamed of owning. But most gave the money to their children and grandchildren, having never previously earned enough to offer their offspring any kind of head start.

*

Now it is all over, a number of us former Fairbridge children look back and try to extract what we gained from our experiences at the school.

Bob Stephens said his time in Molong drove him, as an adult and father, to make sure his children would never experience the trauma and poverty he had to go through. Bob married his wife, Lorna, after she fell pregnant when she was only sixteen or seventeen and he was nineteen. They had seven children, all of whom have grown up to excel professionally. Eventually Bob started his own business, buying a laundrette in Tamworth in north-east New South Wales. He later became the owner of a successful art gallery and is one of only a few Fairbridge kids who ended up actually owning a farm. 'I had no education,' he says. 'I had no money and no qualifications. At the end of the day it was a determination that I never wanted my children to ever go through what I did that drove me to work hard.'

Margaret Watt, who arrived at Fairbridge when she was ten, said she learned to be tough there, and that helped her in adult life:

> I worked, first of all, as a trainee nurse at Manly Hospital . . . I was so young . . . then I worked for the Red Cross blood transfusion service . . . then a secretary for the bank . . . I've done so much in my life after I was married and after I had three children, and all the adventures I've had, I think Fairbridge made me tough . . . and made me stand up for myself – and I think it's brought a lot to my life.

Many may have negative views about their Fairbridge experience but just about all of us feel good about Australia and believe we did, and do, have better opportunities here than we would have had in Britain. I've often reflected on how unlikely it would have been for a kid like me from a poor, working-class family, and brought up by a single parent on a housing estate, to have played a significant leadership role in the national affairs of Britain. Yet in Australia I've been the head of the State Rail Authority, the chairman of the national football association, the chairman and managing director of the Australian Broadcasting Corporation and a member of the Senate of the University of Sydney, Australia's oldest university. For me that proves there are far greater opportunities in Australia than those that exist in the UK, where social division and class have always been more significant.

As Ian Bayliff said:

> Fairbridge and Australia were like different planets. While Fairbridge was bad, Australia and the Australian people were very good to me. At Fairbridge I didn't get a good education and I have absolutely no professional qualifications. But in Australia I'm far better off than I would have been in England. I own my home outright, I regularly buy a new car, and I can now even help out my children – and my grandchildren. As many working people feel, life here is much better and less of a financial struggle than it would have been had I stayed in England.

Many of the former Fairbridge children, particularly those who have never regained contact with their parents in the UK, have remained close to other Fairbridgians, who are very much like an extended family. They have stayed in touch with each other, worked together, shared houses, attended each other's weddings and christened each other's children. Most are members of the

Old Fairbridgians Association (OFA), which organises regular reunions and publishes a newsletter every six months.

In 2013 John Harris, who had been the chairman of the association and on its executive for more than forty years, and in that time would invariably take the side of Fairbridge the institution, was replaced by Derek Moriarty, who was elected by the OFA members as the new president. The election of Moriarty changed the OFA from being an organisation comfortable denying what had happened to one that actively participated in the uncovering of the truth and supporting the case of the abuse victims.

Derek is a popular figure among Fairbridgians. He was at the school for more than eight years, having arrived there as an eight-year-old with his younger brother, Paul, and was regarded as one of the more rebellious boys. For well over a decade Derek helped me with Fairbridge research and he never missed a day in court during our long legal case in Sydney.

He thinks the quest we've all been through in the past years, the process of obtaining compensation and a recognition of what the system put thousands of children through, have resulted in far greater camaraderie among us. What has followed, he says, is more of a willingness to be part of the OFA. He does not want to be critical of the organisation but has acknowledged that in previous decades it tended to staunchly defend the institution of Fairbridge, and to dismiss the claims of abuse of the children. 'This story has brought the Fairbridge kids closer together,' he said. 'They now look out for each other more. I think a lot of them previously thought the Old Fairbridgians Association was a little exclusive and they didn't feel that welcome. There is certainly a greater level of inclusiveness and a sense of ownership of the association than previously.'

He also considers that the Fairbridge kids are stronger and more confident now in continuing to speak out about what happened to them.

Sadly, the old Fairbridge village, with the farm, the children's cottages, village hall, kitchens, guest houses, chapel, hospital, bakery, dairy and various other buildings, is now very much a ghost town and falling into disrepair. A few years ago many of us felt it was important to commemorate the journeys of the children who ended up in Molong. In 2018 it was the eightieth anniversary of the opening of the farm school and that March many former Fairbridgians travelled to Orange and Molong to reunite. It was then we proposed the idea of some kind of monument to Fairbridge.

We began fundraising to build a park dedicated to the Fairbridge children by asking former farm school kids to make a donation, and we very quickly collected $25,000. Over the next few months we successfully raised half a million dollars from the state government, largely because of the sympathetic ear of Deputy Premier John Barilaro, who kicked in a further $100,000 a year later when we were running short of cash. We raised almost another half-million from a host of other donors, including the federal government, and had the benefit of professional services donated free of charge and valued at a further million dollars.

In 2020 the Old Fairbridgians Association opened a beautiful five-acre park on the site of Fairbridge Farm. It was designed by acclaimed Australian landscape architect Leonard Lynch, who had worked on the project for three years free of charge. I was the chairman of the project team, and my brother Dudley supervised the park's construction.

Located down the hill from the old village, the park is dedicated to the almost one thousand child migrants who went through the school. It sits between the Mitchell Highway and Molong Creek on the northern border of the old farm: its location is symbolic because most Fairbridge kids have the fondest memories of that creek. It is where we played, camped, swam; caught, cooked and ate yabbies; enjoyed boiling a billy of tea and went rabbiting.

The park has four linked areas, each of which tells the story of the children's origins in, and their journey from, England; their voyage across the seas; life on Fairbridge farm; and finally their leaving, on their own and with no family, to go out into the wider world. As Lynch said, 'Many former Fairbridge kids see this park as a way to publicly identify as Fairbridgian. It's a living legacy through which their families and future visitors will come to know their story.'

The park includes a memorial saluting those who later served in the military. Ninety-six — or nearly ten per cent — of the boys who went to the farm school ended up joining the armed forces. Fifty-five of them served overseas during the Second World War, the Korean War, the Malayan Emergency and Vietnam. Three were killed in active service.

On 14 March 2020 about a hundred of us gathered to cut the ceremonial gold ribbon to officially open the park. It was an inspiring and uplifting event, which saluted our achievements and was cathartic for all of us.

In 2021 the park won three major landscape-design and heritage awards. The opening of the park, and its impact, made me realise that good had come from it all. I realised that the journey we had been on together since 2006 had empowered many who, for most of their lives, had felt disempowered. They now felt heard, vindicated, believed, emboldened. Many now believe they can slay some of their dragons.

Finally, what has it all meant to me?

It is more than fifteen years since I began working on the Fairbridge story and going through what became a reckoning, a quest for justice. I have been strengthened over the years by the support I received from so many of the Fairbridge kids, many of whom, like Smiley Bayliff, were friends all those years ago when we were at the farm school. I have always been close to my brothers but now feel even closer. Both of them have continued to support me and both donated money to the building of the Fairbridge Children's Park. My wife, Stergitsa, and my son, Damian, have remained my greatest source of strength throughout what has been a long journey. In 2007 Damian was six years old and had to stand on a chair to reach a microphone to introduce me when we launched *The Forgotten Children*. He will help me launch this book.

I had no idea when I started to research *The Forgotten Children* that it would be such a long and emotionally exhausting journey. I am angry that multiple governments and institutions enabled terrible abuse, and allowed it to continue even when they were aware that young children were being maltreated, sexually and physically assaulted, and neglected. I am angry that for decades afterwards officials were prepared to deny any of that happened, and conspired to lie and to cover it all up. I am angry that no one was ever charged with any crime and no one was publicly named for the great wrongs they did to the children. I am at least glad that we have now named the major villains.

The longer I have been on the journey, the more confronting it has become. I thought that the stories and knowledge would become easier the more familiar I was with them, but the reverse is true. I was completely unaware of the extent of the sexual abuse of Fairbridge children while I was at the school and for decades after I left. But the more I reconnected with people who'd been there, the more I learned of the suffering so many of them had endured. I have found it particularly difficult dealing with the recollections of the suffering of the smallest children, who were the most vulnerable, the least protected and the most abused.

I had little knowledge of sexual abuse before I started on the Fairbridge story and very little understanding of how pervasive and permanent the scars are on its survivors. I'll never forget the evidence of a man who went to the farm school in Pinjarra and told the UK inquiry in 2017:

> See, this is the thing. That is what was branded on my mind all the time. I've had to live with this for about sixty-two years now. I live it seven days a week, twenty-four hours a day. But you can't get it out of your mind because it's imprinted on your mind. There's no way you can get away from it.[3]

I had never encountered that kind of personal suffering up close and on such a horrific scale. It reached a stage where I could see it in people's eyes, even when they were not ready, or able, to talk about it. Seeing the terrible hurt of so many of my fellow school-mates has deeply affected me. I have been shaken to the core by the experience.

However, on the positive side, it is satisfying that we managed to expose much of the awful truth and that, against the odds, we brought powerful institutions, including governments, to account. I think now, as a result of this story and others like it, there will be a greater sensitivity to the dangers of institutional care, and a deeper awareness of the need to provide children with security and safety, wherever they are. Above all, hopefully we have learned to hear, listen to, and believe, our children.

At least I'd like to think so.

The justice that, together, the former Fairbridge kids and I have achieved reminds me of something Ernesto Che Guevara once said. After the Cuban revolution he received a letter from Señora Maria Rosario Guevara in Morocco asking if it were possible they were related. 'I don't think you and I are very closely related,' he wrote back, 'but if you are capable of trembling with indignation each time that an injustice is committed in the world, we are comrades, and that is more important.'

ACKNOWLEDGEMENTS

I am grateful to a large number of people for their assistance with this book. It is a book I could not have written alone and without a lot of support from my family, friends and all the former Fairbridge kids.

A very big thanks for the continuing support of my wife, Stergitsa, and son, Damian, who have lived with this story for nearly fifteen years since I started writing *The Forgotten Children*. I also want to thank my brothers, Dudley and Richard, for the strength of their support. I can never thank them enough.

I was lucky to have the ongoing advice and guidance of Michael Georgeson, a very dear friend and retired lawyer, who patiently helped me navigate the complex legal issues of this story in both Australia and the UK.

Thanks to everyone at Penguin Random House, particularly publisher Justin Ractliffe and editor Catherine Hill, who were always there with helpful guidance and good advice. Catherine edited *The Forgotten Children* and has continued to show a remarkable empathy with, and understanding of, the Fairbridge story. *Reckoning* is a far better book than it otherwise would have been because of her involvement.

I am grateful for the widespread and growing support in the community of the central west of the state, where most of this story takes place. When *The Forgotten Children* was first published, many local people would not accept the dark side of the Fairbridge story. Now, there is widespread acceptance and a willingness throughout the community to confront the truth of what happened, supported by local media, including the *Molong Express*, the *Central Western Daily* and the local ABC radio.

But my greatest debt is to the Fairbridge kids, many of whom were at the farm school while I was there, particularly my late, very dear friend Ian 'Smiley' Bayliff, and the president of the Old Fairbridgians Association, Derek Moriarty. This is essentially their story and without their stories there would be no book. I know it took a lot of courage for many to speak up because it is often easier to keep the secret of abuse buried deep inside. I am particularly indebted to those who were the first to talk about being sexually abused, which in turn gave others the strength to follow.

SOURCES AND NOTES

References to files of the Fairbridge Foundation relate to papers formerly held in the King Street, Sydney offices of the New South Wales Fairbridge Foundation. When the Fairbridge Foundation wound up in 2015, the papers were transferred to the New South Wales State Archives and Records collection. Most of the Fairbridge Foundation papers can now be found in the Ian Baylifff Papers, at baylifffairbridgepapers.com. Some are also held by David Hill. The photographs in this book, as well as many more historical images of life at the school in Molong, can also be found in the Ian Bayliff Papers.

Preface
1   Memorandum by the Department of Health, Child Migrants (CM 129), 1997; publications.parliament.uk/pa/cm199798/cmselect/cmhealth/755/8052002.htm

Chapter 2: The Fairbridge Child Migration Scheme
1   Poor British children had been sent to work on farms in British colonies – especially Canada – for much of the nineteenth century, but Kingsley Fairbridge was the first to build a farm training school.
2   Kingsley Fairbridge, *The Autobiography of Kingsley Fairbridge*, Oxford University Press, Oxford, 1927, chapter 1
3   Ibid., p. 171
4   Ruby Fairbridge, *Pinjarra: The Building of a Farm School*, Oxford University Press, Oxford, 1937, p. 12
5   A. O. Neville, Colonial Secretary's Office, 352 1967/13, State Records Office, Western Australia
6   Ruby Fairbridge, *Pinjarra*, p. 168
7   Colonial Office, Overseas Settlement Department, original correspondence, CO 721/12 ff 8:9, 1919, National Archives, Kew, London
8   G. Sherrington and C. Jeffery, *Fairbridge: Empire and Child Migration*, UWA Press, Perth, 1998, p. 108
9   Senate Inquiry into Child Migration, 'Submission by the Department of Immigration and Multicultural Affairs', December 2000, p. 29

Chapter 4: A Working School
1   Eddie Scott, IICSA, London, 2 March 2017, p. 82; iicsa.org.uk/key--documents/1095/view/public-hearing-transcript-2nd-march-2017.pdf
2   M. Baker, 'Report on the Food Service of the Fairbridge Farm School, Molong', 9 December 1953, Fairbridge Foundation, Sydney
3   F. K. S. Woods, 'Principal's Comments of Report by Dietitian', (undated), Fairbridge Foundation, Sydney
4   Kingsley Fairbridge, 'The Immigration of Poor Children to the Colonies', speech read before the Colonial Club at Oxford in 1909, reprinted by the Child Immigration Society, 1930, Fairbridge Society archives D296 A2, University of Liverpool, UK

Chapter 5: Suffer the Little Children
1   Eddie Scott, IICSA, London, 2 March 2017, p. 73; iicsa.org.uk/key-documents/1095/view/public-hearing-transcript-2nd-march-2017.pdf
2   Ibid., p. 81

3   In the 1950s, when a farm labourer was paid more than £12 a week, a
    Fairbridge cottage mother was paid less than £10. Once tax, board and
    lodgings were deducted, she was left with £8, two shillings and sixpence a
    week. The situation did not improve over the years. By 1970 (and after the
    introduction of decimal currency) a farm labourer was being paid about
    $40 a week but a cottage mother only $25 a week.

4   Eddie Scott, IICSA London, 2 March 2017, p. 78; iicsa.org.uk/key-
    documents/1095/view/public-hearing-transcript-2nd-march-2017.pdf

5   Minutes of meeting of UK Fairbridge Society, 22 July 1965, D296/B3/1/1-2,
    University of Liverpool Special Archives, UK

6   Letter from Dr Calov to Lord Slim, 22 July 1965, Fairbridge Foundation,
    Sydney

7   Letter from the secretary of the Fairbridge Council Council to F. K. S.
    Woods, 22 September 1965, Fairbridge Foundation, Sydney

8   Fairbridge Farm School, New South Wales annual report, 1966, Fairbridge
    Foundation, Sydney

Chapter 6: Fear and Shame

1   Witness statement 'A82', IICSA, London, 8 March 2017; iicsa.org.uk/key-
    documents/1145/view/public-hearing-transcript-8th-march-2017.pdf

2   Royal Commission into Institutional Responses to Child Sexual Abuse,
    'Identifying and disclosing child sexual abuse', volume 4, Commonwealth
    of Australia, 2017, p. 30; childabuseroyalcommission.gov.au/sites/default/
    files/final_report_-_volume_4_identifying_and_disclosing_child_sexual_
    abuse.pdf

3   Jim Schembri, 'Tuesday TV: The Long Journey Home', *Sydney Morning
    Herald*, 16 November 2009

4   Eddie Scott, IICSA London, 2 March 2017, p. 76; iicsa.org.uk/key-
    documents/1095/view/public-hearing-transcript-2nd-march-2017.pdf

5   Ibid., p. 75

6   Vivian Bingham's reports, 16 October, 3 November, 6 November 1959,
    personal papers of Vivian Bingham

7   Damien Murphy, 'Revered governor-general accused of abuse', *Sydney
    Morning Herald*, 28 April 2007

8   Author unnamed, 'Slim pickings', *Australian*, 3 May 2007

9   Ibid.

10 Letter to the editor, *Australian*, 4 May 2007

11 'Slim pickings', *Australian*

12 Ibid.

13 Sherryn Groch, 'William Slim Drive in Canberra to be renamed in wake of
    sexual abuse claims', *Canberra Times*, 6 June 2019

14 Sally Pryor, 'William Slim Drive in Canberra should be renamed in the wake of revelations of sexual abuse, victims say', *Canberra Times*, 2 March 2018

15 Ibid.

16 Ibid.

17 Letter to the editor, *Canberra Times*, 22 February 2021

18 Ian Bushnell, 'Gentleman keeps promise to rename William Slim Drive to prevent further hurt', Riotact, 17 February 2021

Chapter 7: Every Childhood Lasts a Lifetime

1 See the UNSW report 'No Child Should Ever Grow Up Like This', which included child migrants: forgotten australians.unsw.edu.au/sites/default/files/uploads/LOW%20RES%20 12859_UNSW_FASS_ForgottenAustralians_Report_Nov16_LR_FA.pdf

2 Letter from W. B. Hudson to F. K. S. Woods, February 1953, D296 J3/2/10, University of Liverpool, UK

3 Fairbridge Farm Annual Report, 1959, Fairbridge Foundation, Sydney

4 Report by Fairbridge Council members H. A. Andrews and P. R. Le Couteur, 3 March 1954, Fairbridge Foundation, Sydney

5 Letter from Sir Percival Halse Rogers to Sir Charles Hambro, 24 February 1944, Fairbridge Foundation, Sydney

6 New South Wales Education Department report on Fairbridge Primary School, nos. 366–69, 25 February 1951

7 NSW Department of Education, 51/92/31578, State Archives and Records, Sydney

8 Report of Sub-Committee Education and Training, undated, Fairbridge Foundation, Sydney

9 Memorandum for Education and Training, P. Le Couteur, 15 September 1955, Fairbridge Foundation, Sydney

10 'Comments on Memorandum re Education and Training', F. K. S. Woods, 20 November 1955, Fairbridge Foundation, Sydney

11 Minutes of meeting of the Fairbridge Council, 26 May 1956, Fairbridge Foundation, Sydney

Chapter 8: Reuniting

1 John Moss, 'Child Migration to Australia', report for the British Home Office, HMSO, London, 1953, para 15

2 Letter from W. B. Vaughan to E. H. Johnson, 10 September 1956, DO 35/6383, National Archives, Kew, London

3 Syd Lee, Graham Lee, Stewart Lee and Ian Bayliff all had the same father, Sydney Lee

4 Letter from Dora Lee, UK Fairbridge Society, 5 September 1954, personal papers of Ian Bayliff

5 Ibid.

6 Letter from F. K. S. Woods to W. B. Vaughan, 7 November 1955, personal papers of Ian Bayliff

7 Letter from G. C. Watson to W. B. Vaughan, 28 August 1958, personal papers of Ian Bayliff

8 Ibid., 22 January 1959, personal papers of Ian Bayliff

9 'The Fairbridge Society: To Provide a New Life in the Commonwealth', c. 1958, Fairbridge Foundation, Sydney

10 Memo from Bill Phillips to F. K. S. Woods, undated, Fairbridge Foundation, Sydney

11 Ibid.

12 Letter from A. C. Thomas to the secretary of the Fairbridge Council, 17 January 1964, D296 B3/1/1-2, University of Liverpool Special Archives, UK

Chapter 9: Cover-ups

1 Letter from W. D. Stewart to Sir Charles Hambro, 1 October 1940, Fairbridge Foundation, Sydney

2 Len Tuder, *A Pommie Kid*, unpublished biography of Len Cowne, 2003, chapter 3

3 E. Heath, special report, May 1943, Fairbridge Foundation, Sydney,

4 Ibid.

5 Letter from Sir Claude Reading to Sir Charles Hambro, 5 February 1946, D296/19/25, University of Liverpool Special Archives, UK

6 Letter from Ruth Woods to Miss Hart, December 1945, D296/19/25, University of Liverpool, UK

7 Ibid., 29 January 1946

8 Letter from W. B. Hudson to Sir Charles Hambro, 16 March 1948, D296/19/25, University of Liverpool, UK

9 V. A. Heffernan, 'Investigation at Fairbridge Farm School', 5 March 1948, D296/19/25, University of Liverpool, UK

10 Ibid.

11 Letter from A. C. Thomas to secretary of Fairbridge Council, 17 January 1964, D296 B3/1/1-2, University of Liverpool, UK

12 Ibid.

13 Letter from R. H. Hicks to W. B. Hudson, 30 December 1957, 10/37271, NSW State Archives and Records, Sydney

14 Letter from W. B. Hudson to R. H. Hicks, 24 February 1958, 10/37271, NSW State Archives and Records, Sydney

15   Ibid.

16   W. J. Garnett, 'Report on Farm Schools in Australia', October 1944, Fairbridge Foundation, Sydney

17   Ibid.

18   Ibid.

19   Ibid.

20   Gordon Green, response to the Garnett Report, August 1945, Fairbridge Foundation, Sydney

21   Ibid.

22   Gordon Lynch, 'Pathways to the 1946 Curtis Report and the post-war reconstruction of children's out-of-home care', Taylor Francis Online, 27 April 2019; tandfonline.com/doi/full/10.1080/13619462.2019.1609947

23   Child Migration Programmes, 'The Curtis Report', Independent Inquiry Child Sexual Abuse, 4: 13–16, February 2017; iicsa.org.uk/publications/investigation/child-migration/part-b-child-sexual-abuse-child-migration-programmes/curtis-report

24   Ibid., 4: 13–17

25   Ibid., 4: 30

26   'Anxiety for 300 Child Migrants', *Daily Mail*, 5 April 1948

27   Ibid.

28   Letter from H. T. Logan to Lord Scarborough, 19 March 1948, D296/10/2, University of Liverpool, UK

29   London Fairbridge Society, Minutes of meeting, 14 December 1948, D296 B1/2/6, University of Liverpool, UK

30   *Canberra Times*, 13 March 1950

31   John Moss, 'Child Migration to Australia', report for the British Home Office, HMSO, London, 1953, para 15

32   Commonwealth Relations Office files, 28 July 1955, DO 35/6380, National Archives, Kew, UK

33   Ibid.

34   Memo to Sir Saville Garner, 2 August 1958, DO 35/6382, National Archives, Kew, UK

35   'Child Migration to Australia; Report of a Fact-Finding Mission', paragraph 7, Commonwealth Relations Office file, 28 April 1956, Public Records Office; iicsa.org.uk/key-documents/4643/view/CMT000397.pdf

36   Letter from Hudson to Woods, 2 February 1956, Fairbridge Foundation, Sydney

37   'Child Migration to Australia: Report of a Fact-Finding Mission', paragraph 14, Commonwealth Relations Office file, 28 April 1956, Public Records Office; iicsa.org.uk/key-documents/4643/view/CMT000397.pdf

38 Ibid., paragraphs 31 and 38(3)

39 Letter from M. K. Ewans to Cyril Costley-White, 10 May 1956, DO 35/6381, National Archives, Kew, UK

40 Commonwealth Relations Office memo, June 1956, DO 35/6981, National Archives, Kew, UK

41 Letter from Cyril Costley-White to I. M. R. McLennan, 11 May 1956, DO 35/6831, National Archives, Kew, UK

42 Commonwealth Relations Office memo, 9 June 1956, DO 35/6831, National Archives, Kew, UK

43 Memo from Shannon to Sir Saville Garner, June 1956, DO 35/6981, National Archives, Kew, UK

44 Memo from R. J. Whittick to G. E. B. Shannon, 22 June 1956, DO 35/6382, National Archives, Kew, UK

45 Addenda to Fact-Finding Mission report, DO 35/6382, National Archives, Kew, UK

46 Ibid.

47 The institutions in Category C that 'passed muster' were; Dr Barnardo's, Burwood, Sydney; Dr Barnardo's, Normanhurst, Sydney; Northcote School, Bacchus Marsh, Victoria; St John's Church of England Home, Canterbury, Melbourne; Burton Hall Farm School, Tatura, Victoria; Methodist Homes, Burwood, Victoria; Clarendon Church of England Home, Kingston Park, Tasmania; and Hagley Area Farm School, Tasmania. Category B was made up of: Melrose United Protestant School, Pendle Hill, Sydney; Murray Dwyer Roman Catholic Orphanage, Mayfield, New South Wales; Goodwood Roman Catholic Orphanage, Goodwood, Adelaide; Clontarf Roman Catholic Boys Town, Clontarf, Perth; St Joseph's Roman Catholic Home. Leederville, Perth; Methodist Home, Victoria Park, Perth; Swan Church of England Homes, Midland Junction, Western Australia; and Nazareth House, East Camberwell, Melbourne.

48 Memo from R. J. Whittick to G. E. B. Shannon, 22 June 1956, DO 35/6382, National Archives, Kew, UK

49 Armstrong's account is contained in a memo from R. H. Johnson to Costley-White and G. E. B. Shannon and follows a phone call to Johnson from Armstrong, 2 July 1956, DO 35/6382, National Archives, Kew, UK

50 Memo from Costley-White to Shannon, 3 July 1956, DO35/6382, National Archives, Kew, UK

51 Memo from Shannon to Costley-White, 5 July 1956, DO35/6382, National Archives, Kew, UK

52 G. Lynch, *UK Child Migration to Australia, 1945–1970: A Study in Policy Failure*, Palgrave, London, 2021, p. 277

53 Hudson to Hambro, 7 September 1956, Fairbridge Foundation, Sydney
54 Fairbridge Society (Inc): renewal of agreement, signed by the Secretary of State for Commonwealth Relations and director of Fairbridge W. B. Vaughan, 1957 and 1960, DO 35/10251, National Archives, Kew, UK

Chapter 10: First Steps to Justice

1 Frank Bongiorno, 'The Forgotten Children', *Sydney Morning Herald*, 6 June 2007
2 Paul Ham, 'Orphans of the Empire', *Sunday Times*, 29 July 2007
3 David Hill et al., *The Long Journey Home* (documentary film), Follow Productions, 2009
4 *Australian*, 14 May 2007
5 Ibid.
6 David Hill et al., *The Long Journey Home*
7 Ibid.
8 Limitation periods (that is, the maximum period of time which can elapse from the time of a cause of action arising until the commencement of court proceedings relating to that cause of action) exist but vary in length depending on the cause of action. As recommended by the Royal Commission into Institutional Responses to Child Sexual Abuse, the New South Wales government passed legislation in 2016 abolishing the time limitations on claims for child sexual abuse, 'serious' child physical abuse and connected child abuse. The government of Victoria passed similar legislation a year earlier. The recommendation of the Royal Commission was undoubtedly a reaction to the examples it had seen of defendants seeking to avoid responsibility by hiding behind the defence of expired time limitations.
9 Parliament of Australia, Community Affairs References Committee, 'Child Migration', 22 March 2001
10 Lorna Knowles, 'Class action to begin over alleged abuse of child migrants at Fairbridge Farm School', ABC News, 14 March 2014

Chapter 11: The First Big Win

1 Denise Cuthbert and Marian Quartly, 'Forced Child Removal and the Politics of National Apologies in Australia', *American Indian Quarterly*, vol. 37, nos. 1–2, winter/spring 2013, pp. 178–205; jstor.org/stable/10.5250/amerindiquar.37.1-2.0178
2 Gordon Brown, 'Child Migration', *Hansard*, British Parliament, 24 February 2010, column 301; publications.parliament.uk/pa/cm200910/cmhansrd/cm100224/debtext/100224-0004.htm

3   David Hill, 'Child abuse action on the one hand, apathy on the other', *Sydney Morning Herald*, 16 May 2013

4   David Hill, submission to the Royal Commission into Institutional Responses to Child Sexual Abuse, April 2014; childabuseroyalcommission. gov.au/sites/default/files/file-list/Issues%20Paper%205%20-%20 Submission%20-%2037%20David%20Hill.pdf

5   Submission by Counsel Assisting, Public Inquiry into the Response of the State to Complaints Made and Litigation Instituted by Former Residents of Bethcar Children's Home, Brewarrina, New South Wales, sections 18–24, October and November 2014; childabuseroyalcommission.gov.au/sites/ default/files/file-list/Case%20Study%2019%20-%20Submission%20- %20Bethcar%20Childrens%20Home%20-%20Submissions%20of%20 Counsel%20Assisting%20the%20Royal%20Commission.pdf

6   Ibid., section 25

7   Ibid., section 75

8   Ibid., section 236

9   Ibid., section 244

10 Ibid., section 243

11 Transcript of evidence of the Bethcar case study, Royal Commission into Institutional Responses to Child Sexual Abuse, 23 October 2015, p. 10181; childabuseroyalcommission.gov.au/sites/default/files/file-list/Case%20 Study%2019%20-%20Transcript%20-%20Bethcar%20Childrens%20 Home%20-%20Day%2097%20-%2023102014.pdf

12 New South Wales government, Communities and Justice, 'Model Litigant Policy' (accessed August 2021); justice.nsw.gov.au/legal-services- coordination/Pages/info-for-govt-agencies/model-litigant-policy.aspx

13 Evidence, Bethcar case study, 30 October 2014; childabuseroyal commission.gov.au/sites/default/files/file-list/Case%20Study%2019%20 -%20Transcript%20-%20Bethcar%20Childrens%20Home%20-%20 Day%20101%20-%2030102014.pdf

14 Evidence, Bethcar case study, 24 October 2014; childabuseroyal commission.gov.au/sites/default/files/file-list/Case%20Study%2019%20 -%20Transcript%20-%20Bethcar%20Childrens%20Home%20-%20 Day%2098%20-%2024102014.pdf

15 Ibid.

16 Rachel Browne, '$24 million payment for Fairbridge Farm abuse victims', *Sydney Morning Herald*, 29 June 2015

Chapter 12: The British Inquiry

1   Memorandum of the UK Department of Health (CM129); publications. parliament.uk/pa/cm199798/cmselect/cmhealth/755/8052002.htm

2   Ibid.

3   Beauchamp was dismissed in 1940, and not 1938 as Haynes suggested.

4   Minutes of evidence, examination of witnesses, question 240 to Nigel
     Haynes, Select Committee on Health, Parliamentary Business (UK),
     22 June 1998; publications.parliament.uk/pa/cm199798/cmselect/
     cmhealth/755/8061121.htm

5   The Welfare of Former British Child Migrants, conclusion, Select
     Committee on Health, Parliamentary Business (UK), 2 July 1998;
     publications.parliament.uk/pa/cm199798/cmselect/cmhealth/755/75512.htm

6   Ibid., para 49

7   Senate Committee, terms of reference for child migration inquiry and
     report, 7 September 2000; aph.gov.au/parliamentary_business/committees/
     senate/community_affairs/completed_inquiries/1999-02/child_migrat/
     report/c01; Australian Senate report, 'Lost Innocents: Righting the
     Record', section 1.18, 30 August 2001; aph.gov.au/parliamentary_business/
     committees/senate/community_affairs/completed_inquiries/1999-02/
     child_migrat/report/index

8   Community Affairs Senate Reference Committee, 'Child Migration',
     Official Committee *Hansard*, 22 March 2001, p. 7; aph.gov.au/binaries/
     hansard/senate/commttee/s4608.pdf

9   Ibid., p. 29

10   Ibid., written submission number 43

11   Australian Senate report, 'Lost Innocents: Righting the Record',
     para 2.116, 30 August 2001; aph.gov.au/parliamentary_business/
     committees/senate/community_affairs/completed_inquiries/1999-02/
     child_migrat/report/index

12   Ibid., para 4.134

13   Ibid., para 4.112

14   Senate Committee, terms of reference for child migration inquiry and
     report, 7 September 2000; aph.gov.au/parliamentary_business/committees/
     senate/community_affairs/completed_inquiries/1999-02/child_migrat/
     report/c01

15   Ibid.

16   IICSA, 'Statement by the Chair of the Independent Inquiry into Child
     Sexual Abuse', update-statement, 27 November 2015, p. 6; iicsa.org.uk/
     sites/default/files/update-statement-november-2015_0.pdf

Chapter 13: The London Hearings

1   David Hill, opening statement, IICSA hearings, 27 February 2017, p. 50;
     iicsa.org.uk/key-documents/997/view/iicsa-cms270217.pdf

2 Ibid.

3 David Hill, IICSA hearings, 8 March 2017, pp. 93 ff; iicsa.org.uk/
key-documents/1145/view/public-hearing-transcript-8th-march-2017.pdf

4 Ibid., pp. 103 ff.

5 Ibid.

6 Ibid., pp. 110 ff.

7 Ibid.

8 'Abuse inquiry: Australian orphanage was "feast of kids"', BBC News,
1 March 2017

9 Ibid.

10 All excerpts from these transcripts of the IICSA hearings on 20 July 2017
can be found at: iicsa.org.uk/key-documents/2396/view/public-hearing-
transcript-20th-july-2017.pdf

11 Nigel Haynes, transcript of evidence, IICSA hearings, 19 July 2017, pp. 7
ff.; iicsa.org.uk/key-documents/2239/view/public-hearing-transcript-19th-
july-2017.pdf

12 Ibid., pp. 53 ff.

13 Ibid., pp. 54–5

14 All excerpts from these transcripts of the IICSA hearing on 19 July 2017
can be found at: iicsa.org.uk/key-documents/2239/view/public-hearing-
transcript-19th-july-2017.pdf

15 All excerpts from these transcripts of the IICSA hearings on 20 July can be
found at: iicsa.org.uk/key-documents/2396/view/public-hearing-transcript-
20th-july-2017.pdf

Chapter 14: The British Government Agrees to Pay Compensation

1 IICSA, 'Child Migration Programmes Investigation Report', March 2018,
p. vii

2 Ibid.

3 Ibid., p. ix

4 Ibid., pp. 7 and 14

5 Ibid., p. ix

6 Ibid., pp. 58 and 77

7 Owen Bowcott, 'Inquiry urges payouts for victims of postwar UK child
migration scheme', *Guardian*, 2 March 2018

8 IICSA, 'Child Migration Programmes Investigation Report', March 2018,
p. 150

9 Ibid.

10 'IICSA inquiry says UK government should pay Australia child migrants',
BBC News, 1 March 2018

11 Gordon Lynch, 'Britain sent child migrants overseas – it's running out of time to make reparations', The Conversation, 23 October 2018

12 Ibid.

13 Lisa Nandy, 'Child Migration Programmes (Child Abuse)', TheyWorkForYou, 3 July 2018; theyworkforyou.com/whall/?id=2018-07-03b.94.0

14 Sarah Marsh, 'UK child migrants sent to Australia offered $36k compensation', *Guardian*, 1 February 2019

15 'Government response to the Interim Report by the Independent Inquiry into Child Sexual Abuse', Secretary of State for the Home Department, December 2018; assets.publishing.service.gov.uk/government/uploads/system/uploads/attachment_data/file/765917/CCS207_CCS1218194158-001_Gov_Resp_to_IICSA.PDF

Chapter 15: Redress from the Fairbridge Society

1 David Hill, IICSA hearings, 20 July 2017, p. 97; iicsa.org.uk/key-documents/2396/view/public-hearing-transcript-20th-july-2017.pdf

2 IICSA, 'Child Migration Programmes Investigation Report', March 2018, p. 94

3 Ibid.

4 Letter from Dame Martina Milburn to Alexis Jay, 4 July 2017

5 Martina Milburn, IICSA Inquiry, 12 July 2017, p. 16; iicsa.org.uk/key-documents/1620/view/public-hearing-transcript-12th-july-2017.pdf

6 Ibid., p. 4

7 Ibid., p. 7

8 Ibid., p. 9

9 AAP, 'Prince's Trust "covering its backside" over child migrant abuse, David Hill says', *Guardian*, 11 July 2017

10 'Redress and Civil Litigation Report', Royal Commission into Institutional Responses to Child Sexual Abuse, Commonwealth of Australia, 2015, p. 31; childabuseroyalcommission.gov.au/sites/default/files/file-list/final_report_-_redress_and_civil_litigation.pdf

11 Ibid.

12 Megan Neil, 'Victims still in fight to join scheme', *Canberra Times*, 16 May 2020

13 AAP, 'Abuse survivors sent from UK to Australia as children given fresh hope of redress from Prince's Trust', *Guardian*, 17 May 2020

14 Senator the Hon. Ruston, 'National Redress Scheme Update', Ministers for the Department of Social Services, 1 July 2020; ministers.dss.gov.au/media-releases/5946· The other institutions were the Australian Air

League, the Boys' Brigade NSW, Lakes Entrance Pony Club, the Jehovah's Witnesses and Kenja Communications.

15 Prime Minister Scott Morrison, statement, House of Representatives, 22 October 2020; pm.gov.au/media/statement-house-representatives-act

16 Ibid.

17 Michael McGowan, 'Dozens of child abuse claims remain from organisations refusing to sign on to national redress scheme', *Guardian*, 28 November 2020

18 Simon Major to David Hill, email, 25 May 2021

19 Senator the Hon. Anne Rushton, 'Five Fairbridge farm schools to join the National Redress Scheme', Ministers for Social Services, 24 March 2021; ministers.dss.gov.au/media-releases/6861

20 Simon Major to David Hill, email, 23 November 2020

21 Ibid., 5 June 2021

22 Joint Select Committee on Implementation of the National Redress Scheme, 'Second Interim Report of the Joint Select Committee on Implementation of the National Redress Scheme', Commonwealth of Australia, November 2021, p. 85

23 Simon Major to David Hill, emails, 5 May 2021, 11 May 2021, 28 May 2021, 5 June 2021, 6 August 2021, 23 September 2021, 8 October 2021. Chris Laverty to David Hill, emails, 29 July 2021, 1 August 2021, 3 September 2021, 10 September 2021, 20 October 2021, 2 December 2021

Chapter 16: Reckoning

1 Lennie Magee to David Hill, email, 22 September 2020

2 IICSA hearings, 28 February 2017; iicsa.org.uk/key-documents/1046/view/public-hearing-transcript-28th-february-2017.pdf

3 Ibid.

INDEX

INDEX